# AFRICA SINCE 1800

# AFRICA SINCE 1800

BY

ROLAND OLIVER

AND

ANTHONY ATMORE

CAMBRIDGE
AT THE UNIVERSITY PRESS
1969

Published by the Syndics of the Cambridge University Press
Bentley House, 200 Euston Road, London N.W. 1
American Branch: 32 East 57th Street, New York, N.Y. 10022

© Cambridge University Press 1967

Library of Congress Catalogue Card Number: 67–11527

Standard Book Numbers:
521 05864 3 clothbound
521 05863 5 school edition

First published 1967
Reprinted 1969

Printed in Great Britain
at the University Printing House, Cambridge
(Brooke Crutchley, University Printer)

# CONTENTS

vi                    *Contents*

# LIST OF MAPS

## ACKNOWLEDGEMENTS

The authors wish to record their thanks to Professor J. D. Fage of the University of Birmingham, Dr A. Adu Boahen of the University of Ghana and Mr Philip Harris for their valuable comments on the manuscript of this book.

# 1

## AFRICA NORTH OF THE EQUATOR

*The Sahara and Islam: the bonds unifying northern Africa*

The geography of the northern half of Africa is dominated by the Sahara desert. Throughout its vast area, seventeen hundred miles from north to south and nearly five thousand from east to west, rainfall is less than five inches a year. Except round a few oases, where underground supplies of water reach the surface, the only people living there until modern times have been nomadic herdsmen. Only in the last few years have oil and natural-gas fields been found under the desert. Nomads have become technicians and workers, living in the oil towns which draw their essential water supplies from far underground by deeply bored artesian wells. To the north of the desert lies the temperate Mediterranean coastland, its rainfall concentrated mostly between January and March. Southward are the tropics, the land of the summer rains. Racially as well as geographically, the Sahara marks a frontier. In the desert and north of it live Berbers and Arabs, fair-skinned peoples of Caucasian stock. South of the desert is the 'land of the blacks'—to the Greeks 'Ethiopia', to the Berbers 'Akal n'Iguinawen' (Guinea), to the Arabs 'Bilad as-Sudan'.

The Sahara, therefore, has been a barrier against large-scale migrations. But it has not stopped the movement of small numbers of men carrying their ideas and skills from one side to the other. The desert has always been a formidable obstacle to human communications, but for two thousand years at least, since the introduction of the horse and the camel made travel easier, men have persevered in overcoming its difficulties. Before the days of the motor-car and the aeroplane it took two months or more to cross. Nevertheless people did cross it, not merely in the course of isolated journeys of exploration, but regularly, year after year, in the course of trade, education and pilgrimage. Long before any sailing-ship from Europe reached the Atlantic coast of West Africa, the Sudanic lands immediately to the south of the desert were in touch with the lands to the north. Between the eleventh century and the sixteenth, at least the townsfolk of the Sudanic countries began to be Muslims, like the Arabs and Berbers to the north. Their learned and pious men studied Arabic, the language of the Quran, the Holy Book of Islam, and made the pilgrimage to the holy cities of Mecca and Medina. Above all, the merchant caravans kept touch with developments in the outside world. The rulers and the rich men on both sides of the desert worshipped the One God, read the same books, shared the same luxuries, discussed the same things.

It is debatable just where the southern frontier of northern Africa lay at different times in its past history. Until the twelfth and thirteenth centuries it probably included little more than the open grasslands, forming a belt three or four hundred miles wide to the south of the desert margin, from the Senegal to Lake Chad, and eastward through Darfur and Kordofan to the Ethiopian highlands. Throughout this region beasts of burden could circulate, and troops of armed horsemen could control and levy tribute upon the populations of quite large states. To the south again lay the woodland belt, thickening progressively into dense equatorial rain-forest. Here, because of tsetse fly in the woodlands and lack of fodder in the forest, all goods had to be carried by porters, and soldiers fought on foot. Markets and states were smaller, and there were no towns where Islamic religion and learning could get a foothold. Nevertheless, by the fourteenth and fifteenth centuries at least, some northern influences were beginning to penetrate even these southern lands. When the Portuguese discovered the West African coast they found that the trading frontier of the Sudanic kingdoms had already reached the sea. During the three following centuries the European traders, operating from the Atlantic coastline, pushed the economic frontier northwards again, but only by a matter of two or three hundred miles. By 1800 there was still far more of West Africa south of the Sahara which looked northwards for its contacts with the outside world than southwards to the Atlantic coast and the trade of Europe. And, of course, through the whole vast region to the east of Lake Chad there remained no other source of outside contacts but the northern one. The civilisation of the Sudanic belt exercised some influence as far south as the equatorial forests and the Nile swamps.

At the beginning of our period, therefore, the whole of Africa north of the Equator can be considered together. All this part of the continent was in some sense within the range of Muslim civilisation. All but a fraction of it looked northwards and

Highlands
Limits of Desert
Limits of rain forest
Line of 15ins annual
average rainfall—
limits of normal
cultivation

1  Northern Africa: geographical features and vegetation

eastwards for its outside contacts, and in this it differed from most of the southern part of the continent.

### Countries of the Mediterranean coast

By the end of the eighteenth century men in the Muslim world as a whole had lost much of the energy and sense of purpose that had driven them to produce such a brilliant culture in the early centuries of Islam. They had failed to keep abreast of the new inventions and techniques being discovered in western Europe, particularly in military affairs and transport (such as the improvements made in sailing-ships). This failure to make progress affected all parts of Africa considered in this chapter in one way or another. It applied in particular to the lands north of the Sahara from Egypt in the east to Mauretania in the west. All these countries except Morocco had formed since the sixteenth century a part of the Turkish Ottoman empire (so-called after Othman, the founder of the ruling dynasty), with its capital at Istanbul. (Istanbul had earlier been called Byzantium when it was the capital of the eastern Roman empire.) By the eighteenth century Ottoman power had declined considerably from the peak reached two centuries earlier. Provincial rulers now acted almost independently of the Sultan at Istanbul. ('Sultan' is an Arabic word for the secular authority of a ruler. There were many sultanates in the Muslim world; the Ottoman was the greatest.)

Egypt at this time was ruled by the *amirs* (commanders) of the *mamluks*. These were slaves who had been captured as boys from the lands on the fringes of the Muslim world, from the Christian lands around the Caucasus. Unlike slaves in most other societies, however, they enjoyed a highly privileged position. They were given a special education as Muslims and as cavalry soldiers. At the end of their military service they were freed, and could reach the highest positions as *amirs* in the Ottoman military and civil service in Egypt. These *amirs* themselves recruited fresh slave troops to form their own armed supporters, and so, generation after generation, new *mamluks* were brought to Egypt. They had governed the country since 1260, and the Ottoman conquest in 1517 had done little to reduce their power. To the peasant millions of Egypt who toiled and were taxed, *Mamluk* rule was a harsh one. But it supported a leisured and educated class which made Cairo, at least, one of the greatest centres of luxury and learning in the whole of the Muslim world.

West of Egypt, the countries of Tripoli, Tunis, Algeria and Morocco were known to the Arabs collectively as *al-Maghrib* (the West). Here, in contrast with Egypt, the authority of governments rarely extended far beyond the main cities. In the hinterland of all these countries lived fierce nomadic tribes, both Berbers and Bedouin (Arabic *bedawi*, tent-dwellers) Arabs. These could only be rather loosely controlled by playing off one against another. In Tripoli the Ottoman government had been represented since 1711 by the local Karamanli family, which had concentrated its efforts mainly on developing the trans-Saharan trade from Bornu and the Hausa states. By this route came a steady supply of Negro slaves, who were distributed by the merchants of Tripoli to Istanbul, Damascus, Cairo, and all over the western part of the Muslim world. Tripoli was likewise a distributing centre for the splendid leatherwork of the Hausa cities, already well known in western Europe as 'Morocco', and for the kola-nuts brought by the Hausa merchants all the way from the Ashanti forests. These were one of the few stimulants permitted by Islam, and were served as a luxury throughout the Middle East.

Tripoli, however, had no monopoly of the trans-Saharan trade. Perhaps the greatest centre of the desert trade was at the oasis of Ghadames, where Tunisia, Algeria and Libya now meet. The town stood where caravan routes from the central and the western Sudan met, and Ghadames merchants were well known alike in Hausaland and Timbuktu. From Ghadames some of the Sudan trade was carried to Tunis and Algiers. These were busy ports from which merchants could more easily reach the markets of western Europe than from Tripoli. The *Beys* (rulers) of Tunis had been drawn since 1705 from the local Hussainid family, whose armed forces protected a large settled population from the attacks of the nomadic Berbers of the eastern Atlas. These peasant farmers of the Tunisian plain were some of the greatest wheat producers of the whole Mediterranean area. In the coastal towns a sophisticated middle class of merchants and administrators, enjoying a long tradition of Islamic civilisation and learning, ran a more orderly system of government than was possible in any other Maghrib country.

The Ottoman rulers of Algiers were known as the *Deys*. Unlike the rulership of Tunis, this office had not fallen into the hands of a single family, to be passed down from father to son. It was filled on the death of the reigning Dey by election from among a group of merchants and soldiers who were the most influential men in the city. The merchants, called *Corsairs* by Europeans (from an Italian word meaning to chase), traded by sea with the European countries. Occasionally they committed acts of piracy against European shipping, for which they became famous. During the seventeenth century Algiers had been one of the richest and most attractive cities of the Mediterranean. Dr Shaw, an English traveller early in the eighteenth century, commented favourably on the surroundings of the city:

The hills and vallies round about Algiers are all over beautified with gardens and country-seats, whither the inhabitants of better fashion retire, during the heats of the summer season. They are little white houses, shaded with a variety of fruit-trees and ever-greens; which, besides the shade and retirement, afford a gay and delightful prospect towards the sea. The gardens are all of them well stocked with melons, fruit, and pot-herbs of all kinds. The natives of Algiers live extremely happy, for though the government is despotic it is not so in reality.

> (T. Shaw, 'Travels and observations relating to Barbary', in Pinkerton, *Voyages*, vol. xv.)

Even at the time of its surrender to the French in 1830 it was described as 'perhaps the best regulated city in the world'. The French conquerors found that the majority of the Algerines were better educated than the majority of the local Frenchmen. This was after half a century of grave political disorders due to revolts among the Arab and Berber tribes who roamed over the high plateaux of the interior behind the coastal plains. These tribes were led by *marabouts*, the Muslim holy men, and they carried their attacks to the very outskirts of the cities on the Mediterranean shore.

In Morocco the extent of territory paying tribute into the Sultan's treasury had greatly declined since the late sixteenth and early seventeenth centuries. Then, for a few years, the kingdom had stretched right across the desert to Timbuktu. Increasingly, as in Algeria, tribal groups from the high Atlas and the desert fringes penetrated the settled areas and extorted tribute from the peasants of the plains. The inefficient armies of the Sultan could do little to prevent them. Nevertheless Morocco was still the terminus of a considerable trade to the south. Morocco continued to control the production of most of the salt consumed in the western Sudan, and it was the need for salt which kept the gold of the Upper Senegal–Niger region flowing northwards across

2 Northern Africa in 1800

the desert rather than westwards to the Atlantic, where the French at St Louis, on the mouth of the Senegal river, were so anxious to receive it. (The exchange of gold and salt had been a major item of trade since the early Middle Ages.) Slaves from Timbuktu still went northwards to Morocco in great numbers. Despite the direct sea-routes, a great many European manufactures, especially English cotton goods, were distributed over West Africa by Moroccan merchants who bought them at the port of Mogador. Commercially and culturally, if not politically, Mauretania belonged to Morocco. Arabic-speaking Moors lived all over the western edge of the Sahara as far south as the banks of the Senegal. Their holy men practised the characteristic Maghribi forms of *maraboutism*, becoming followers of such Muslim religious orders as the Ramaniyya, which was founded in 1770 in Kabylia (Algeria), and the Tijaniyya. This was established in 1781 by Sidi Ahmad Tijani at Ain Mahdi, near Laghouat on the edge of the desert in southern Algeria. Tijani's teaching was accepted by the great Moroccan university at Fez, and his order prospered in Mauretania, and among the Tuareg tribesmen of the central Sahara.

### States of the Sudan region

Most of the states to the south of the Sahara were affected in some degree by the stagnation of the Islamic world as a whole. Generally there was less security for traders and pilgrims than there had been, and, in consequence, less wealth, less learning and less religion. Among the states most affected was Ethiopia, which, though Christian in religion, lay close to the Arabian heartlands of Islam and suffered severely from the decline in Red Sea trade. Ethiopia was still at the end of the eighteenth century disturbed on its southern frontier by the invasions of pagan Galla which had been going on since the early sixteenth century. The Galla were a people whose language and origins were similar to the Somalis. The capital of Ethiopia had been fixed, in the seventeenth century, at Gondar, but this attempt at centralisation had not been successful. When emperors moved about their whole kingdom, they could keep an eye on what was going on. But afterwards, the authority of the monarch was acknowledged only locally around Gondar. Governors of the outlying provinces were able to rule independently of his control. Since the expulsion of the Jesuit missionaries in 1632 virtually the only foreigners to be permitted entry had been the handful of skilled artisans from eastern Europe who were always employed about the court. The country had turned in upon itself, and the result had been nearly ruinous. Jesus II (1730–55) was the last of the eighteenth-century emperors to exercise any real authority. After that, rival emperors became a regular feature; and by the early nineteenth century one of them had fallen into such abject poverty that, when he died, there was not enough money in the treasury to pay for a coffin.

West of Ethiopia lay the Funj sultanate, with its capital at Sennar on the Blue Nile, which during the sixteenth and seventeenth centuries had been a considerable centre of trade and learning. When the Scotsman James Bruce, who wrote a marvellous description of his dangerous travels in Ethiopia, passed through the country on his way down the Blue Nile in 1770, there was still a standing army of 1,800 horse and 14,000 infantry. The sultans had by then lost control of Nubia and of Kordofan, and the rich trade in ivory, which had formerly been exchanged for Indian cottons at Jidda, on the Arabian side of the Red Sea, had now shrunk to a trickle. Bruce was not impressed by what he saw there. 'War and treason', he wrote, 'appear to be the only occupations of this horrid people, whom Heaven has separated by almost impassable deserts from the rest of mankind.'

More prosperous than the Funj sultanate were now those of Darfur and Wadai, one on each side of the modern frontier between the Sudan Republic and Chad. Though nominally Muslim, it is clear from the early nineteenth-century accounts of Muhammad al-Tunisi, one of the *ulama*, or religious dignitaries of Cairo and a lecturer in the French medical school there, that here, as in many states of the western Sudan, the ancient pagan ideas of divine kingship still persisted. Al-Tunisi describes an annual ceremony of re-covering the royal drums, when a boy and a girl were sacrificed; and he also describes the sultans taking part in almost Pharonic rituals of seedtime and harvest:

At the beginning of the planting season the Sultan rides out in great pomp, escorted by more than a hundred young women, by his slave boys and by a troop of flute-players. When he reaches the open fields, he dismounts from his horse, takes different kinds of seeds, and sows them, while a slave hoes the ground. (*Voyage au Darfour*, p. 159.)

The wealth of these two states consisted of slaves raided by their armies of horsemen from among the defenceless pagan tribes to the south, and also in the rich copper deposits of Hofrat an-Nahas accessible from both of them. The main trade-route for the region was the *Darb al-'Arba'in* (the Forty Days Road) leading due northwards to reach the Nile at Asyut.

The ancient empire of Kanem-Bornu, with its wide territories to the east and west of Lake Chad, was probably, at the end of the eighteenth century, the most civilised of the Sudanic states. It was no longer as powerful as it had been at two earlier periods of its history; but its rulers were still at least pious and literate Muslims, and justice was administered according to Islamic law. The capital at this time was the brick-built town of N'gazargamo, some sixty miles west of Lake Chad, the ruins of which can still be seen, and cover a circular area nearly two miles in diameter. Here the *mais* (kings) lived a dignified but secluded existence supported by the tribute collected for them by their provincial governors from the peasantry of a kingdom measuring perhaps 600 by 300 miles.

Commercially, however, the most active part of the central Sudan was not Bornu but the city-states of Hausaland lying along its western flank. Though never politically united, these Hausa cities were unique in the Sudan in possessing manufacturing industries on a really important scale. Weaving, dyeing, leather-work, glass-making, smithing and metal-work of every description were carried out. At the end of the eighteenth century Katsina was still the leading city: soon it was to be Kano, already second, with Zaria a close third. It was from these cities rather than from N'gazargamo that the great caravan-routes radiated out across the Sahara to Tripoli and Ghadames and on to Tunis. Bornu with its cavalry armies supplied most of the slaves exported northwards. The manufactures were from Hausaland and their distribution covered the whole of northern Africa.

South of the Sahara from the Maghrib, the powerful empires of the western Sudan of medieval times had broken up by the end of the eighteenth century into many little weak kingdoms. (Medieval times or the Middle Ages: the period from roughly the tenth to the sixteenth centuries.) The great empire of the Songhay Askias, which had stretched in the sixteenth century from the upper Senegal to the frontiers of modern Nigeria, had come to an end with the Moroccan invasion of 1591. At the battle of Tondibi the Moroccans used fire-arms for the first time against Sudanese cavalry and foot-soldiers armed only with bows and spears. The conquerors settled down, and their descendants formed a new ruling-class, the *arma* (shooters, gunmen), which soon became independent of the Sultan of Morocco, the soldiers electing their own *pashas* at Timbuktu and their *kaids* in the garrison towns around the loop of the Niger bend from Jenne to Gao.

After the Moroccan conquest what remained of the ruling-class of Songhay retreated down the Niger and set up an independent government in the southerly province of Dendi. Upstream from Jenne, on the western side of the Niger bend, the Mande subjects of the Songhay empire broke up into an immense number of little village states, although here and there in Mandeland, families and clans of pagan war-lords, getting fire-arms in exchange for slaves, set up some larger kingdoms like those of Segu and Kaarta. However, the really vital region of the western Sudan during the seventeenth and eighteenth centuries was the far west. Here, in Futa Toro on the south bank of the lower Senegal, there had grown up in the medieval period an extraordinarily virile people of mixed Berber and Negro descent, known as the Fula (French: *Peul*; Hausa: *Fulani*). Unlike any other negroid people of the western Sudan, the Fulani were mainly specialised pastoralists. The constant need to find fresh grazing grounds for their cattle caused many of them to leave their homelands. As early as the fifteenth century they were spread out in small groups all over the savanna belt of West Africa as far to the east as Hausaland. Until the eighteenth century these scattered Fula were mostly pagan. However, those Fula who remained in their Futa Toro homelands were converted to Islam by *marabouts* from Mauretania in the sixteenth and seventeenth centuries and formed Muslim brotherhoods, full of zeal for their new faith. One Fula clan, the Torodbe, became the missionary and clerical leaders of the whole of the Fula nation. Wherever Fula were dispersed, there Torodbe preachers were to be found, and with the belief in conversion by *jihad*, or holy war. It was, of course, but a short step from religious revival to political revolution. The two bases of the Fula movement were Futa Toro, and Masina, a Fula-led state south-west of Timbuktu, once tributary to Songhay, which became independent after the Moorish conquest. From Masina in the eighteenth century Torodbe missionaries carried the *jihad* to Futa Jallon, the mountain country on the borders of Guinea and Sierra Leone, and eastwards across the Niger bend to Say. From this background of missionary zeal and holy war, the great Fulani *jihad* of the early nineteenth century arose.

It is often said that the seventeenth and eighteenth centuries were a period of decline in the western Sudan, and certainly this was a time of great political disorder. But, thanks to the Torodbe and other clans of religious leaders, much of the learning of the medieval Sudan was kept alive. It is possible that by the end of the eighteenth century both Islam and Arabic education were more widely spread than they had been during the great days of the medieval empires. Despite the political disorders, trade continued to flow. There seems to have been a breakdown in communications between the western and the central Sudan. This was because, after the defeat of Songhay, no other power was able to control the fierce Tuareg nomads living to the north and east of the Niger bend. But the routes running north-west from Timbuktu and north from the Senegal remained open and active until well into the nineteenth century—more active by far than the routes from Timbuktu westwards to the Atlantic coast.

### States of the woodland and the forest

It was among the states of the woodland and forest zones to the south of the savanna belt that the coming of the Europeans and the Atlantic trade had made by the eighteenth century a crucial change. In origin these states were offshoots of the kingdoms to the north of them. In all probability the Akan states of modern Ghana and the Ivory Coast were offshoots of the Mande kingdoms in the region west of the Niger bend, whilst the states of the Edo- and Yoruba-speakers in southern Nigeria, the Fon-speakers of Dahomey, and of the Gur-speakers of northern Ghana, Upper Volta and western Niger, were all in some sense the offspring of pre-Islamic kingdoms in the Hausa region. These woodland and forest states were more backward than their parent kingdoms to the north. The dense tropical vegetation made them difficult to reach, and the tsetse fly prevented the use of cattle and horses. They were rather isolated from outside influences until they were caught up in the Atlantic slave-trade. As Samuel Johnson, the historian of the Yorubas, pointed out:

It should be remembered that light and civilisation with the Yorubas came from the north. . . The centre of light and activity, of large populations and industry, was therefore in the interior, whilst the coast tribes were scanty in number, ignorant and degraded, not only from their distance from the centre of light, but also (later) through their demoralising intercourse with Europeans and the slave trade.

It was the same in Ghana and the Ivory Coast as it was in Nigeria. The most important of the woodland and forest states had at first been those on the northern side. The smallest and the most backward, populated only by fishermen and salt-makers, had been the little states on the coast.

The Atlantic slave-trade, which was begun by the Portuguese early in the sixteenth century, when a trickle of Africans was shipped across the ocean to work in the Spanish and Portuguese colonies in South America and on the islands of the Caribbean, had developed by the end of the seventeenth century into a steady flood. Most of the European maritime countries took part in it, especially Britain and France. The brisk competition for slaves among the European powers meant that the states on and near the coast had easy access to fire-arms, which they exchanged for slaves from the Europeans. In the eighteenth century a typical payment for 'a man and a girl' was

> One roll tobacco, one string pipe coral,
> One gun, three cutlasses, one brass blunderbuss,
> Twenty-four linen handkerchiefs, five patches (of cloth),
> Three jugs rum, twelve pint mugs, one laced hat.
> (From the log-book or journal of a slaving ship.)

The fire-arms were used against the formerly more important states inland. Within the woodland and forest states there had been by the end of the eighteenth century a considerable change in the balance of power. The rising states were those based near the coast, especially Ashanti and Dahomey, which had grown by the use of fire-arms acquired through the Atlantic slave-trade. The most dramatic demonstration of this shift in power occurred in 1745 when the musketmen of Ashanti defeated the armoured cavalry of Dagomba, who in any earlier period would have chased them mercilessly out of any open country they had dared to enter. This process, begun in the seventeenth and eighteenth centuries, was to be carried much farther in the nineteenth.

### The encircling power of Europe

The only real colonial power operating in the northern half of Africa at the end of the eighteenth century was Ottoman Turkey. Its dependencies in Egypt, Tripoli, Tunis and Algiers were, admittedly, almost 'self-governing', but they did at least contribute revenue to the Sultans at Istanbul. The European powers trading with North and West Africa had, in contrast, nothing but a few footholds, in the shape of fortified trading factories scattered along the West African coast from St Louis on the Senegal to Whydah in Dahomey. These forts, whether British, Danish, Dutch, French or Portuguese, were designed mainly to protect the operations of one group of European traders from the competition of another group. Few of the castles could have withstood a determined attack by the local Africans, and their governors had to be cautious in exercising jurisdiction outside the walls. They carried on their trade with the help of middlemen living in the coastal towns. Though they were exporting by the end of the century around 100,000 slaves a year from West Africa alone, the Europeans seldom captured a single slave for themselves, and save for the French on the Senegal it was the rarest thing for any European to venture a dozen miles inland. Nor did there seem to be at any time in the eighteenth century the slightest likelihood of a change in the pattern of these relationships, which were satisfactory to the Europeans and the Africans alike. It is true that by the end of the century the slave-trade was under attack in one or two European countries. A judge in an English court had declared in 1772 that there was no such thing as slavery on English soil. And 15 years later a group of philanthropists in England—men who were inspired by the religious revival started by John Wesley to improve the condition of the poor and down-trodden—bought a few square miles of the Sierra Leone peninsula for the purpose of settling Negro slaves freed in England and across the Atlantic in Canada. From this tiny beginning, the result of the stirring of the consciences of a few distinguished men, truly 'a cloud no bigger than a man's hand', sprang the ever-growing flood of European interference in tropical Africa during the century to come. But nobody at the time could have foreseen this.

To contemporaries the change in the balance of power in the Mediterranean must have seemed much more impressive than any growth of European power in tropical Africa. To Britain, and therefore to France, India and the routes to India were already a matter of the most serious strategic importance. When these two powers were locked in combat at the end of the century, it seemed a natural move that Britain should forestall the French by seizing the Cape of Good Hope from the Dutch. That Napoleon should reply by occupying Egypt was surprising only in that it finally showed the weakness of the Ottoman empire in relation

to European military might. The Mamluk armies surrendered to
the French in a single battle fought near the Pyramids in 1798.
The French were removed three years later only through the
powerful assistance of the British. It was all very well for al-
Jabarti, a citizen of Cairo, and an eyewitness of these events, and
the last of the traditional Muslim chroniclers of Egypt, to write:

> The presence of the French in Cairo was intolerable...Muslims died of
> shame when they saw their wives and daughters walking the streets un-
> veiled, and appearing to be the property of the French...It was bad
> enough for them to see the taverns that had been established in all the
> bazaars and even in several mosques...The scum of the population was
> doing well, because it benefited from the new freedom. But the *élite* and
> the middle class experienced all sorts of vexation.

What had happened once, could happen again. It was only
surprising that it did not happen for another 80 years.

## 2

## AFRICA SOUTH OF THE EQUATOR

### The lands of the Bantu

The geography and climate of Africa south of the Equator is much
less simple than that of the northern half of the continent. Very
briefly, however, high and rather dry steppe country runs south
from the Ethiopian highlands through East Africa. It then crosses
over towards the western side of the subcontinent, ending up in
the Kalahari Desert and the dry lands of the Orange Free State
and Basutoland on one side of it, and of South-West Africa on
the other. On the other hand, low-lying and distinctly humid
country extends from the Cameroons right across the northern
half of the Congo basin to Lakes Tanganyika and Nyasa. From
there it continues down the Zambezi valley to the Indian Ocean
and round through southern Mozambique into Natal. In general
the steppe country is too dry for agriculture, whilst the dense
forests of the humid region make farming difficult. The best
conditions for human occupation are found in the borderlands
between the two zones, and therefore in the very middle of the
subcontinent. This is where the dense populations still are; and

this is where political institutions first developed, and where at the end of the eighteenth century they were most flourishing.

There is one particularly striking fact about the peoples who live in Africa south of the Equator, which is that nearly all of them speak very closely related languages belonging to a family known as Bantu (from the common word *muntu*, a man, plural *bantu*, people). The exceptions to this rule, the people who speak languages which do not belong to the Bantu family, are all found in the dry zones of the north-east (parts of Kenya and Tanzania) and the south-west, where the practice of agriculture is difficult. It looks therefore as though the Bantu-speakers were the first agriculturalists in this part of Africa. From the study of language relationships it seems as though the 'cradle-land' from which they dispersed was the present-day Katanga, south-west of Lakes Tanganyika and Mweru. Starting perhaps 2,000 years ago, the early Bantu spread from this central area in all directions. There were four main regions where dense populations grew up and powerful states arose: the light woodlands south of the Congo rain-forest, including the Katanga itself; the interlacustrine lands (or lands between the East African Lakes); the hilly region on either side of the lower Congo river; and the southern Rhodesian plateau.

(1) *The Luba–Lunda states.* In the light woodland region extending for five or six hundred miles to the south of the Congo forest—that is to say, in the southern half of the Congo basin, up to and including the Congo–Zambezi watershed—conditions were almost ideal for human occupation. Rainfall was adequate, but not excessive. There was excellent fishing in the northward-flowing tributaries of the Congo river system, and hunting in the strips of forest which lined the river-banks, with plenty of open country suitable for agriculture in between the streams. The rich mineral deposits of the Katanga were being extensively exploited as early as the eighth and ninth centuries, and metal-working in iron and copper had even then reached an advanced stage. The earliest large states in this region would appear to have been those of the Luba peoples in the northern half of the Katanga. By the end of the eighteenth century, however, the two most important kingdoms were those of the Lunda, farther to the west and south. These were the kingdom of the Mwata Yamvo, which occupied the whole south-western corner of the modern Congo Republic, and the kingdom of the Mwata Kazembe, astride the Luapula

3 Africa south of the Equator: geographical features and vegetation. Parts of central Tanzania and around Lake Rudolf in Kenya have less than 15 ins. annual average rainfall.

river in southern Katanga. These great states, however, were but the centre of a whole cluster of smaller ones, which filled up most of the southern Congo, the interior of Angola and north-western and north-eastern Zambia.

The rulers of the two great Lunda kingdoms and of several of the more important outlying states were kings who were regarded as divine. These were very like those in Darfur and Wadai, described in Chapter 1. The courts of these kings, and the rituals connected with them, provided the centres for larger and more progressive societies than would have been possible without them. The capitals of the Lunda kings, though not as permanent as West African towns, were considerable centres of government and trade. The palace population was large because the kings took hundreds of wives and concubines drawn from all the main family groups in the country. The court officials were numerous. So also were the skilled craftsmen—potters, smiths, weavers, basket-makers, brewers, wood-carvers, huntsmen and traders— the majority of whom congregated round the capital, and lived off the tribute paid in foodstuffs by all the surrounding country- side. Describing such towns as late as 1906, the German explorer Leo Frobenius wrote:

When I penetrated into the region of the Kasai and the Sankuru I found villages still existing whose principal streets were lined on both sides, and for miles on end, with four rows of palm-trees, and whose charmingly decorated houses were each of them a work of art. There was not a man who did not carry sumptuous weapons of iron or copper, with inlaid hilts and damascened blades. Everywhere there were velvets and silken stuffs. Every cup, every pipe, every spoon was a piece of artistry, fully worthy of comparison with the creations of Europe.

(2) *The interlacustrine kingdoms.* 'Interlacustrine' means 'be- tween the lakes' and is the region bordering upon the eastern edge of the great Congo forest and taking in all the country between Lake Albert, Lake Victoria and the northern part of Lake Tanganyika. This region today covers southern Uganda, north-west Tanzania, Rwanda, Burundi and adjacent parts of the eastern Congo. All of it is pleasant, easy country to live in. The average rainfall is between 30 and 40 inches, and the rains are well-distributed throughout the year. Not only has the popu- lation there grown by natural increase, but like all rich countries it has attracted waves of foreign conquerors. These came mostly from the Ethiopian borderlands and from the plains and swamps of the Nile and its tributaries in the southern Sudan. They were Nilotes and Nilo-Hamites, physically and linguistically distinct from the Bantu. By the end of the eighteenth century six large neighbouring states had grown up here—Buganda, Bunyoro,

4   Africa south of the Equator in 1800

Ankole, Karagwe, Rwanda and Burundi—which are shown on
Fig. 4. Though not as big as the great states of the Sudanic
belt of the northern part of the continent, all of them probably
had populations of half a million or more people. As with the
pre-Islamic states of the Sudan, they were ruled by divine kings

who governed through an elaborate hierarchy of court officials and provincial chiefs. As with the kingdoms of the Mwata Yamvo and the Mwata Kazembe, many smaller states clustered around these big ones, some of them paying tribute to one or other of the large kingdoms, but most in practice independent of all of them.

The first European travellers who came upon this region in the mid-nineteenth century felt that they were entering a new world. They had walked seven or eight hundred miles from the East Coast along tortuous footpaths never more than a few inches wide, through sparsely inhabited country where provisions were hard to come by and even drinking water was often a problem. Along most of their route every day's march had brought them into the territory of some new petty potentate with whom they had to negotiate permission to pass. And then suddenly they found themselves in a world of plenty and of order. Here a ruler's writ or authority could run for a hundred miles from his capital. His messengers sped along wide, well-beaten roads to the provincial or district headquarters to which they were going. Speke and Grant in 1862 stayed with the 'ever-smiling' King Rumanika of Karagwe while runners were sent to announce their arrival to Kabaka Mutesa of Buganda. Once their passport was granted, they were accompanied for the rest of their journey by royal guides, and food and lodging was arranged at the end of each day's march.

(3) *The Kongo kingdom.* To the south of the estuary of the Congo river, in what is today northern Angola, lay the kingdom of Kongo, which, when discovered by the Portuguese at the very end of the fifteenth century, was at the height of its power. A sixteenth-century Roman Catholic priest described the authority of the Kongo monarchy in the following terms:

At the head of the Kongo kingdom is a king of kings who is the absolute lord of all his realm, and none may intervene in any of his affairs. He commands as he pleases. He is not subject to any law. The village chiefs have above all to take care to collect from their subjects the taxes which are due to the king, and which they each of them carry to the governor of their province. The governor presents himself twice in each year at the royal capital in order to pay in the tribute, and if the king is satisfied, he replies with the one word *wote*, which means 'you have done well'. In this case the governor esteems himself highly favoured and makes many clappings of his two hands. As a sign of his joy he throws himself on the ground, covering his body with dust. His servants do the same, and then take him on their shoulders, and go through all the city crying his praises. But if the king does not say this word *wote*, he retreats greatly discomfited, and another time he takes care to bring a larger tribute. The tribute is not fixed as to quantity: each brings as much as he can. But if the governor does not do better, the king addresses to him a strong reprimand, and takes away his post. Such a man then becomes as poor as the most miserable of all the blacks.

(Vatican document quoted in J. Cuvelier and L. Jadin, *L'ancien Congo d'après les archives romaines* (Brussels, 1954), pp. 33–4.)

By the end of the eighteenth century the kingdom was very weak compared to its previous magnificence. It had fallen apart into the provinces that had formerly owed allegiance to the king, who by then exercised little power even over the lands immediately surrounding his capital. The region as a whole was, however, a densely populated and even prosperous one. Inland from Kongo, on the north bank of Stanley Pool, there was the kingdom of the Bateke, with its ruler who bore the title of Makoko. And to the north of the estuary, between the Bateke and the sea, there were the kingdoms of the Luango coast, which had once paid tribute to Kongo, but had long since become independent. All this region was an exception to the general rule that the most important states were to be found in the interior of Bantu Africa, and the reason would seem to be largely geographical. To the west of the Congo forest, both north and south of the cataracts and falls of the lower Congo between its estuary and Stanley Pool, there is a belt of high grassland and light woodland. This really forms an extension of the geographical conditions of the southern Congo. Probably these kingdoms were founded by migrants from the east, who moved round the southern margins of the forest from Lubaland; but it is possible that these kingdoms had had connections with the states of West Africa from ancient times.

(4) *Mwenemutapa.* The fourth and last region of Bantu Africa which had developed a dense population and a system of powerful states was the region of the southern Rhodesian plateau, and the neighbouring parts of the Zambezi valley and the lowlands of southern Mozambique. This was a region rich in gold and ivory, where at least from the fifteenth century onwards a series of Shona-speaking states had recognised the paramount authority of a great king called the Mwenemutapa. This ruler had his capital on the southern edge of the Zambezi valley some sixty or seventy miles north-east of modern Salisbury. When the Portuguese

colonised the lower Zambezi valley from the late sixteenth century onwards, they gave protection to successive Mwenemutapas who were their inland neighbours. Gradually the Mwenemutapas became so dependent upon the Portuguese that outlying parts of their empire broke away and became independent. By the end of the eighteenth century, therefore, they were ruling only a small remnant of their former kingdom and this only with Portuguese support and protection. But other, formerly dependent, states were still in existence round about, including one, the Rozwi kingdom of the Changamires, that had its capital at Great Zimbabwe. Here the earlier buildings go back as far as the eleventh century, and were probably built by the ancestors of the Mwenemutapas, before their capital moved north to the Zambezi in the fifteenth century. The more impressive and well-built structures at Great Zimbabwe, such as the conical tower and the great girdle-wall, are now recognised to be the work of the later Changamire dynasty.

### The trade-routes of Bantu Africa

With the exception of the Lower Congo region, therefore, the most populous and politically advanced parts of Bantu Africa ran in a great crescent through the centre of the subcontinent. This belt ran from the interlacustrine region in the north through the southern Congo region to that of Rhodesia and southern Mozambique. The most striking fact about these Bantu states was that, unlike their counterparts in the Sudanic belt of Africa, they were almost wholly cut off from the outside world. The great Bantu states completely lacked, until after the eighteenth century, the Islamic influence which was so important in the more powerful states of the Sudan. Trade-links with the outside world were difficult to establish and slow to develop. So far as we know at present, the only trade-route deep into any part of Bantu Africa during medieval times was up the Zambezi valley from the southern part of the east coast. Here the Arabs were trading cloth and beads for gold and ivory at least by the tenth century and possibly earlier. The Mwenemutapa's state used this line of approach to the Indian Ocean. In the sixteenth century the Portuguese replaced the Arabs on the Zambezi, and henceforward this line of communication ran through their hands.

The more important part of the Portuguese contribution, however, was their opening of the Atlantic coast of Bantu Africa to sea-borne trade with Europe and South America. Their first venture in this direction was with the Kongo kingdom, where they made the Kongo kings their allies. They also supplied them with Christian missionaries and technical and military aid. In the course of a hundred years, however, their interests had shifted southwards to Luanda and Benguela, where they found it easier than in Kongo to obtain slaves, which were needed in ever increasing numbers to work the sugar plantations of their colony of Brazil. The demand of the Portuguese for slaves was mainly supplied by the almost continuous wars which they fought against the Mbundu peoples of central Angola. They also sent African trading agents (*pombeiros*) to open commerce with the interior. The slave-trader Barbot observed in 1700 that:

These slaves have other slaves under them, sometimes a hundred, or a hundred and fifty, who carry the commodities on their heads up into the country. Sometimes these pombeiros stay out a whole year, and then bring back with them four, five, or six hundred slaves.

(Barbot, *A Description of the Coasts of North and South Guinea; and of Ethiopia Inferior, Vulgarly called Angola,* 1746.)

In this way the Portuguese made indirect contact with the Lunda kingdom of Mwata Yamvo and its many satellites. By the end of the eighteenth century the main Lunda kingdoms and their related dynasties had acquired guns, cloth and other European luxuries, and their own industries had developed greatly by learning from European examples. Splendid axes and cutlasses were made by the Lunda smiths in the period following the European contact. Manioc (or cassava), the South American root-crop, was introduced by the Portuguese and rapidly became the staple food for the whole of the Southern Congo region.

The important region which remained right out of touch with the outside world until late in the eighteenth century was the interlacustrine region. To the west of it lay the Congo forest; to the north lay the Nile swamps; to the east lay the Kenya highlands, inhabited mainly by nomadic and warlike pastoralists such as the Nandi and the Masai. The easiest line of approach, therefore, was from the south-east, but it was a long time before this was developed. It does not seem that the medieval Arab traders and settlers of the east coast had contact with any but the coastal peoples to the north of the Zambezi. Certainly the Portuguese, when they occupied this part of the coast during the sixteenth and seventeenth centuries, had no knowledge of any part of the interior that lay behind. It was in fact only when the

Arabs of Oman (on the Persian Gulf) seized the northern part of the east coast from the Portuguese at the beginning of the eighteenth century that contacts with the interior began to develop; and even then the main agents of this contact appear to have been the Nyamwezi people, who inhabit most of the western part of modern Tanzania, and who found their way down to the coast with ivory. Throughout the late eighteenth and early nineteenth centuries it was the Nyamwezi who organised and operated most of the carrying trade in East Africa. Their caravans covered the whole region from Katanga to the east coast, marching great distances with heavy loads and usually with very little to eat. The early travellers reported how the Nyamwezi boys used to prepare themselves for this way of life by carrying small tusks on their shoulders as they went about the villages. Traditional history relates that it was in the late eighteenth century that the first consignment of plates, cups, saucers, knives and cotton-goods reached the kingdom of Buganda, at the heart of the interlacustrine region. From this time onwards the traditions tell of a steadily growing trade passing to the south of Lake Victoria and through the Nyamwezi country to the Zanzibar coast.

### South Africa: Bantu and Boer

Another part of Bantu Africa which had almost no contact with the outside world until late in the eighteenth century was the region south of the Limpopo in what is now the Republic of South Africa. Two main groups of Bantu peoples lived here—the Sotho-Tswana (Basotho-Bechuana) on the *High Veld* (Dutch, plateau) to the west of the Drakensberg mountains, and the Nguni peoples (Zulu, Pondo, Tembu, Xhosa) in the fertile and well-watered coastal lowlands of Natal and the Transkei. Perhaps just because these Sotho and Nguni peoples were isolated from outside influence or interference, they did not create any large centralised states. Throughout most of Africa, powerful kingdoms developed in response to the threat of invasion, the desire to control trade-routes, or as the result of the conquest of one group by another. None of these forces operated to any large extent in southern Africa until the beginning of the nineteenth century. Until then these peoples remained organised under a large number of ruling clans or families, who frequently quarrelled amongst themselves. In spite of this political instability, the South African Bantu lived fairly prosperously, especially after the introduction of maize, another South American food-crop, which spread there from the Portuguese trading stations in southern Mozambique. Such European visitors as passed through the land in the sixteenth and seventeenth centuries—mostly survivors of shipwrecks—commented on the large herds of sleek cattle. They noticed, however, that iron tools remained scarce except in the neighbourhood of Delagoa Bay. The Governor of the Cape, Simon van der Stel, wrote a dispatch to his superiors in Holland in 1689, telling them of the journey of the crew of a wrecked vessel, the *Stavenisse*. The country of the 'Magossebe'—Ama-Xhosa—is described as follows:

Their riches consist in cattle and assagais, also copper and iron. The country is exceedingly fertile and incredibly populous, and full of cattle, whence it is that lions and other ravenous animals are not very apt to attack men, as they find enough tame cattle to devour. They preserve their corn in cavities under ground, where it keeps good and free from weavels for years.

In their intercourse with each other they are very civil, polite and talkative, saluting each other, whether young or old, male or female, whenever they meet; asking whence they come, and whither they are going, what is their news; and whether they have learned any new songs or dances. The kings are much respected and beloved by their subjects; they wear the skins of buck and leopard. One need not be under any apprehension about meat and drink, as they have in every village a house of entertainment for travellers, where they are not only lodged but fed also.

It was more than a century before the Dutch colony, planted at Cape Town in 1652, made any contact with these south-eastern Bantu peoples. Most of the western Cape Province was still at this period the country of the Hottentots (Khoi) and Bushmen (San)—the hunting and pastoral predecessors of the Bantu, now driven back into the south-western corner of a subcontinent of which they had once been the principal inhabitants. The Dutch settlers at the Cape expanded slowly into the interior, driving out the Bushmen. They made herdsmen and servants of the Khoi, whose tribal organisation was broken by the double attack of colonists and smallpox. This labour force was supplemented by slaves brought from both the west and east coasts of Africa, and from the Dutch possessions in the East Indies. The Dutch settlers and their slaves increased at an almost equal pace—there were some 17,000 of each at the end of the eighteenth century. Intermarriage between all the racial groups at the Cape—Europeans, Negroes, Khoi and Malays—was beginning to produce the mixed Cape coloured population. Not until about 1770 did Boer (Dutch, farmer) and Bantu face one another across the Fish River, thieving each other's cattle by night and arguing about its return by day. There were frequent armed conflicts. In 1795, when the British first seized the Cape from the Dutch at the time of the Napoleonic wars, the problems on the eastern frontier were threatening and dangerous, but might still have been satisfactorily solved, given understanding and good will on both sides, and a firm decision to maintain a permanent frontier between the two races by the European government at the Cape. But by the time the British returned permanently in 1806, the situation on the frontier had passed beyond the hope of peaceful negotiation and control.

### The east coast

At the end of the eighteenth century, therefore, Bantu Africa was still a very secluded region in comparison with most of Africa north of the Equator. The only part of it which had been for any long period in contact with a literate civilisation and a universal faith was the coastal region of East Africa. Here trading settlements were known to Greek geographers as early as the first century A.D., and stone-built Muslim towns were beginning to be founded by the twelfth century. By the seventeenth and eighteenth centuries not only the Arab settlers, but most of the Bantu inhabitants of the coastal belt, were beginning to be Muslims. They also became conscious of belonging to a society much wider than that of a particular part of tropical Africa. Within East Africa the influence of this Swahili–Arab civilisation was very restricted indeed. Arab traders had preceded the Portuguese on the Zambezi, where both Sena and Tete had been built on the sites of earlier Arab settlements. Here also Arab traders resident at the Mwenemutapa's court had instigated the murder of the first and most famous Roman Catholic missionary, Gonçalo de Silveira, in 1569. Silveira journeyed up the Zambezi, and arrived, we are told, lean, haggard and fever-ridden at the court of the Mwenemutapa. After a month's instruction, the Great King, his favourite wife and sister, and 300 relatives and counsellors were baptised. But this success aroused the jealousy of the Arab traders (called in the Portuguese chronicles 'Moors'). They denounced Silveira as a spy and an evil magician, and the Mwenemutapa had him strangled in his sleep. Elsewhere, however, until late in the eighteenth century, there is scarcely a reference to Arab or Swahili activities more than a few miles from the Indian Ocean coast.

## The Portuguese in Africa

After the Arabs came the Portuguese, whose direct influence was confined to the Kongo kingdom, the Kwanza and Zambezi valleys, and to a few offshore islands, including Luanda, Mozambique, Kilwa and Mombasa. In Kongo some thousands of people, including the royal family, became Christians. The Portuguese king corresponded with the King of Kongo as an equal, addressing him as 'Most high and powerful prince and king my brother'. Many of the Kongo people remained Christians for eight or nine generations, until the last links with Europe were cut by the quarrelling and fighting which broke out inside the country from the end of the seventeenth century onwards. On the Kwanza, and again on the Zambezi, some tens of thousands of Africans came to regard themselves as the subjects of the Portuguese rather than of any indigenous African state. Of these perhaps the majority became in some sense Christians, but only a tiny handful acquired any literary education or became assimilated to the Portuguese way of life and culture. In any case, the example of Portuguese manners and culture in such isolated settlements in Angola and Mozambique was not very inspiring. In one way or another, by conquest or by taking a people under their protection, the Portuguese destroyed most of the African states with which they came into direct contact. Much more important were the indirect effects of their presence. Undoubtedly the opening of the Atlantic slave-trade encouraged the building up of African states in the hinterland of Portuguese Angola and Mozambique, as it had done also in West Africa. It was late in the nineteenth century before any Mwata Yamvo set eyes upon a live Portuguese, and yet the Mwata Yamvo's state, no less than that of Ashanti in West Africa, had grown up as a response to the trade brought to Africa by the Europeans. Whoever had guns had power. Whoever had cloth had prestige. These things were bartered for ivory, which was only obtained in sufficient quantities by properly organised elephant hunting, and which had to be transported safely to the Portuguese frontier markets. These activities could only be performed successfully by the ruler of an organised state, who could command obedience over a wide area. Such states could be, and usually were, established and run on completely African lines. The Mwata Yamvo and the Mwata Kazembe, like the Makoko and the Mwenemutapa, were, as we have seen, divine kings, and their political institutions were of a fully African kind. But the Lunda states would not have flourished where they did, or when they did, but for the Portuguese presence in Luanda and on the Zambezi.

After the Portuguese came the Dutch. But the Dutch settled beyond the Bantu sphere. Only after their colony had been growing for 120 years did it begin to affect the south-eastern Bantu. That was only shortly before the situation had been further complicated by the British annexation of the Cape.

## Madagascar

The island of Madagascar, one of the largest in the world, formed a kind of stepping-stone between Asia and Africa. From at least as early as the fifth century A.D. immigrants from South-East Asia had settled on the island, bringing with them Asian food-crops, such as rice and beans, and their distinctive Malagasy language and culture. Swahili–Arab merchant communities had made contact with Madagascar by the eleventh century, and African peoples, more or less Arabised, settled in the western and southern parts in large numbers. By the thirteenth century the Comoro Islands and some of the coastal regions of Madagascar had become part of the Muslim culture that had developed all round the shores of the Indian Ocean. The island probably supplied the East African coastal region with foodstuffs—otherwise it offered little of value to traders. The Portuguese and the Dutch called there for supplies on their voyages to the Far East. Only after coffee from Arabia had been introduced onto the French islands of Réunion and Mauritius in 1720 did Madagascar become of more commercial importance as a supplier of slaves to work on the coffee estates. These naturally came mainly from the eastern side of the island, which faced Réunion and Mauritius.

At the same time, in the eighteenth century, the western part of Madagascar was being exploited by European and Arab settlers on the east and south-east coasts of Africa, for slaves, cattle and food crops. The response of the Malagasy to this trade was similar to that of African peoples on the mainland. With the aid of European fire-arms, powerful states grew up. The greatest of these was the Merina kingdom of the Hova people, which in the nineteenth century conquered two-thirds of the island. The Hova were a group of almost pure Indonesians—the original settlers perhaps added to by much later arrivals. The Merina state was very small in the eighteenth century, stretching just a few miles around Tananarive. In 1787 King Nampoina came to the throne, and embarked upon a career of expansion. By the time of his death in 1810 the Merina kingdom controlled much of the central plateau, and had conquered many of its rivals. Nampoina had built the foundations of a powerful, centrally administered state.

# 3

## WEST AFRICA BEFORE THE COLONIAL PERIOD, 1800–1875

### The Fula jihads

Historians have often written of the nineteenth century in Africa mainly as a period in which Europeans were increasing their influence and power. So far as the first half of the nineteenth century is concerned, however, this is not really the correct way of looking at the history of Africa. In West Africa during this time the most significant happenings were the holy wars or *jihads* of the Fula. These events had nothing to do with direct European intervention in the region, and yet they affected the whole of the western Sudan.

As we have mentioned in Chapter 1, these *jihads* had their origin in the revival of Islam in the western Sudan, which was brought about by the Arabic-speaking Moors who came into Mauretania from across the Sahara in the fifteenth and sixteenth centuries. The leaders of this revival retired from the hustle and bustle of politics and trade, and went to live in remote places. They trained small bands of devoted disciples both in the study of the Islamic scriptures and legal traditions and in their own methods of prayer and devotion. The disciples were formed into brotherhoods (*tariqa*) called after the name of the founding teacher (for example, the Tijaniyya brotherhood named after Ahmad Tijani). The eighteenth-century *jihads* waged in Futa Toro and Futa Jallon were organised by Fula teachers, most of whom belonged to the ancient brotherhood called the Qadiriyya. Uthman dan Fodio, the leader of the great nineteenth-century *jihad* in northern Nigeria and Niger, was a member of this brotherhood.

Uthman dan Fodio was born into the Torodbe clan in 1754, in Gobir, the northernmost of the Hausa states. He studied under a famous teacher at Agades, the capital of the Tuareg state of Air in the Sahara north of his home. Here he came in touch with the reformist ideas then stirring throughout the Muslim world. These were a part of the great reaction of Islam as a whole to the advance of the Christian West. It had begun in Arabia with the Wahhabi movement in the eighteenth century, and led to the reform of old brotherhoods like the Qadiriyya and to the foundation of new ones. Typical of these new brotherhoods were the Tijaniyya, which became particularly powerful in the western Sudan, and the Sanusiyya in Cyrenaica and the eastern Sahara. There was of course no European menace on the spot to react to in West Africa at this time. However, it does seem that, along with the desire to reform the practice of Islam in the Sudan, the religious leaders did have the sense of a threat to the Islamic world in general from expanding European Christendom. Early European explorers of the Sahara region, for example, encountered Muslim teachers who asked them why the British had conquered India (which had a large number of Muslims amongst its population).

This, then, was dan Fodio's background when he returned from Agades to become tutor to the son and heir of the Hausa *sarki* (ruler) of Gobir. In this position he gained a considerable influence in the councils of the state, which he used to spread his zeal for religious reform. In 1802 dan Fodio's pupil Yunfa became *sarki* on the death of his father. Yunfa proved a bitter disappointment to his former tutor, who now retreated from the court to his native village, where he was soon joined by members of the reforming party. These became so numerous that Yunfa threatened him with military action. Dan Fodio, pointing to the historical parallel of the Prophet Muhammad's flight (*hijra*) from Mecca, then retired to the remote district of Gudu (21 February 1804). At Gudu his supporters rallied round him in such numbers that he found himself at the head of a really formidable army of warriors (Arabic *mujahidun*, from the word *jihad*), all burning with religious fervour and intent on *jihad*. Dan Fodio was unanimously proclaimed *Amir al-Mu'minin* (in Hausa *Sarkin Musulmi*, Commander of the Faithful), which was the traditional title of the caliphs, or successors, of the Prophet. (The caliphs were the rulers of the Arab empire in the early, glorious days of the Muslim era.) After being proclaimed Commander of the Faithful, dan Fodio swore to the disinterestedness of his intentions, saying: 'If I fight this battle that I may become greater than my fellow, or that my son may become greater than his son, or that my slave may lord it over his slave, may the Kaffir (infidel) wipe us from the land.'

After the declaration of *jihad*, dissatisfied men came from all the Hausa states to swear allegiance to the *Amir al-Mu'minin* and to receive in exchange the green banner of the True Believers. The puritanical motives of the leaders of the *jihad* are well described by Muhammad al-Tunisi (see Chapter 1), who was in Wadai in 1810 and heard news of its success:

The Falata (Fula) accuse all other Sudanese of impiety and of heresy, maintaining that only by force of arms can they be brought to repentance. They assert that the other Sudanese have altered and adulterated the principles of Islam, that they have broken the criminal code by allowing compensations of money for criminals, which is illegal and proscribed by the Holy Book. They claim that they have undermined the foundations of religion by proclaiming illegal and criminal innovations to be legitimate, by shameful customs such as adultery, the use of fermented drinks, passion for amusement, song and dance, neglect of the daily prayers, and refusal to offer alms for the poor. Each of these crimes and shameful deeds deserves vengeance and calls for a *jihad*. These ideas kindled the minds of the Fula for years, until suddenly there arose amongst them one renowned for his piety and godliness; the *Zaki* (Hausa, lion) who became a reformer and proclaimed the holy war.

Not all the *mujahidun* were animated by such purely religious enthusiasm. The leaders were drawn for the most part from the educated Muslim Fulas of the towns (Hausa, *Fulanin gidda*), who had come to despise, as al-Tunisi shows, the corrupt, half-pagan conduct of the old Hausa ruling families, known collectively as *Habe*. They were supported by many of the town Hausa, who treated the movement as an opportunity to free themselves from the *Habe* rulers and to fight among themselves. The *jihad* was also supported by virtually all of the pastoral Fula (Hausa, *boroje*) of the countryside. These were mostly still pagan but they felt a racial affinity with the town Fula, and even belonged to the same clans. The main motive of most *boroje* was doubtless the hope of being able to loot the wealth of the Hausa towns.

The revolt swept all over Hausaland, the leading towns of

Katsina yielding to dan Fodio's *mujahidun* in 1807, and Kano in 1809. The *Habe* dynasties were replaced by Fula *amirs*, most of whom had been appointed by dan Fodio in 1804 and 1805. Beyond Hausaland to the east, Adamawa, which had long been penetrated by pastoral Fulani, became part of the new empire after a struggle lasting nearly thirty years. The political intrigues of the Fula religious teachers paved the way for the penetration of the *mujahidun* into Nupe and Yorubaland. They occupied the northern provinces of the old Oyo empire (see below, p. 37) which, as the emirate of Ilorin, became a base for the spread of Islam among the Yoruba. To the north-east the *jihad* was halted only in Bornu, where Muhammad al-Kanemi, a warrior and cleric from east of Lake Chad, successfully drove out the invaders. Al-Kanemi took over control of the affairs of Bornu, but the *mai* of the ancient dynasty was allowed to retain his court ceremonial although deprived of all real power. The Scottish traveller Clapperton, who visited Bornu in 1821, remarked on the position of the *mai*:

The Sultanship of Bornu is but a name; the court still keeps up considerable state, and adheres strictly to its ancient customs, and this is the only privilege left them. When the sultan gives audience to strangers, he sits in a kind of cage, made of bamboo, through the bars of which he looks on his visitors, who are not allowed to approach within seventy or eighty yards of his person.

The conquest period over, Uthman dan Fodio, always more of a scholar than a ruler, returned to his books. His empire was divided into two, his son Muhammad Bello ruling the eastern part from the newly founded city of Sokoto, and his brother Abdallah the western part from Gwandu. After Uthman's death in 1817, Bello was recognised by Abdallah as Sultan of Sokoto, and he ruled there until his death in 1837. By this time the religious fervour of the movement was largely spent. The Fulas had turned from religious reformers into a ruling class. Nevertheless it was under Fula rule that Islam first spread outside the towns into the country districts. Their rule was in general more progressive and more effective than that of their *Habe* predecessors, and their importance was by no means ended when Britain and France began to impose their power.

### The jihad in the western Sudan

The successes of the Fula in Hausaland had important effects farther to the west. In 1810 Hamadu Bari (also known as Ahmadu Lobo), one of Uthman's early followers, led an army westwards across the Niger bend and drove out the Bambara overlords from his homeland, the Fula state of Masina. Here, as in Futa Toro and in Futa Jallon, the ground for reform had been prepared by the *jihads* of the previous century. The whole of this area was now undergoing a further period of revival as a result of the spread of the new and powerful brotherhood of the Tijaniyya. In 1826 a young cleric called Umar from Futa Toro made the pilgrimage to Mecca. He was initiated into the Tijaniyya in the holy city, and then returned slowly homewards through the Bornu of al-Kanemi, the Sokoto of Muhammad Bello (whose sister he married), and the Masina of Hamadu Bari. Known now as Al-Hajj Umar (the pilgrim), he settled in Futa Jallon and began to prepare the fiercest *jihad* of them all. He equipped his force with fire-arms obtained from the Europeans at the coast, and at last in 1850 he launched them on the Bambara kingdoms of Segu and Kaarta and then on Masina. Had he not been checked by the French (see below, p. 41), he would have made for Futa Toro also. As it was, when he captured Timbuktu in 1863, his empire, based now at Hamdillahi near the old Bambara capital of Segu, stretched over the whole of the country from the Niger bend to the upper Senegal.

The empire of Al-Hajj Umar did not last as long as that of Uthman dan Fodio. Umar himself was killed in 1864, and it took his son Ahmadu Sefu nearly ten years to establish his right to rule throughout his father's dominions. Even then his rule lasted only until 1884. Nevertheless, the active survival of Islam under French colonisation throughout most of the region occupied by the Mande-speaking peoples was largely due to the revivalist movements carried forcefully into the whole of this region by Al-Hajj Umar.

### The forest states and the outside world

Unlike the situation in the Sudanic region, the changes in the woodland and forest belt of West Africa came about only slowly and sporadically during the first sixty years or so of the nineteenth century. It is true that the whole attitude of the main trading nations towards West Africa underwent a complete change during the last years of the eighteenth century and the earliest years of the nineteenth. Denmark made the slave-trade illegal for her own nationals in 1805, Britain in 1807, Holland in 1814 and France in 1818. In 1815 and 1817 Spain and Portugal restricted their slave-traders to the seas south of the Equator (as far as Portugal was concerned, this meant the trade between Angola and Brazil). Britain even carried this new anti-slavery policy so far as to establish a naval patrol in West African waters and to declare the freed-slave settlement on the Sierra Leone peninsula a Crown Colony (1808).

If they intended to continue trading in West Africa, all these nations had to seek a new basis for their commerce. This search for trade was one of the main reasons why so many European explorers undertook dangerous and arduous expeditions in West Africa during the first half of the nineteenth century. The first were the journeys of Mungo Park to the upper Niger in 1795 and 1805. The greatest was the long journey of the German, Heinrich Barth, as a result of which he wrote a magnificent description of the central and western Sudanic region. Here, as an example of his penetrating eye for detail, is a little of his description of the Tasawa region of northern Hausaland (not far from Uthman dan Fodio's Gobir), which he entered by the desert route from Agades:

Tasawa was the first large place of Negroland proper which I had seen, and it made the most cheerful impression upon me, as manifesting everywhere the unmistakable marks of the comfortable, pleasant sort of life led by the natives: the courtyard fenced with a 'derne' of tall reeds, excluding to a certain degree the eyes of the passer-by; then near the entrance the cool shady place of the 'runfa' for ordinary business and for the reception of strangers... the whole dwelling shaded with spreading trees, and enlivened with groups of children, goats, fowls, pigeons and a horse or a pack-ox. With this character of the dwellings, that of the inhabitants themselves is in entire harmony, its most constant element being a cheerful temperament, bent upon enjoying life, rather given to women, dance, and song, but without any disgusting excess. Drinking fermented liquor cannot be strictly reckoned a sin in a place where a great many of the inhabitants are pagans; but a drunken person, nevertheless, is scarcely ever seen; those who are not Mohammedans only indulge in their 'giya', made of sorghum, just enough to make them merry and enjoy life with more light-heartedness.

(*Travels in Africa*, vol. II, pp. 24, 25.)

This was a state of affairs very similar to that about which the Fula reformers had complained some fifty years previously, apparently with little effect.

Side by side with the search by Europeans for trade-routes and for objects of a new and legitimate commerce, there was the beginning of the first really unselfish Christian activity in Africa. Some Christians in Europe were deeply concerned for Africans as people with a right to share in the benefits of Christianity as well as the useful skills and knowledge built up by Christian civilisation in western Europe. Earlier Roman Catholic missionary efforts had only touched West Africa briefly and at one or two scattered points. The beginning of the nineteenth century, however, saw the establishment of flourishing Church of England (Anglican) and Methodist missions in Sierra Leone. Their converts were to play a most important part in the later history of the whole of the southern part of West Africa. The 1820s saw the coming of the Presbyterian Basel missionaries to the Gold Coast, and by the 1840s all the main Protestant denominations were represented in the Gold Coast, Dahomey, and in western and eastern Nigeria. Roman Catholic missions followed between the 1840s and 1880s.

Still, all these exploring and missionary activities were only the first stages in the development of European influence. The first half of the nineteenth century, from the point of view of African history as opposed to colonial, saw little more than a continuation, and even a strengthening, of the eighteenth-century pattern amongst the woodland and forest peoples of West Africa. Despite the anti-slavery legislation in European countries, and despite the constant patrolling of the British navy, the slave-trade not only continued, but actually increased in scale. Whereas most authorities have estimated the export of slaves from the whole of West Africa at about 100,000 a year at the end of the eighteenth century, by the 1830s it had risen to about 135,000. Slavery, as distinct from the slave-trade, continued to be legal in the southern states of America until 1863, and throughout this period the illicit trade yielded great profits. The trade to Brazil and Cuba continued, though on a decreasing scale, until the 1880s, and as European and American merchants dropped out of the trade for fear of the punishments involved, their places were taken by Brazilian Negroes (Afro-Brazilians), whose operations were much more difficult to detect and prevent.

It would be wrong, however, to draw from these figures the simple conclusion that all the states of the Guinea forest were irretrievably committed to a continuation of the slave-trade.

Ashanti, at least, had long outgrown its period of active expansion, during which the disposal of war captives had temporarily eclipsed the export of gold-dust and ivory. By the nineteenth century it was concerned mainly to hold its wide dominions. It was the sheer military power of Ashanti, fed by the constant exchange of gold-dust for fire-arms with the Dutch at Elmina, which kept the British and their Fante allies along the central stretch of the Gold Coast in a state of constant alarm. The forts were expensive to maintain. They could pay their way only by the levying of customs dues on legitimate trade. Yet the trade-routes were constantly subject to closure through the military operations of the Ashanti against their tributary states in the interior. Even the Fante were discouraged from agricultural production for export by threats of Ashanti invasion. Officially, British jurisdiction, whether vested in an unofficial Council of Merchants, as it was for most of the time up till 1842, or in a Colonial Office governor, as it was thereafter, was limited until 1874 to the coastal forts. Such informal influence as was exercised upon the coastal states was largely concerned with resistance to Ashanti pressure.

If a militaristic and still partially slave-trading Ashanti continued to dominate the affairs of the Gold Coast, the situation on the Slave Coast to the east of it was even more similar to what it had been in the eighteenth century. Here, as the modern air traveller so clearly sees, the coast is nothing but a narrow surf-hammered beach, behind which a vast system of interconnected lagoons provides secure access for canoes to all the rivers of Togoland, Dahomey and Western Nigeria. The methods of the slave-traders of the 1830s along this stretch of coast were described by Richard Lander:

As soon as a vessel arrives at her place of destination, the crew discharge her light cargoe, with the manacles intended for the slaves, and land the captain at the same time. The vessel then cruises along the coast to take in country cloth, ivory, a little gold dust, etc., and if a British man-of-war be near, the crew having nothing on board to excite suspicion, in most cases contrive to get their vessel searched whilst trading with the natives. They return to the place where the cargoe had been loaded, and communicate with the captain on shore who then takes the opportunity of acquainting his crew with the exact time in which he will be in readiness to embark. The vessel then cruises a second time up and down the coast, till the appointed day approaches, when she proceeds to take in her living cargoe.

(Lander, *Records of Captain Clapperton's Last Expedition to Africa*,
vol. II, 238.)

Dahomey, like Ashanti, had by the nineteenth century reached its full territorial extension. Unlike Ashanti, however, it had no export with which to procure the guns which it needed to maintain its military power. So long as the demand for slaves continued, therefore, the kings of Dahomey continued, however unwillingly, to supply it.

The bulk of Slave Coast slaves did not, however, in the nineteenth century at least, come from Dahomey. They came from Yorubaland, and were exported through Porto Novo, Badagry and Lagos. All these ports were to the east of Whydah on the same lagoon system. Although there was a thriving Afro-Brazilian stronghold at Lagos, the main reason for this was the decline and disintegration of the ancient Oyo empire. This was the result of tensions from both north and south. On the one hand the southern Yoruba states—Egba, Ijebu and Ondo—had been growing steadily in power through access to the coastal trade. On the other hand Ilorin and other northern districts of the empire had been penetrated, as had the Hausa states, by the Fula, and were therefore involved in the *jihad*. The beginning of the end came in 1817, when the great chiefs of Oyo, led by Afonja of Ilorin, sent an empty calabash to the *Alafin* (king), Aole, thus signifying that they no longer acknowledged his authority. Aole accepted the hint in the traditional fashion by committing suicide, but not before he had uttered his famous curse. From the palace forecourt he shot three arrows, one to the north, one to the south, and one to the west, saying:

'My curse be on you for your disloyalty and disobedience, so let your children disobey you. If you send them on an errand, let them never return to bring you word again. To all the points I shot my arrows will you be carried as slaves. My curse will carry you to the sea and beyond the seas, slaves will rule over you, and you, their masters, will become slaves.' Then, smashing an earthenware dish, he shouted, 'Broken calabash can be mended, but not a broken dish; so let my words be irrevocable.'

(Johnson, *History of the Yorubas*.)

The curse seemed to take immediate effect, for shortly afterwards Oyo was abandoned by its inhabitants, and those who stayed in that area became subjects of the Fulani emirate of Ilorin. The majority of the people moved away, however, some founding a new town of Oyo nearly a hundred miles to the south on the edge of the forest, while others settled at Ibadan, which grew to be the greatest Yoruba city within the forest belt. The states and provinces of the Oyo empire became independent of central control, and started to fight each other both for extended frontiers and for control of the trade-routes. The principal gainers from these wars were the Egbas, who founded a new capital city at Abeokuta in 1830, controlling the routes to Porto Novo and Badagry, and the Ijebus, whose territory controlled the main route from Ibadan to Lagos. One result of these destructive, internecine struggles among the Yoruba was that vast numbers of captives were taken as slaves, so that by the 1840s Lagos and Badagry had become the greatest slaving ports in West Africa.

The Yoruba wars were a tragedy, for much of southern Yoruba-land lies within that part of the forest belt where the oil-palm grows wild, and where, therefore, there was an easily marketable alternative to the slave-trade. Because of these wars, the oil-palm in southern Yorubaland was not commercially exploited. It is indeed one of the curious facts of West African history that the one region where a peaceful changeover to legitimate commerce took place was the region where in the past the slave-trade had been most active. This was the region roughly corresponding to the eastern region of Nigeria, which at the end of the eighteenth century had supplied 20,000 slaves a year. Here the Efik and Ijaw villagers of the lagoon area used to take their great war-canoes up the rivers to the Ibo slave-markets, and now they showed an equal enterprise in converting the Ibos to the collection of palm-nuts which were taken down the rivers to be sold to the Europeans. By the 1820s the region was beginning to be known as the Oil Rivers.

The European traders realised that if they could take steam-driven ships (which were starting to be available in the 1820s, though it was not until much later that they replaced sailing-ships on the open seas) up the larger rivers into the forest region where the oil-palms grew, they could buy the produce cheaper and eliminate the coastal middlemen. This was the real significance of the discovery of the Niger mouth by John and Richard Lander in 1830, as the result of a journey down the river by canoe from Bussa to the delta. Eleven years later the British government was persuaded by philanthropists and traders alike to send an ambitious expedition to penetrate the interior using the new water-route. But the west coast was extremely unhealthy for Europeans —it was known as the 'white man's grave'. The reign of the malarial mosquito had still another fifteen years to run before the use of quinine helped Europeans to overcome the fever that was so deadly for them. The Niger expedition of 1841–2 was a failure, over one-sixth of its European members dying in the space of two months. The commercial navigation of the Niger was delayed until the 1860s.

## The beginnings of European intervention

Half-way through the century, therefore, the main characteristics of the societies of the southern, forested part of West Africa had changed very little except in the Oil Rivers district. This was in spite of the legal abolition of the slave-trade by the European powers, in spite of the British navy, and in spite of the small and scattered possessions of the French and the British, the Danes and the Dutch. In general, the slave-trade was still flourishing, and the main military states, Ashanti and Dahomey, were still increasing their strength. The only significant increase of European power, even during the third quarter of the century, was along the coast itself. Here, on the eastern sector of the Gold Coast, Britain in 1850 bought the Danish forts, in order to be able to impose customs duties along a sufficient stretch of coast to pay the expenses of her occupation. In 1872 the Dutch, finding their forts along the western sector of the coast no longer profitable, ceded them freely to the British. Another factor was Britain's intervention in the affairs of Lagos. The British supported the claims of Akitoye to the title of *Ologun* (the ruler of Lagos, at one time appointed by the Oba of Benin), and in 1851 helped him drive out his nephew and rival Kosoko. In return for British help, Akitoye promised to end the slave-trade from Lagos, but he could not keep his hold over the island city without further British support. When in 1861 Dahomey again threatened to attack Abeokuta, Britain rid herself of the Akitoye–Kosoko dispute by annexing Lagos as a colony. From this point an almost inevitable path led forward to further intervention—on the one hand the punitive expedition against Ashanti in 1873 and the incorporation of the coastal states into the Gold Coast colony in 1874; on the other hand the gradual expansion of Lagos along the coast to the east and the west, and the increasing interference of the British Consuls in the affairs of the Oil Rivers states.

In the French colony on the Senegal a new phase of active intervention began with the appointment as governor of Louis Faidherbe in 1854. Since its reoccupation by the French in 1817

*5a*  West Africa, 1800–1875: western half

(it had been in British hands during the Napoleonic Wars) the
colony had consisted of nothing more than a circle of agricultural
villages around the port of St Louis. The only active trade was
that in gum arabic with the Moorish tribes living in the desert to
the north of the river. Trade with the interior, which the French
so much wanted to develop, was prevented by the powerful Fula
state of Futa Toro higher up the river on the southern side.
Convinced that the Senegal would prove the commercial highway
for the trade of the whole of the western Sudan, the French had a
clearer motive for interior conquests than the British at any of
their coastal bases. Conquest of the lower Senegal valley was
therefore Faidherbe's declared policy, and in ten years he had
carried it out, encouraging economic crops—especially ground-
nuts—in the conquered lands, and establishing schools as well as
administrative centres in each newly acquired district.

   Any kind of European intervention on African soil was likely
to lead to more. Britain's creeping protectorates along the Lagos

5*b*   West Africa, 1800–1875: eastern half

and Gold Coast stretches of the West African shore were one example. Faidherbe's policy of military conquest inland was another. It was, however, more difficult to call a halt to this inland conquest than to the growth of Britain's coastal possessions. The farther the French advance went inland, the more sharply it came into conflict with the Muslim states of the interior of the western Sudan. Already by 1857 Faidherbe was involved with the forces of al-Hajj Umar. The Muslim leader of the *jihad* temporarily checked the French advance south-east up the Senegal, but was unable to prevent their attacking Futa Toro to the south of the river. The French conquest of Futa Toro was a blow to the prestige of al-Hajj Umar. Most of his *mujahidun* were emigrants from Futa Toro, which had been the original Fula *jihad* state. Clearly this was a situation which could end only in the defeat of the French and their retreat to St Louis, or else in the defeat of the Muslims and the French advance to Timbuktu and beyond.

In West Africa, therefore, events were tending by the third quarter of the nineteenth century to increasing intervention by both France and Britain. There was still in 1875 nothing that could suggest the speed of events that were to follow in the next 25 years, however. Had France and Britain not been pushed by other European powers into a scramble for outright partition, their intervention would undoubtedly have proceeded much more slowly than in fact it did. Still, European armies—the outward sign of imperialism—had already been in action against African states before 1875. In West Africa at least the broad pattern that the partition was to follow had been laid down, and could lead only to an ever-growing area of colonial occupation.

# 4

## WEST-CENTRAL AFRICA, 1800–1880

The region we call 'West-Central Africa' is the region of the Congo forest and of the light woodland country to the south of it. Today this is the area occupied by Angola and the states of Congo (Kinshasa), Gabon, Congo (Brazzaville) and the Central African Republic. In terms of the older African states, it includes the area of the Luba-Lunda and the Lower Congo kingdoms. The Portuguese were the most active external influence in this region, but were not the only one. During the first three-quarters of the nineteenth century the northernmost frontier of Angola was at the Loge river, and from here northwards to the Cameroons, and up both sides of the Congo estuary, there was a kind of commercial 'no-man's-land', the shore dotted with the trading factories of English, Dutch, American, French and Spanish as well as Portuguese firms. During the second half of the nineteenth century, an even more important source of external influence was that of the Swahili-Arabs and Nyamwezi from East Africa. Only during the colonial period was the region as a whole reconnected with its natural ports of exit on the Atlantic coast.

### The pombeiros and the Mwata Kazembe

During the early part of the century Portuguese influence reached the interior by two main routes, one of which started in Luanda, the other in Benguela. The Luanda route was the older, and by the beginning of the nineteenth century it led in a sense right across the continent. Portuguese Luanda merchants themselves seldom left Luanda: indeed the Portuguese government always did its best to prevent them from doing so. It knew that relations with the peoples of the interior went much more smoothly if trade was handled by the *pombeiros*. These, as we noted in Chapter 2, were Negro, or sometimes Mulatto, agents from the colony. They were employed by the Portuguese government or by private traders to lead caravans into the interior and to reside at the *feiras*, or garrisoned market-places. Peoples living beyond the Portuguese borders would bring their produce for sale to these markets. The most distant *feira* on the Luanda route was about 300 miles up country at Kasanje. It had been founded in the seventeenth century at the capital of a tributary state, the inhabitants of which were a people called the Imbangala, who had originally formed a part of the Luba-Lunda dispersion. The *pombeiros* did not normally go beyond Cassanje. From there to the Mwata Yamvo's kingdom trade was organised by the Imbangalas. The Mwata Yamvo sent his own caravans still further inland to the Mwata Kazembe's capital on the Luapula river. And by the end of the eighteenth century the Mwata Kazembe in his turn was in commercial contact with the Portuguese station at Tete on the Zambezi—the usual carriers on the last stretch of the route being the Bisa people of the north-eastern part of modern Zambia. At the end of the eighteenth century and several times during the early nineteenth century the Portuguese tried to survey this route. They hoped by this means to extend their own power and influence from coast to coast. In 1798 an expedition commanded by Lacerda reached the Kazembe's capital from Tete, but had to turn back. In 1806, however, two *pombeiros* called Pedro Joao Baptista and Amaro Jose were sent out from Luanda and accomplished the double journey to Tete and back on foot with no greater hardship than that of being detained for nearly four years on the outward journey at the court of the Mwata Kazembe. Baptista wrote of the king in his journal:

6   West-Central Africa, 1800–1880: trade routes

The Kazembe is powerful in his capital, and rules over a great many
people. His place is rather smaller than the Mwata Yamvo's. His orders
are harsh, and he is feared by all the great chiefs, who are also lords in
their own lands...When there are no travellers trading at his capital, he
will order slaves and ivory to be collected, and will go with his ambassadors to
chastise such chiefs as stop the way to traders coming from Tete to his country.
The territory of Kazembe is supplied with provisions all the year round—
manioc flour, millet, maize, beans, bananas, sugar-canes, potatoes, yams,
gourds, ground-nuts, and much fish from the rivers Luapula and Mouva
which are near. He owns three salt districts...He possesses victuals and
oxen...which he sends and buys from the Huizas (Bisas) in exchange for
slaves...King Kazembe has tea-pots, cups, silver spoons and forks...and
gold money. He has a Christian courtesy: he doffs his hat and gives good day.

The *pombeiros* noticed that the Kazembe, whose capital was
almost in the middle of the continent, would normally export his
slaves westwards via the Mwata Yamvo's kingdom to Luanda

7   West-Central Africa, 1800–1880: tribal areas and migrations

while he sent his ivory eastwards to Tete. This was probably a just reflection of the market for slaves and ivory in the trade of the Atlantic and Indian Oceans at that time.

## The Ovimbundu and the Chokwe

By the middle of the nineteenth century great changes had taken place along the old transcontinental route. On the one hand, as we shall see, the trade eastward from Kazembe's had changed its direction from the Portuguese on the Zambezi to the Swahili-Arabs of the Zanzibar coast. On the other hand the old Luanda route to the Mwata Yamvo's, using the Imbangalas as inter-mediaries, had been superseded by a more southerly route from Benguela. Trade on this route was in the hands of the Ovimbundu of the Bihe plateau. The Ovimbundu, like the Imbangalas, were people who had been organised into small states by conquering migrants from the Lunda area. From the eighteenth century on they had been joined by considerable numbers of European refugees, some escaped convicts, some deserters from the Portuguese army. These people had passed on to their hosts their own skill with fire-arms and had thus helped to make them the greatest traders of the whole of the dry, upland region of the Congo–Zambezi watershed to the south of the Mwata Yamvo's kingdom. By 1850 their caravans, usually numbering 200 or 300 porters, had penetrated south-eastwards into the Lovale and Lozi countries of the upper Zambezi valley, eastwards as far as the Lamba of the Zambian copper-belt, and northwards right across the Mwata Yamvo's country and down the Kasai as far as the southern fringes of the Congo forest.

In part, the decline of the Luanda route and the rise of the Benguela one reflected a change in the commodities exported. The Luanda route had been above all a slaving route, and the Imbangalas had for two and a half centuries been specialists in the supply of slaves. Luanda continued to export slaves openly and actively until 1838, when slavery was officially abolished in all the Portuguese possessions. Illegal shipments continued for another two decades, but of course from lesser ports and not from the capital of the colony. Hence the downfall of the Imbangalas. And simultaneously with the abolition of the slave-trade the Portuguese lifted the government monopoly of the ivory trade. This opened up new trading opportunities, which the Ovimbundu were better placed to exploit than the Imbangalas. The Ovimbundu were traders rather than hunters. But their eastern neighbours, the Chokwe, were the great ivory-hunting specialists of the mid-nineteenth century. Their methods were ferocious in the extreme. They were well-supplied with fire-arms, and were continuously on the war-path. They lived by pillage, taking slave-prisoners and incorporating them in their own war-bands, seizing stocks of dead ivory, and hunting out the elephants systematically in one region after another. The Ovimbundu traders, in fact, advanced behind a screen of Chokwe hunters and warriors, buying their ivory and supplying them with fire-arms in exchange. Thus the Chokwe, a small and almost unheard of people in 1800, had by the end of the century conquered large areas between the upper Zambezi, the Kwango, the middle Kasai rivers and the western Katanga, and it was they who in 1885 at last made an end of the great kingdom of the Mwata Yamvo.

## The Nyamwezi and the Arabs

While the Ovimbundu and the Chokwe were displacing the Lunda and the Imbangala at the western end of the transcontinental route, the Mwata Kazembe, in the centre of it, was likewise being displaced by newcomers from East Africa. The story of the Nyamwezi and Swahili-Arab penetration of East Africa during the nineteenth century will be told in Chapter 6: here we are concerned only with that part of the movement which affected West-Central Africa. As early as 1832 the Kazembe rebuffed a Portuguese trade mission which visited him, saying that he was already getting all the foreign goods that he needed from the Zanzibar coast, and that he no longer wished to trade with the Portuguese on the Zambezi. If he had foreseen the consequences of these new East African trading contacts, he might have been more cautious in rejecting the Portuguese proposals. For, about 1856, a Nyamwezi merchant, Msiri (the Mosquito), who had already made several trading expeditions to the Katanga, settled down with an armed following at Bunkeya, on the northern edge of the Kazembe's kingdom. There he steadily built up his power and influence until he was strong enough to defy the Kazembe and to make himself the effective overlord of a large region which included the whole of the north and west of the Kazembe's kingdom. He also spread into the Luba kingdoms to the north of it. Msiri, with his Nyamwezi warriors, known in Katanga as the Bayeke, now added to his trading profits with regular tribute in ivory, salt and copper levied from the chiefs who had formerly paid it to the Kazembe or to the Luba kings. Like the Kazembes before him, he traded these products in many directions. The salt and copper (cast in small bars or crosses) went down the Kasai and the Lulua rivers to the peoples of the forest margin like the Kuba and the Songye, who traded it for ivory. The ivory Msiri exchanged for guns, obtained both from the Ovimbundu and the Portuguese in the west and from the Swahili-Arabs in the east. Msiri's empire, known to the early European explorers as Garanganze, lasted until the coming of the Belgians in 1891, when Msiri himself was shot in a scuffle with a Belgian officer. His Bayeke followers continued, and still continue, to form an important element in the politics of the Katanga. Godfrey Munongo, for example, who was Minister for the Interior in Tshombe's Congolese government, was a Yeke—and a grandson of Msiri himself.

What Msiri was doing in southern Katanga was being done at the same time in northern Katanga and the Kivu region by other groups of East Africans, led in this case mostly by Swahili-Arabs from the Zanzibar coast. These had first crossed Lake Tanganyika about 1840 from their lakeside ferry-port of Ujiji. By about 1860 there was a regular Arab settlement at Nyangwe on the Lualaba (the upper Congo). Soon they were trading and raiding over the whole area between Lake Tanganyika and the Lomami river, where they met the sphere of the Chokwe raiders coming from the west. Like the Chokwe, they could penetrate where they wished, as the possession of fire-arms made them all-powerful and the ancient Luba and Songye kingdoms were even more defenceless than the Lunda kingdoms to the south. Like the Yeke invaders to the south of them and the Chokwe to the south-west, they were ruthless and rapid in their exploitation of the ivory resources of the country. They hunted elephants in armies, and the armies lived off the local populations and savaged them, levying tribute in foodstuffs and ivory, and burning and looting the villages at the slightest signs of resistance. Nevertheless, behind the first line of advance of the elephant-hunters, the invaders of the eastern Congo settled down to an organised way of life. Their townships, many of which still exist, were equipped with mosques, and the principal houses had all the little luxuries of urban life on the East African coast—beds, furniture, coffee-tables, even the beautifully carved doorways of Zanzibar. Around their settlements the Arabs developed thriving agricultural plantations. Europeans were much impressed by these Arab achievements, as can be seen from the following description of Kasongo, written by Sidney Hinde, the English medical officer of the Congo Free State forces that conquered the Arab lands of the eastern Congo in 1893:

Kasongo was a much finer town than even the grand old slave capital Nyangwe. During the siege of Nyangwe, the taking of which was more or less expected, the inhabitants had time to carry off all valuables, and even furniture, to places of safety. At Kasongo, however, it was different. We rushed into the town so suddenly that everything was left in its place. Our whole force found new outfits, and even the common soldiers slept on silk and satin mattresses, in carved beds with silk mosquito curtains. The room I took possession of was eighty feet long and fifteen feet wide, with a door leading into an orange garden, beyond which was a view extending over five miles. We found many European luxuries, the use of which we had almost forgotten; candles, sugar, matches, silver and glass goblets and decanters were in profusion. The granaries throughout the town were stocked with enormous quantities of rice, coffee, maize and other food; the gardens were luxurious and well-planted; and oranges, both sweet and bitter, guavas, pomegranates, pineapples, mangoes and bananas abounded at every turn. The herd of cattle we found in Kasongo was composed of three distinct breeds.

I was constantly astonished by the splendid work which had been done in the neighbourhood by the Arabs. Kasongo was built in the corner of a virgin forest, and for miles round all the brushwood and the great majority of trees had been cleared away. In the forest-clearing fine crops of sugar-cane, rice, maize and fruits grew. I have ridden through a single rice-field for an hour and a half.

(S. L. Hinde, The Fall of the Congo Arabs, London, 1897.)

## Tippu Tib

In the early days each of these Arab settlements was ruled by its founder and followers, who exercised a kind of loose political authority over the local African chiefs. The man who brought the Arabs of this region together, to recognise his own supremacy and, ultimately, that of the Sultan of Zanzibar, was Muhammed bin Hamed, more generally known by his nickname of Tippu Tib. He was born in 1830 in Zanzibar, and his mother was a pure Muscat Arab of the ruling class. His father and his paternal grandfather were coastal Swahilis who had taken part in the earliest trading expeditions to the interior. His paternal grand-mother had been the daughter of a Nyamwezi chief, and Tippu's own earliest journeys were with Nyamwezi caravans travelling round the south end of Lake Tanganyika to Katanga. He was for a time associated with Msiri, but later left him and set up his own headquarters at Kasongo on the Lualaba, where he described himself as Sultan of Utetera. This was in the late 1860s and the early 1870s. From then on, for 20 more years, Tippu Tib was the most powerful man in the eastern Congo. He was loyal to the Sultan of Zanzibar, yet, unlike most of the Arabs, he maintained excellent relations with the Nyamwezi. The Nyamwezi territory lay between him and the east coast, controlling his line of com-munications with Zanzibar. In 1877 he met the explorer Stanley at Nyangwe and accompanied him down the Lualaba to Stanley Falls (later Stanleyville), thus extending his ivory-hunting and other trading activities into the Ituri forest region. By the 1880s Tippu Tib was said to have 50,000 guns at his command. His territory touched that of the Chokwe in the south-west, while his station at Stanley Falls was only a fortnight's journey for the river-steamers which Stanley, by then in the employment of King Leopold of the Belgians, had launched at Stanley Pool. Tippu Tib realised that the European powers were closing in on tropical Africa. From 1883 to 1886, therefore, he made a great effort to rally the Arabs of the eastern Congo to acknowledge the political authority of the Sultan of Zanzibar, in the hope that the Sultan's dominion over East Africa would be recognised by the Europeans. In this way Tippu Tib hoped that his rule in the eastern Congo would become more permanent. But his efforts were in vain: the European powers at the Berlin Conference (see Chapter 9) did not uphold the Sultan's claims over the interior of East Africa. Tippu Tib's last years in the Congo (1887–92) were spent in the im-probable role of King Leopold's 'governor' at Stanley Falls. After his eventual retirement to Zanzibar, his former lands had to be conquered, as we have seen, by European forces. However, as with Msiri's Katanga, the Belgians took over many of the institu-tions of Arab rule in the eastern Congo and employed many Swahili in positions of subordinate authority. In fact, the Swahili language, known locally as Kingwana, remains the common language of this part of the Congo to this day.

### The Lower Congo region and the Congo river route

The part of West-Central Africa least known to Europeans at the beginning of the nineteenth century was the region north and south of the Lower Congo, which at the end of the century was to be the main centre of interest and of the struggle for political control. The most important factor in this region was the geo-graphical one. The Congo river and its tributaries that converge upon Stanley Pool provide something like 4,000 miles of water-ways which are navigable without interruption. But the 250 miles of river between Stanley Pool and the Atlantic Ocean passes through a district of steep and broken hill country in a series of cataracts and waterfalls. This country is as hard to travel through as any in the world. Only with immense difficulty did Stanley and other officials of the Congo Free State have a road cut across the stony hills and forested valleys to transport parts of steamships up to Stanley Pool to be reassembled for use on the navigable waterways. But previous to this, so long as water transport on the upper river was by canoe, and so long as head porterage was the only means of transport over the cataract region, the economic possibilities of the Congo river system were limited. At the beginning of the century, when the Portuguese government maintained its monopoly of the ivory-trade, a certain amount of ivory and other traffic used the northward-flowing tributaries of the Congo in order to by-pass Portuguese territory. This trade did not come together at Stanley Pool, which was not yet, as it later became, a commercial 'bottle-neck'. Instead it passed from the rivers to the scores of European trading factories scattered along the coast to the north of the Portuguese possessions in Angola, along numerous side-routes through the forest and down the streams that flowed directly into the Atlantic. The staple or main product of this trade was ivory, but, as the nineteenth century went on, it came to include also palm-oil and palm-kernels, beeswax, coffee, raw cotton, and rubber. By the 1870s the volume of British trade alone from the West-Central African coast rivalled that from the Oil Rivers district of southern Nigeria.

It was ivory, however, which formed the backbone of the trade. It was ivory which had the highest value and which did not deteriorate in transport. It was ivory therefore which came from farthest afield—from the Lunda-dominated countries of the Kwango and the Kasai, and from the forest peoples of the main river. Among these, the Teke from the northern shores of Stanley Pool acted as the main traders and carriers for the whole region below Bolobo. Above Bolobo the Bobangi took their place as far as Irebu, and beyond that the Ngala, who traded as far as Lisala, a thousand miles from the sea. This was the farthest point from the west coast where Stanley found European merchandise during his journey down the Congo in 1877. The European guns and cloth which he saw here had taken five years to reach their destination. North of the main river, in the region between the Ubangi and the coast, the part taken by the Chokwe farther south was played by the Fang (French, Pahuin) people. These were immigrants into West-Central Africa from the interior of the Cameroons. They had moved southwards from the savanna into the rain-forest and had become the pre-eminent ivory-hunters, exchanging their ivory, generally through African middlemen, for European goods, especially guns, at the factories on the Gaboon coast. The Fang at this time were very fierce and were widely reputed as cannibals, and Mary Kingsley, a courageous Englishwoman who travelled through their country in 1894, described how the inhabitants of a Fang village started to sell her their store of elephant tusks and india-rubber:

I did not want these things then, but still felt too nervous of the Fangs to point this out firmly, and so had to buy. . . I found myself the owner of balls of rubber and some tusks, and alas, my little stock of cloth and tobacco all going fast. . . To be short of money in a Fang village is extremely bad, because these Fangs, when a trader has no more goods to sell them, are liable to start trade all over again by killing him and taking back their ivory and rubber and keeping it until another trader comes along.

The whole of this pattern of trade which found its way by lateral or side-routes to European trading factories scattered along the coast from the Cameroons to Angola was, however, placed in danger by Stanley's journey down the Congo in 1877, and by his demonstration that above the Lower Congo cataracts there were thousands of miles of smoothly flowing waterways, easily navigable by steamers. The British government was satisfied with the old pattern of trade, and took no action when Stanley returned to England and told of his discoveries. However, King Leopold of the Belgians, who had by this time spent nearly twenty years studying the colonial activities of other nations and looking for an opportunity to establish an empire of his own, listened with interest to Stanley's stories. Already Leopold's eyes were fixed upon the Congo basin, though he was planning to approach it from the east, using the Swahili-Arab routes. With Stanley's report before him, he completely changed his plans: he would by-pass the cataracts on the lower river with a railway and launch steamers on the upper river. At once the Congo would become a bottle-neck, funnelling the trade of the whole vast river basin into his net. The Arab and Nyamwezi empires would be rolled back. The Chokwe would cease to be of any commercial importance. Under a European reorganisation of its trade, the region as a whole would resume its natural unity.

King Leopold's design, as we shall see, did more than anything else to spark off the European scramble for Africa. It brought to an end an old chapter of African history. When the Portuguese first came to West-Central Africa in the fifteenth century, they had opened its trade to the westwards—to the coast and to the lands across the Atlantic Ocean. Through their subsequent con-centration on the slave-trade, however, and through their un-enlightened attempt to hold down the price of ivory by a royal monopoly, they allowed the East Africans during the first three-quarters of the nineteenth century to divert most of the ivory trade away from its natural Atlantic outlets into the trading system of the Indian Ocean. From the point of view of geography this was all wrong. Stanley Falls and Bunkeya (Msiri's capital) were both much nearer to the west coast than to the east. But it took Stanley's journey and King Leopold's commercial vision to reverse the swing of the pendulum, which otherwise would have left West-Central Africa a dependency of East-Central Africa and a part of the Muslim world.

# 5

## SOUTHERN AFRICA, 1800–1885

### *The conflict between Boer and Bantu*

In tropical Africa the basis for the early meetings between Africans and people from the rest of the world was trade. In South Africa such encounters were usually over land. In tropical Africa European and African merchants, even those engaged in the wretched slave-trade, met on an essentially equal footing. They treated each other with a mixture of suspicion and respect. Europeans and Arabs were careful to acknowledge the authority of African rulers, and to pay attention to the manners and customs of African peoples. In South Africa the Europeans were present from the beginning not as traders but as settlers. As their numbers grew, and as they pushed inland from their first foothold on the Cape Peninsula, they cast an envious eye upon the land of the local people. During the seventeenth and most of the eighteenth centuries this land was that occupied by the Bushmen hunters and by the Hottentot herdsmen. Thereafter, it was the much more densely settled land of the Bantu, who were agriculturalists as well as pastoralists. The only way the Boers could gain possession of the fertile land of the eastern Cape province was by conquest. Such a conquest might take the form of a party of frontier farmers, on horseback and armed with their hunting rifles, driving out the inhabitants of a nearby Bushman or Hottentot encampment or Bantu village. Or it might be carried out by the official forces of the colony, involved in a frontier war which was the consequence of the raids and counter-raids of Dutch and African farmers.

Naturally the conquerors felt superior to the conquered, and justified their actions on the grounds of their superiority.

The Boers' feeling of superiority is illustrated in an English traveller's account of a frontier farmer who was flogged and imprisoned by the British military authorities in 1798 for ill-treating a Hottentot servant:

For the whole of the first night his lamentations were incessant; with a loud voice he cried, 'Myn God! is dat een maniere om Christian mensch te handelen'. (My God, is this the way to treat a Christian man.) His, however, were not the agonies of bodily pain, but the burst of rage and resentment on being put on a level with one of the Zwarte Natie (Black Natives), between whom and themselves the Boers conceive the differences to be fully as great as between themselves and their cattle.

(Sir J. Barrow, *An Account of Travels into the Interior of Southern Africa*, vol. I.)

Here we have the origins of the race attitudes characteristic of South Africa.

We have seen (Chapter 2, p. 26) that during the first thirty or so years after the Boers and Bantu met on what came to be known as the Eastern Frontier of the Cape Colony in the 1770s a solution to the conflicts arising out of cattle stealing and demands for more land might have been found if the two groups had been kept apart. An agreement to halt further expansion, and the creation of a frontier properly defended by soldiers, like those which exist between modern states, might still have been possible. After the first or second decade of the nineteenth century no solution along these lines had any real chance of success. The demands of people on both sides of the frontier for land could not be satisfied. The struggle for control of the land of southern Africa had to be fought out until one side or the other emerged as victor.

### Shaka and the Zulu nation

When the first clashes between White and Black people took place along the Fish river, the population of the Nguni-speaking Bantu was increasing like that of the Boers. On the Bantu side of the frontier there was less and less available land on which people could live and graze their cattle. Cattle, which required a large area of pasture, were an essential feature in the lives of the South African Bantu; they were the outward sign of their wealth and power, and no man could marry without handing over cattle to his bride's family. In earlier times this pressure of man and beast upon the land would have been met by further expansion along the coast in a south-westerly direction, at the expense of the more thinly settled Hottentots of the western Cape. This line of expansion was now blocked by the Boer farmers, who, as we have seen, were also hungry for fresh land. Thus any Bantu people seeking to enlarge its territory could do so only at the expense of its neighbours. In the early years of the nineteenth century one Nguni group expanded in this way, with the result that most of South Africa was plunged into a period of destruction and violence known to Africans as the Time of Troubles (Sotho, *Difaqane*; Zulu, *Mfecane*).

The Zulus were originally a small clan living in the territory of one of the Nguni rulers in Natal, Dingiswayo. Shaka, who was born in 1787, was one of the sons of the Zulu clan-chief. He quarrelled with his father and took refuge at the court of Dingiswayo, where he grew up to become a regimental commander. In 1816, after the death of his father, he was made chief of the Zulu clan by Dingiswayo. Two years later Dingiswayo was murdered and Shaka took over the military empire that he had started to build up. Shaka proved to be a military leader of outstanding genius. He reformed the organisation, weapons and tactics of Dingiswayo's *impis* (Zulu, regiments). The young warriors were formed into a regular army, and were not allowed to marry until they had completed their military service. Delegorgue, a French traveller in the 1830s, wrote of the transformation brought about by Shaka (the older spelling of his name was with *Ch*):

Before Chaka the Zulus wore sandals, and in their battles they hurled the *assagai* (Zulu, spear), as the Amakosa (Xhosa) still do. Above all, they charged in a mass, and without observing any orderly arrangement. Chaka formed regiments of a thousand men each. He did away with the sandal, in spite of the thorny nature of the vegetation, and ordered every warrior to take but one assagai, which was to be exhibited after a fight, stained by the blood of an enemy. The struggle could only be hand to hand. This new way of fighting, unknown to the neighbouring nations, greatly facilitated Chaka's conquests. (Quoted in Bird, *Annals of Natal*, vol. i.)

Shaka experimented with the new *assagai* before making it the standard weapon of his *impis*; a trader, Henry Fynn, who first visited the great king in 1824, heard of the 'sham-combat' and recounted it in his diary, as an example of Shaka's thoroughness and of his ruthlessness:

Chaka disapproved of the custom of throwing the assagai. To substitute a different mode of attack, he assembled two divisions of his followers, who were ordered to supply themselves with a reed each from the river-bank, that he might be convinced of the effect which only one weapon would produce when used at close quarters. The two divisions then opposed each other, the one throwing their reeds, the other rushing on and stabbing their opponents. The result of this collision met with Chaka's entire satisfaction; few in the first division escaped being wounded, and several severely. Chaka then ordered six oxen to be slaughtered, and collecting the assagais of his followers, he ordered the shafts to be broken and used in cooking the meat. The prime parts were given, hot, to those who had been conspicuous for courage: the inferior parts, after being soaked in cold water, were given to those who had been seen to shrink in the combat.

Shaka's *impis*, which in battle encircled the enemy like the horns of a buffalo, were so effective and so highly disciplined that they proved almost irresistible. The neighbouring Nguni chiefs were defeated, and their lands used by the Zulus for grazing cattle. Many of the young men and women, however, were incorporated into the Zulu nation, which under Shaka and his successor Dingane, who murdered his royal brother in 1828, came to dominate most of the area of modern Natal. As we shall see (p. 60), it was the existence of this aggressive and rapidly expanding kingdom in the rear of the Cape Colony's eastern frontier which made the policy of separation along the line of an agreed and stabilised frontier impossible to carry out.

### The Time of Troubles: Moshesh and the Basuto

The effects of the Zulu expansion were felt throughout southern Africa. In the hope of escaping from Shaka and his *impi*, fugitives from Natal streamed across the Drakensberg mountains. Under their impact the Sotho-Tswana peoples of the High Veld clashed upon one another like an avalanche of stones rolling down a hillside. Thousands of displaced people wandered over the Veld or sought refuge in the mountains. Some were driven by famine to live by violence and pillage, and set out like the Zulu on campaigns of conquest. The brunt of the invaders' onset was borne by the Batlokwa, who were ruled by a redoubtable chief-tainess called Mantatisi and later by her son, Sikonyela. Assimi-lating many of the refugees from Natal, Sotho peoples struck out against the Batswana peoples of the western Transvaal and Bechuanaland (Batswanaland) and threw them into utter disorder. Only towards the end of the century did one group, the Bamangwato, re-emerge as a stable chiefdom. One Sotho group, the Bafokeng or Makololo, were driven northwards by Mantatisi. Their leader, Sebetwane, is said to have appealed to his people in 1823 in the following words:

My masters, you see that the world is tumbling about our ears. We and other peoples have been driven from our ancestral homes, our cattle seized, our brothers and sons killed, our wives and daughters ravished, our children starved. War has been forced upon us, tribe against tribe. We shall be eaten up one by one. Our fathers taught us *Khotso ke nala*—peace is prosperity—but today there is no peace, no prosperity! What are we to do? My masters, this is my word: Let us march! Let us take our wives and children and cattle, and go forth to seek some land where we may dwell in tranquillity.

(Quoted in Edwin W. Smith, *Great Lion of Bechuanaland*.)

Thereupon he led the Makololo northwards, in a running struggle with their great enemies, the Matabele, to the east of them. Finally, about 1840, they settled on the upper Zambezi, after having overcome the Lozi people of the Barotse kingdom and made them their subjects. Their rule over the Barotse only lasted some twenty years, but this was time enough for their Sotho language to become the language of Barotseland.

In two other areas refugees from the *Difaqane* were gathered together by very able chiefs who merged them into new nations strong enough to withstand pressure from the Zulus and, later on, even from the Europeans. One of these was the Swazi kingdom, created by Sobhuza and his successor Mswazi. The other was Lesotho. The creation of this kingdom was the life's work of Moshesh, one of the greatest leaders southern Africa has ever known. His character, and the steps he took to build Lesotho, were described by Eugène Casalis, the French missionary who first entered the country in 1833, and who spent many years as Moshesh's adviser on 'foreign affairs'. Casalis wrote of Moshesh in the rather pompous language characteristic of many Europeans at that time: 'Moshesh has an agreeable and interesting countenance, his deportment is noble and dignified, his features bespeak habits of reflection and of command, and a benevolent smile plays upon his lips.' Casalis was told of the peaceful times before the *Difaqane*:

At the time of Moshesh's birth (about 1790) the country of the Basutos was extremely populous. Disputes arose from time to time between the various communities, but generally little blood was shed. The green

3-2

8   The *Mfecane*: Nguni and Sotho migrations

pastures of Butobute, Moshesh's home, and the steep hills where he and
his companions hunted, are still celebrated in the national songs of the
Basuto. At the moment when it was least expected, these favourite sports
were suddenly interrupted by disastrous invasions from Natal. Desolation
was carried into the peaceful valleys of Lesuto, fields remained uncultivated, and the horrors of famine were added to those of war. Nearly all
the influential men in the country were swept away by the tide of war.
Moshesh breasted the stream. Being of a very observant disposition, he
knew how to resist and how to yield at the right moment; procured himself

allies, even among the invaders of his territory; set his enemies at variance with each other, and by various acts of kindness secured the respect of those even who had sworn his ruin.

In their struggles against both Zulus and Boers the Basuto were aided by the mountains of their country, which provided them with defensive positions almost impregnable even by troops armed with rifles. Moshesh's great tactical and diplomatic skill, which enabled the Basuto to exercise an influence quite out of proportion to their numbers and military strength, is shown in the way he treated Mzilikazi's Ndebele after they had failed to capture his mountain fortress of Thaba Bosiu in 1831:

Accustomed to victory, the Zulus advanced in serried ranks, not appearing to notice the masses of basalt which came rolling down with a tremendous noise from the top of the mountain. But soon there was a general crush— an avalanche of stones and a shower of spears, which sent back the assailants with more rapidity than they had advanced. The chiefs who were seen rallying the fugitives, and snatching away the plumes with which their heads were decorated, and trampling them under foot in a rage, led their men again towards the formidable rampart. But in vain. The next day the Zulus retired. At the moment of their departure a Mosuto, driving some fat oxen, stopped before the first ranks, and gave this message. 'Moshesh salutes you. Supposing that hunger had brought you into this country, he sends you these cattle, that you may eat them on your way home.' Moshesh was never troubled by these people again.

(Eugène Casalis, *The Basutos.*)

Some Zulu groups, whose leaders had quarrelled with Shaka, left Zululand to make their own conquests elsewhere. Soshangane took his people, the Shangane, into Gazaland in southern Mozambique, where they conquered and largely absorbed the Thonga, who were the earlier inhabitants of that region. Next, Zwangendaba and his warriors swept northwards across the Limpopo and onto the Rhodesian plateau, where they destroyed the old Rozwi kingdom of the Changamires, the later builders of Zimbabwe. Before long, however, Zwangendaba and his 'Ngoni' moved on, to settle finally in the highlands east and west of Lake Nyasa. Some of the farthest-flung of these Ngoni *impi*, always gathering fresh recruits from the peoples they defeated, campaigned as far north as the southern shores of Lake Victoria and as far east as the Indian Ocean. As we shall see in Chapter 6, they had a considerable effect on events in East Africa. Lastly, Msilikazi led his Ndebele (Sotho, *Matebele*) Zulu across the Drakensberg and on to the High Veld, in the wake of Mantatisi and Sebetwane's Sotho groups, until they were defeated near modern Pretoria by the invading Boers in 1837. The Ndebele then retreated north, across the Limpopo, and settled on the western part of the Rhodesian plateau (Matabeleland), making many of the local Shona people, the former subjects of the Rozwi kingdom, into their tribute-paying subjects.

### The expansion of the Boers: the Great Trek

Refugees also fled from the Zulu armies into the eastern Cape province, increasing the frontier conflicts with the Dutch farmers, whose numbers were increased by 5,000 British settlers in 1820. The lawlessness on the frontier, and the rough treatment by the Boers of their semi-servile labourers, shocked the humanitarians and missionary societies in Britain. These, during the early years of the nineteenth century, forced the British government to adopt a more responsible concern for the non-white peoples of the British empire. The most outspoken of the Christian missionaries in South Africa was John Philip of the London Missionary Society. Mainly through his efforts, the Hottentots of the Cape Colony were brought under the protection of the law in 1828. Later, after the abolition of slavery in 1833, he extended his campaign to include the former slaves. In the eyes of the Boers the British government was more concerned with giving legal protection to their servants than with helping them to expand at the expense of the Nguni tribes. Every Dutch farmer's son considered it his birthright to possess a 6,000 acre ranch when he got married, and in this wasteful way the available land within the colony's borders was soon exhausted. In 1836 a large area of land on the eastern frontier which had previously been annexed to the colony was returned to the Africans, because the British government was not prepared to meet the expense of administering it. This was more than the Boers would endure, and many *trekked* (Dutch, *trek*, a journey, a migration) out of British territory and across the Orange river to the north. Anna Steenkamp, the sister of one of the leaders of the Great Trek, gave as one of their reasons for leaving the Cape:

The shameful and unjust proceedings with reference to the freedom of our slaves: and yet it is not so much their freedom that drove us to such lengths as their being placed on an equal footing with Christians, contrary to the laws of God and the natural distinction of race and religion, so that it was intolerable for any decent Christian to bow down beneath such a yoke; wherefore we rather withdrew in order thus to preserve our doctrines in purity.      (Quoted in J. Bird, *Annals of Natal*, vol. I.)

Livingstone later commented: 'The Boers determined to erect themselves into a republic, in which they might pursue without molestation the "proper treatment of the blacks". This "proper treatment" has always contained the element of compulsory unpaid labour.'

The Trekkers had learned from hunters and traders that fertile parts of Natal had been virtually depopulated by the Zulus and turned into grazing-lands. They planned to infiltrate the Zulu lands by moving across the Transvaal and descending through the Drakensburg passes into Natal. By this means they hoped to outflank the densely settled Nguni between the Fish river and Natal. At first the Zulu king Dingane successfully resisted this encroachment. By 1839, however, the Boers under Pretorius had defeated them and had set up a republic in Natal. This action brought them into conflict once again with the British government, which would not allow the existence of a rival European state on the shores of the Indian Ocean. It also rightly feared the effects of Boer penetration into Natal on the encircled Nguni of the eastern Cape. Natal was therefore annexed by Britain in 1845. Frustrated in this way, most of the Natal Boers returned to the High Veld, where other groups of farmers had already driven the Ndebele across the Limpopo. The British government half-heartedly followed the Boers north of the Orange river, but in 1852 and 1854, respectively, recognised the independence of the Boer republics of the Transvaal and the Orange Free State.

In the middle years of the nineteenth century therefore South Africa consisted of two British colonies, the Cape and Natal, the two Boer republics, and many independent African kingdoms and chiefdoms, of which the Basuto and Zulu kingdoms were the largest. The total white population was little more than 300,000; the African population was between one and two million. In 1853 the Cape Colony was granted a constitution with an elected parliament, and in 1872 full internal self-government, with ministers responsible to parliament. The franchise was non-racial; that is, representatives were elected by people of all races, provided they owned property of a certain value, or received a certain amount in wages. This liberal political attitude of the Cape was not shared by the other Europeans in South Africa. In the Boer republics only white people were recognised as citizens, and only white males exercised the vote.

### The end of the independent African states

The discovery of great diamond deposits near the junction of the Orange and the Vaal rivers in 1868 hastened the inevitable process whereby the self-governing African peoples and states lost their independence and were brought under European rule. Already in 1856–7 the situation had seemed so desperate to the Xhosa and Tembu living immediately to the east of the Cape Colony that they followed the prophecy of a girl, Nongqause. She stated that if, on a certain day, the cattle were killed and the grain destroyed, the tribal ancestors would drive the Europeans into the sea. The result, of course, was a disastrous famine, in which thousands died, while thousands more abandoned their land and went to seek work and food in the Cape. The opening of the diamond mines greatly increased the demand for labour, and Africans converged upon Kimberley from all over southern Africa. In the early days of the mining the companies regularly paid these workers in rifles and ammunition, and so thousands of Africans returned to their homes armed with guns. This led to exaggerated fears on the European side of a 'united native rising'. Fortunately for the white men in South Africa the wars that did break out were no such thing, but they were extremely destructive because Africans as well as Europeans were using fire-arms.

In 1871 the Cape government assumed control over the Basuto, who had been involved in a bitter land struggle with the Free State farmers. Next, in 1877–8, it finally broke the fighting power of the Xhosa and other Nguni tribes on the eastern frontier— though at a great cost in men and money. Again, in 1877 the British government took over the Transvaal, where the forces of a poverty-stricken Boer government could make no headway in the war which had broken out against the Bapedi under their chief Sekukuni. This involved the British (who in Natal had been friendly with the Zulus) in a quarrel which the Transvaal Boers had with Cetshwayo (pronounced Ketshwayo), the nephew and successor of Dingane. Cetshwayo was now provoked by Sir Bartle Frere, the British High Commissioner in South Africa, to armed conflict. The Zulus defeated one British army at Isandhlwana before being crushed by the reinforcements which the British hurriedly sent into Natal. The following year, 1880, saw the outbreak of a long war between the Cape government and the Basuto, sparked off by an attempt to disarm the Africans. The Cape had to be rescued from this disastrous war in 1884, when the British government took over direct responsibility for administering Basutoland. These were not the only troubles. Whites were also involved in clashes with some of the Tswana tribes, and with the Korana Khoi on the lower Orange river. In South-West Africa the mutual enmity of the Herero (Bantu) and Nama (Khoi) peoples, both pastoralists in a dry land, was inflamed by the activities of European traders, who took sides in their disputes and supplied them with both fire-arms and liquor.

Just before the outbreak of all these wars, and while they were in progress, attempts were made, in Britain by the Colonial Secretary, Lord Carnarvon, and in the Cape by Frere, to unite the white states in South Africa into a single large territory under one government. By the end of the 1870s this attempt at confederation had failed. The Boers in the Orange Free State had never forgiven the British annexation of the diamond-bearing district of Griqualand West in 1871. At the end of 1880 the Transvaalers rose against the government imposed upon them by Britain three years previously, and in 1881 defeated a British force sent to put them down in an action at Majuba Hill.

## The road to the north

Much of the hostility between the British government and the Boers was due to the presence of the Christian missionaries, whose activities among the Africans were regarded by the Boers with great suspicion. Missions were well established within the colonial borders of the Cape and Natal, though they could make little headway among the still independent and warlike Nguni peoples, especially the Zulus and the Ndebele. They were more influential among the Sotho and Tswana groups, however. The Paris Missionary Society established a close relationship with Moshesh, as we have seen, and, although neither he nor his successor was converted, many thousands of the Basutos became literate and Christian. Robert Moffat of the London Missionary Society had worked among the Griqua (a group of mixed Khoi and European descent) and Tswana peoples at Kuruman, beyond the northern frontier of the Cape, since the 1820s. Here Boer encroachment upon Tswana lands during and after the Great Trek added to the dislike of the missionaries for the Transvaal

Caption below figure:

9 Southern Africa, 1800–1885: African migrations

Labels within the map:

BAMANGWATO

Bechuanaland
Protectorate
1884

Limpopo

Missionary Road

Kolobeng
(Livingstone)

Marico
(Boers beat
Ndebele 1837)

Pretoria

Makololo

Ndebele (Mzilikazi)

Ngoni (Zwangendaba)

Shangane (Soshangane)

SWAZI
(Sobhuza)

Kuruman
(Moffat)

Vaal

Sotho Groups

(Sebetwane)

(Mzilikazi)

ZULU
(Shaka)

Isandhlwana

Buffalo

Tugela

GRIQUAS

Kimberley

Bloemfontein

GRIQUAS

(Thaba
Bosiu)

(Adam Kok)

Orange

Caledon

BASUTO
(Moshesh)

(Cape 1871–1884,
annexed by
Britain 1884)

Port Natal
(Durban)

PONDO

TEMBU

Bushmen

CAPE

COLONY

Great Fish

Kei

XHOSA

9th Kaffir War
1877–1878

Hottentots

Port Elizabeth

1820 British
settlers

Legend:

The Mfecane:
African migrations

African nations or
tribal groups

Land partially emptied
by Mfecane

Limpopo

Missionary 'road'

Kolobeng
(Livingstone)

×Marico
(Boers beat
Ndebele 1837)

●Pretoria

Annexed by Britain
1877-1881

Delagoa
Bay (P.

Kuruman
(Moffat)

T R A N S V A A L   (1852)

Boers

Marico

Vaal

Boers

Majuba
Hill  ×

Buffalo

● Isandhlwana

Tugela

Boers

NATAL

Annexed by
Britain 1845

Diamonds

● Kimberley

O R A N G E   F R E E   S T A T E   (1854)

Boers

Bloemfontein

Caledon

Orange

Port Natal
(Durban)

Frontier of British
Colony of Natal

Great Trek

Eastern frontier

CAPE
COLONY

Great Fish

Kei

Queen Adelaide
Province annexed
1834,
abandoned 1836

● Port Elizabeth

The Great Trek—
Boer migration

Boer Republic

10   Southern Africa, 1800–1885: Boer migrations

government, and made them determined to keep open a way to the north which was free from Boer control. Livingstone began his career in Africa as a missionary and explorer, working to open up this 'missionary road'—the narrow strip of habitable Bechuanaland between the Transvaal and the Kalahari desert, which led northwards to Matabeleland and Barotseland. Through Livingstone's great journey from Barotseland to Luanda, and from there across Africa to the Zambezi mouth (1853–6), European governments, traders and missionaries were made aware of the possibilities for Christianity and commerce in the lands north of the Limpopo. The British government in particular realised the vital importance of the 'missionary road' between South Africa and the interior. As soon as the Germans annexed the South-West African coast in 1883, the British replied by declaring a protectorate over Bechuanaland. This paved the way for Rhodes's occupation of Rhodesia a few years later.

# 6

## EAST-CENTRAL AFRICA, 1800–1884

East Africa, for the purposes of this chapter, includes not only the modern states of Kenya, Uganda and Tanzania, but also northern Mozambique, Malawi, Burundi and Rwanda. All these lands were to come under some kind of European rule before the end of the century, but from 1800 till 1884 the predominant outside influences were not European, but Swahili-Arab or Egyptian-Sudanese. Before 1884 only a handful of Europeans attempted trading ventures of their own in the interior. In general, European and American enterprise was limited, like that of the Indians from the British empire in India, to supplying Arab and Egyptian merchants with manufactured goods, especially cloth and fire-arms, in exchange for ivory and a few less-important products such as hides, beeswax and gum arabic. It was the Muslim merchants who traded directly with the African peoples. The work of Christian missionaries was the main European activity in East Africa before the partition took place. The missionaries, however, arrived in this region much later than the Muslim traders, and their work was still in the pioneer stage when the colonial period began. They were not responsible for the establishment of European political control which came, when it did, mainly as the result of happenings outside East Africa.

### The Arab penetration of the interior

The evolution of the Swahili-Arab population in the coastal belt of East Africa and on Zanzibar and the other offshore islands has been described in Chapter 2, as has the origins of trade between the interior and the coast. This trade from the interlacustrine kingdoms and from Katanga, most of which was carried originally by the Nyamwezi, seems to have been mainly a peaceful activity. Early European travellers were much impressed by the prosperity and sufficiency of many of the inland districts they visited. For example, Sir Richard Burton, who was by no means prejudiced in favour of African achievements, wrote after his journey to Lake Tanganyika in 1858: 'The African is in these regions superior in comforts, better dressed, fed and lodged than the unhappy Ryot (peasant) of British India. His condition, where the slave-trade is slack, may indeed be compared advantageously with that of the peasantry in some of the richest of European countries.' Traditions among peoples who were to suffer from the violence that was to come recall, in the exaggerated way that people often do, the good old days:

In the old times, long long ago, in their old homes, the Yao were in accord and united. If a quarrel arose they used to fight without rancour, avoiding bloodshed. If strangers came to a village, would they have to pay for their food? No, it was bestowed on them free; directly a man heard that a stranger was at his door, he would rejoice and say 'I have the plant of hospitality at my door, bringing guests'.

(Y. B. Abdallah, *The Yaos* (1919), p. 11.)

As the nineteenth century approached, however, two factors combined to hasten changes in the old way of life. The first was the rapidly growing demand at the coast for ivory and slaves. The second was the great desire of the peoples in the interior for more and more fire-arms. There was still, as there had always been, a ready market for domestic and plantation slaves in all the east coast settlements, as well as in Oman and the other states of Arabia and the Persian Gulf. From the mid-eighteenth century until the mid-nineteenth the French added greatly to the demand with their labour requirements for the sugar and coffee plantations in Réunion (and, until the Napoleonic wars, in Mauritius).

11  East-Central Africa, 1800–1884

In the early nineteenth century the Portuguese, because of the restrictions imposed on the West African slave-trade north of the Equator, shipped an increasing number of slaves round the Cape from Mozambique to Brazil and Cuba. And, above all, the nineteenth century saw a vast development of the plantation agriculture of the Swahili-Arabs, and with it a growing demand for slaves from the interior. But, as the nineteenth century went on, the demand for ivory—and therefore the prices paid for it— became even greater than that for slaves. The age-old market for East African ivory was the Asian one. By the middle of the nine-teenth century, however, demand in Europe and America had very greatly increased. Wealth derived from the industrial and commercial changes taking place in their countries had developed an almost insatiable appetite for the luxury objects made from ivory, such as knife-handles, piano-keys, billiard balls and orna-ments of every kind.

A few of the Swahili-Arabs who had been settled on the coast for centuries began to respond to these opportunities at the end of the eighteenth century, soon after the Nyamwezi traders had pioneered the routes. The great advance of the coastmen, how-ever, developed only during the long and brilliant reign (1806–56) of Seyyid Said, Imam of Muscat and hereditary overlord of the Arab settlements along the Zanzibar coast. Said was both an able commander and an economic genius, and it did not take him long to see that his East African empire was more worthy of his attention than the rocks and deserts in his little state of Oman on the western shores of the Persian Gulf. But first he had to reconquer it. He possessed efficient armed forces. The ships of his navy had been provided by Britain under the terms of a treaty made with him, and his army consisted of Baluchi mercenaries recruited from the borders of Persia and India. With these he occupied Zanzibar, and made effective his nominal control over the coastal towns, from Warsheikh in the north to Lindi in the south, including the important cities of Mombasa and Kilwa, which had for long been practically independent. Under Said's influence Zanzibar became the central market for the whole of the East African coast. After his introduction of the clove-tree from the East Indies, the islands of Zanzibar and Pemba soon came to grow most of the world's supply of cloves. The planta-tions were (naturally) worked by slaves who were imported from the interior. In 1840, after a series of increasingly long visits to his

African dominions, Said actually transferred his capital from Muscat to Zanzibar, where he was usually given the title of Sultan. After his death in 1856, the scattered empire was divided, one son taking Oman, and another, Majid, becoming Sultan of Zanzibar.

Sultans Said and Majid encouraged Arabs to settle in Zanzibar as plantation owners, and they also encouraged the coastal people to trade in the interior. The sultanate provided the background of security necessary for large-scale trade: debts could be collected at Zanzibar and contracts enforced. The financial arrangements for the trade were made by Indian merchants of Zanzibar and the coastal towns, who had strong commercial ties with their fellow countrymen across the ocean in India. They supplied credit to Arab traders to enable them to stock up caravans with goods and journey up-country, sometimes not returning with their purchases of ivory and slaves until several years later. In a letter dated 21 November 1872 (which was sent back to England with his body) Livingstone wrote of these Indian traders: 'The Banians have the Custom House and all the public revenue of Zanzibar entirely in their hands and by their money, arms, ammunition and goods a large and cruel Slave trade had been carried on' (quoted in Zoë Marsh, *East Africa*). The Nyamwezi traders resisted the competition of the newcomers, and were able to retain a near monopoly of trade-routes from central Tanganyika to Katanga. But the Arabs were better organised and armed and had greater financial resources behind them. They were able to supply African rulers with guns and ammunition, which were beyond the means of the Nyamwezi traders. As the century went on, and as European armies were re-equipped with more and more modern varieties of fire-arms, so more and more of the out-of-date models found their way on to the African market. By the end of the 1830s Arab traders had penetrated to Lake Tanganyika, and in 1844 the first Arab visited the court of Buganda. So extensive was the Arab trading in the interior that it was said as a joke that 'when they pipe in Zanzibar, people dance on the shores of the great lakes'. Arabs established settlements at certain key points, such as Tabora in the Nyamwezi country and Ujiji on Lake Tanganyika. These were mainly commercial depots, but in time they grew to exercise a certain military and political control over the surrounding countryside. Burton and Speke visited Tabora in 1858, and wrote:

The Arabs live comfortably, and even splendidly. The houses, though single-storied, are large, substantial and capable of defence. Their gardens are extensive and well planted; they receive regular supplies from the coast; they are surrounded by troops of slaves, whom they train to divers crafts and callings; rich men have riding asses from Zanzibar, and even the poorest keep flocks and herds.

Generally the Arabs obtained their ivory and slaves from the local rulers, who, armed with the imported guns, sent their warriors to hunt elephants and to raid the forests of neighbouring peoples, often capturing slaves in the process. In most of East Africa, however, slaving was more a by-product of the ivory rush than the primary object of the trade. Only the country around Lake Nyasa was primarily a slaving region, where the powerful Yao chiefs raided the ill-organised and defenceless peoples of the eastern lakeshore. The Bemba, and later the Ngoni, did the same on the west. It was along the trade route from Lake Nyasa to the coast that Livingstone noted some of the worst atrocities that he witnessed in all his long travels:

We passed a woman tied by the neck to a tree and dead...We saw others tied up in a similar manner, and one lying on the path shot or stabbed for she was in a pool of blood. The explanation we got invariably was that the Arab who owned these victims was enraged at losing his money by the slaves being unable to march...Today we came upon a man dead from starvation...One of our men wandered and found a number of slaves with slave-sticks on, abandoned by their master from want of food... We passed village after village and gardens, all deserted.

Elsewhere, however, the emphasis was on ivory, though slaves were bought and sold at every stage along the trade-routes. The Nyamwezi, for example, were great buyers of slaves, whom they employed in agricultural work while they themselves were absent on long trading journeys.

## The Ngoni and Mirambo

The situation in Tanganyika was complicated towards the middle of the nineteenth century by the incursions of the Ngoni from the south. Bands of warriors who had broken away from Shaka's Zulu kingdom (see Chapter 5) were swollen by the attachment of the remnants of peoples they had defeated on their long northward trek. They spread across much of western and southern Tanganyika to the east and west of Lake Nyasa, where they finally settled as ruling aristocracies. Far beyond the range of their settlement, their outlying raiders and their military tactics were absorbed into the new groupings of tribes that were taking place in Tanganyika. Warrior bands, called *ruga-ruga* in Nyamwezi country, and *maviti* and *magwangwara* elsewhere, roamed the countryside, usually pillaging on their own account, but ready to be employed by ruthless war-lords or Arab traders. Sometimes their raids caused their victims to combine against them. The centralised state of the Hehe, for instance, in south-central Tanganyika, was formed in this way. On the other hand a young Nyamwezi chief, Mirambo, actually took groups of Ngoni *ruga-ruga* into his service and used them to build up and extend his hereditary chiefdom in the western part of Unyamwezi. Mirambo became powerful enough, in the 187('s, to rival the Arab merchant princes. By 1880 he had gained control of the Ujiji trade-route to Lake Tanganyika and was able to threaten even the route leading north-westwards to Buganda. It was with Mirambo, and not with his fellow Arabs, that Tippu Tib allied himself in his commercial exploitation of the eastern Congo, which was described in Chapter 4.

### The interlacustrine region

North of the Nyamwezi country, the trade with the rich inter-lacustrine region developed, from the 1840s on, mainly under the control of Swahili-Arab merchants. The main trade-route ran from Tabora through Karagwe, where there was a large Arab commercial settlement at Kafuro near the capital, to the Kagera river. Here it divided, a westerly branch leading off through the plains of eastern Ankole to Bunyoro, and an easterly branch following near the shoreline of Lake Victoria towards the capital of Buganda. The Tutsi kingdom of Rwanda, though still at the height of its power, would admit no strangers within its frontiers, and such outside trade as there was passed by Rwanda caravans to and from Karagwe. Ankole was nearly as hostile to foreigners as Rwanda. The big trading countries were Bunyoro and Buganda. For, in addition to her powerful armies, Buganda was the chief naval power of Lake Victoria, and, as the nineteenth century went on, fleets of the great Buganda canoes made of planks sewn together, with their high prows visible far over the water, came regularly to the southern shores of the lake, competing with the overland trade-routes. In this way Kabakas Suna and Mutesa, who reigned through the middle years of the century from about 1832 till 1884, steadily built up their stocks of cloth and guns, and used them to arm and pay ever more efficient armies, which harried the Basoga to the east and the Bahaya to the south, and nibbled more cautiously at the renewed military power of Bunyoro to the north-west.

It was not only from the south-east, however, that the outside world was forcing itself upon the interlacustrine states. As we shall see in the next chapter, the trading frontier of the Egyptian Sudan had been established since the 1840s in the Bari country to the south of the Nile swamps, and by the 1860s the Khartoum-based ivory-traders were operating among the Acholi people of the northern province of modern Uganda. The Egyptians established their first contacts with Bunyoro by intervening in the succession struggle following the death of the ruler, Kamurasi, in 1869. In that year the Khedive Ismail of Egypt sent the British explorer Samuel Baker to be governor of this 'Equatorial Province' of the Sudan. Baker tried unsuccessfully to occupy Bunyoro, and had to be content with establishing forts along its northern edge. In 1873, however, he was succeeded by Charles Gordon, who had definite instructions to extend the Egyptian dominions to the Great Lakes. Thus in 1874 Gordon's emissaries reached the court of Kabaka Mutesa of Buganda.

Mutesa knew enough of the outside world to guess what was afoot. An Egyptian garrison was detained by the Kabaka, and given a taste of Buganda's power to hurt, and then allowed to retire unharmed. Meanwhile Mutesa strengthened his links with the strangers from the east coast, buying more arms, listening to the Islamic teachings of his Arab friends, even learning to write the Swahili language in Arabic characters. His fears of the Egyptians were described by the Anglican missionary Alexander Mackay a few years later, in his biography which was written by his sister:

Egypt had always been an object of great suspicion in the eyes of the Baganda. Captain Speke, who formed Mtesa's acquaintaince a dozen years before Stanley, tells how the king objected to his passing through Uganda to Egypt via the Nile...The Egyptian station of Mruli was regarded by Mtesa with very jealous feelings, and the Arabs lost no opportunity to fan the flame. Knowing well that with the presence of the white man the hope of their gains was gone, they told him that Colonel Gordon and the Turks (as they called the Egyptians) would soon come and 'eat the country'. The Baganda constantly had the word *Baturki* on their lips. Mtesa never wearied in narrating to Mackay all his intercourse with white men: how

Speke brought Grant, and then sent Baker; how Colonel Long (Gordon's agent) came and was followed by Stanley. 'What do they all want?' asked Mtesa. 'Are they not coming to look for lakes, that they may put ships and guns on them? Did not Speke come here by the Queen's orders for that purpose?'

It was almost certainly the presence of a second Egyptian delegation at his court at the time of the explorer Stanley's visit in 1875 which caused him to encourage Stanley to let it be known in Europe that he would like Christian missionaries to come and settle in his country. Mutesa was an exceptionally intelligent and open-minded man, and no doubt he was genuinely impressed by what his European visitors—first Speke (1862) and then Stanley—had told him of Christianity and European civilisation. As a statesman he realised that if Buganda was really threatened by the Egyptian advance from the north, it would be wise to increase the number of his other foreign contacts, so as to be able to play them off against the Egyptians. Church of England missionaries from Britain therefore arrived in Buganda in 1877, and Roman Catholic missionaries from France in 1879, and, so long as the Egyptian threat lasted, both received a warm welcome. In the course of the next six or seven years Christianity became so deeply established among a minority of the court circle in Buganda that it was able to survive a brief, but terrible, persecution at the hands of Mutesa's successor, Mwanga, in 1885–6.

### Peoples and trade-routes of Kenya

Right up until the colonial period the main trade outlet of Buganda and the other interlacustrine states remained the south-easterly one, linking up with the trans-Tanganyikan route at Tabora. It was difficult to set up a more direct route from Buganda to the coast at Mombasa because of the nomadic and warlike way of life of so many of the peoples, notably the Masai, in what became Kenya. With the Masai, it was not merely that they attacked strangers: throughout the nineteenth century they fought almost continuously among themselves. Thus the whole region of the Kenya highlands was in a perpetual state of unrest. Traders could only pass through this country at great danger to themselves and to their goods, and no regular trading links could be set up by the Swahili-Arabs with the densely populated lands of the Luo and the Abaluhya in the Kavirondo region to the north-east of Lake Victoria until several decades after they had taken over the Nyamwezi routes to the south and west of the lake. The equivalent among the Kenya peoples of the Nyamwezi were the Kamba, who lived some 200 miles inland from Mombasa. They made trading contacts with the Kikuyu on one side and with the coastmen on the other as early as the 1830s, when a series of disastrous famines caused them to leave their homelands in search of food. The German missionary traveller Johann Krapf noted how: 'The Swahili purvey to the Wakamba cotton fabrics (Americani), blue calico, glass beads, copper and brass-wire, red ochre, black pepper, salt and blue vitriol (zinc), and receive in exchange, chiefly cattle and ivory' (J. L. Krapf, *Travels in Eastern Africa* (1860), p. 353). The Kamba continued to monopolise trade between Kikuyuland and Mombasa until, in the 1880s, the Arabs with their superior organisation and weapons drew off the Kikuyu trade into their own routes. The Arabs did not thrust into the hinterland of any part of the Kenyan or north Tanganyikan coast until the 1860s, when they managed to open routes to the Chaga of the Kilimanjaro region. Thence they were able to work their way across the narrowest part of the Masai plain and on westwards to Kavirondo. By about 1880 these Arab ivory-traders and hunters had reached the country to the west of Lake Rudolf. Here, in the last unexploited ivory district of East Africa, they came into contact with Egyptians from the southern Sudan, and with Ethiopians, all concerned with enriching themselves from the ivory trade.

### The summit of Swahili-Arab power in East Africa

We have seen that the most important development during the first three-quarters of the nineteenth century in East Africa was the commercial penetration of the whole region by the Swahili-Arabs from the East Coast. And now for a brief period in the late 1870s and early 1880s it seemed that the commercial empire of Zanzibar might turn itself into a political one. In the eyes of the British Consul-General at Zanzibar, Sir John Kirk, this was a development very much to be hoped for. Kirk had been in Zanzibar since 1864 and had built up a remarkable degree of influence, first with Sultan Majid and then with his brother, Sultan Barghash. Neither Kirk nor his masters in London wished for direct British intervention in East Africa. In their view a friendly and easily influenced Sultan of Zanzibar would be both the cheapest and the most effective means of achieving their two objectives, which were to end the East African slave-trade and to avoid the intervention of other European powers in the area. In 1873 Barghash was persuaded to abolish the slave-trade within his dominions, and from then onwards, so far as the British government was concerned, the wider the Sultan's dominions, the better. Inspired by Kirk, Barghash engaged a British officer to enlarge and train his army, and in the late 1870s he began to set up garrisons along the line of the main trans-Tanganyikan trade-route. As Kirk watched the growing interests of other European powers, especially of King Leopold of the Belgians, so he spurred Barghash to greater efforts. The Arab traders in the far interior were encouraged to turn from commerce to conquest, and did so —first Tippu Tib in the region round Lake Tanganyika; next the Arabs who were settled round the north end of Lake Nyasa; and finally the Arabs in Buganda. In 1887 a special representative of Sultan Barghash arrived in Buganda, where the previous year the Kabaka Mwanga had executed a number of Christians at his court. This representative plotted with the Muslim party in the kingdom to depose Mwanga in 1888, and then to seize power for themselves. A younger brother of Mwanga was declared to be Kabaka. This Muslim success, however, was short-lived. By 1890 Mwanga had regained power, with the support of the Christian Baganda, in spite of his previous persecution of their religion.

The achievements of Tippu Tib and other Arab chiefs marked the summit of Arab power in East Africa; and to the European missionaries living scattered about in the interior this appeared in a very different light from that in which it had been conceived by Kirk at Zanzibar. Where Kirk had imagined a Zanzibar dominion recognised by the powers and responsive to British influence, the missionaries saw burning villages and starving refugees, and a new, anti-European and anti-Christian attitude among the Arabs. The experience made them long for, and in some cases work for, European colonial occupation. In the event, however, Swahili-Arab imperialism did not last long. Before any missionary condemnation of it had time to take effect, a handful of German adventurers had shown that the Sultan's power in the interior of East Africa was nothing but a hollow sham. Neither Carl Peters nor his associates in the Society for German Colonisation had ever set foot in East Africa before 1884; but they had grasped the essential fact, that a mere 30 or 40 miles inland from the coast there were African communities which owed no allegiance to the Sultan of Zanzibar. They realised that the rulers of these could be persuaded without too much trouble to sign pieces of paper placing their lands under the protection of a European power. From that moment onwards Kirk's plan was doomed. The European scramble for East Africa had begun.

## Madagascar

King Nampoina's conquests at the end of the eighteenth and the beginning of the nineteenth centuries laid the foundations for the great Merina state. This must rank as one of the most remarkable political creations in the whole of Africa in the pre-colonial period. Nampoina's successor, Radama I (1810–28), transformed the warrior chiefdom into a nation comparable in many ways to the smaller states of Europe. He rounded off Nampoina's conquests, so that by the end of his reign two-thirds of the island was under Hova domination. The rich kingdom of Betsileo, in the highlands around Fianarantsoa to the south of Tananarive, recognised the control of Radama. The Merina army was equipped with fire-arms, largely supplied by the British from the Indian Ocean island of Mauritius, and Radama was advised on military matters by a strange trio—a Scotsman, a Jamaican and a Frenchman. The King, however, did not confine his attentions to conquests and military reforms. In 1820, with royal permission, the first Christian missionaries, belonging to the British London Missionary Society, arrived in Merina. The fruits of their efforts were astonishing—after seven years it was estimated that 4,000 Hova could read and write their own language, and many had been trained to perform European trades.

The pagan priests and the older Hova upper class naturally felt their positions threatened by the new religion and the young educated men, and there followed an almost inevitable reaction. Radama I was succeeded in 1828 by the first of the queens of nineteenth-century Merina, Ranavalona. In 1835 she closed the London Missionary Society's schools, and only allowed those foreigners to enter her kingdom who could contribute directly towards its military and economic power. But the seeds of Christianity and of Western education could not easily be up-rooted. After a violent struggle for power at the death of Queen Ranavalona in 1861, a most remarkable man became prime minister—Rainilaiarivony, who remained in office until the coming of the French expedition in 1894. He made certain of his position by becoming the husband of three successive queens. Missionary work was resumed, and in 1868 Rainilaiarivony himself became a Christian. By the 1880s (by which time French Roman Catholic missionaries were also active) there had been a massive conversion to Christianity, and the proportion of Malagasy children at school was comparable with that in western Europe. Pagan beliefs, however, did not wither away, and, indeed, continued to flourish, in many cases among converts to Christianity.

This continuation of traditional beliefs was one sign of the considerable strain that was building up within the Merina state. Its subject peoples resented the often harsh rule of the Hova aristocracy, and many of the Hova resented the huge personal power of the Prime Minister. Although the majority of Christians were converts of the London Missionary Society, and although Britain kept close diplomatic links with Merina, a great amount of the external trade of Madagascar was in French hands. The Hova were proudly independent, and had no wish to be under the 'protection' of either Britain or France. However, the French were determined to secure their commercial interests, and in 1885, after the first of the Franco-Malagasy wars, forced a treaty upon Merina. Like the Wichale Treaty between Italy and Ethiopia (see Chapter 10), the French and Malagasy versions of this treaty differed. The Malagasy considered that they had maintained their independence; the French thought that they had secured control over the external affairs of the island, and had thereby set up a protectorate over it. As in the case of Ethiopia, the misunderstandings arising out of this treaty led to increased friction between France and the kingdom of Merina.

# 7

# NORTH-EAST AFRICA BEFORE PARTITION

## *Political decline and commercial stagnation*

As we saw in Chapter 1, the states of North-East Africa at the end of the eighteenth century were suffering, without exception, from a serious decline in their political power and a stagnation in the economic and cultural activities of their subjects. The authority of rulers was much less than it had been in former times. Every-where nomadic peoples were overrunning the lands of the settled agriculturalists, on whose production the power of kingdoms and chiefdoms very largely depended. North of the Swahili coast, the Somalis with their herds of camels and goats (which were particu-larly destructive of vegetation) were steadily extending the desert region, which could only support a nomadic pastoral way of life. Behind them, all round the core of the Ethiopian highlands, the Galla were still spreading by infiltration and conquest into the Sidama kingdoms and other neighbouring areas which had once been part of the Ethiopian empire. What was left of Christian Ethiopia had fallen apart into the regions that had formerly been united under the rule of the Emperors—these were Shoa and Lasta, Amhara and Tigre, and many more. The Red Sea was full of pirates, and the lack of security had reduced the flow of pilgrims to the holy places of Islam to a mere trickle. With the breakdown of orderly government, the trade of the whole region had suffered severely, especially that of Egypt, the Funj kingdom and Ethiopia. A further reason for commercial decline was that the trade of all these states had been linked to the larger trade of the Indian Ocean, which was now increasingly diverted round the Cape of Good Hope to western Europe.

### *Muhammad Ali (1805–49): the revival of Red Sea trade*

The turn of the tide in the fortunes of all the states in this part of Africa was Napoleon's invasion of Egypt in 1798. The French occupation, though it lasted little more than two years, showed up the weakness of the Muslim world in relation to the countries of Christian Europe which were forcing themselves upon it. In particular, it revealed the inability of the Ottoman Sultan to control and defend the southern part of his vast empire. Above all, Napoleon's invasion threw up in Egypt an outstanding leader, who was able to understand these events and to apply the lesson he had learned. The history, not only of Egypt, but of the whole of North-East Africa and the Red Sea area, was dominated during the first half of the nineteenth century by the figure of Muhammad Ali Pasha. This remarkable man combined the talents of an oriental despot with a shrewd understanding of the very different world of Europe. Muhammad Ali was a man of great charm and utter ruthlessness, an able administrator, and a cunning diplomat. Although he himself was not an outstanding military leader, several of his many sons were extremely efficient commanders. He was concerned above all to secure his position as Ottoman viceroy in Egypt, and to make the office hereditary within his own family. In addition, however, he restored the beginnings of order and prosperity to the Red Sea area, and provided Egypt with the framework of a modern state.

Muhammad Ali was born in 1769 in Macedonia, one of the Ottoman territories in the Balkans, and first entered Egypt as an officer in the Ottoman forces sent there to deal with the French invasion. With the support of a body of Albanian soldiers loyal to him personally rather than to the far-off Ottoman Sultan, he made himself by 1805 the most powerful military boss in Cairo. The following year he was appointed *vali* (Turkish, viceroy, governor) by the Sultan. His power was at first very uncertain, there being many other military groups opposed to his own. In 1811 he dealt with this opposition with characteristic ruthlessness by inviting the principal Mamluk *amirs* to a banquet in Cairo and then having some 300 of them massacred in a narrow alley leading out of the citadel on their way home. His power in Egypt was now secure, and for the next eight years he devoted his main efforts to the pacification of the Red Sea area. First and foremost, this involved the suppression of the Wahhabis, the followers of a fanatical Muslim sect which had arisen among the Bedouin tribesmen of the Arabian desert. The Wahhabi leaders denied the authority of the Ottoman government, and disrupted the annual pilgrimage caravans travelling to the holy cities of Mecca and Medina. Muhammad Ali's armies cleared the Hijaz of the Wahhabis, and in 1818 finally overcame the fanatical tribesmen in the heart of Arabia. The holy places were restored by Muhammad Ali to the authority of his overlord. The Ottoman garrison towns of Suakin and Massawa, on the African side of the Red Sea, remained under Ottoman control until the end of the Viceroy's reign, when, in 1846, they were leased by the Sultan to Egypt; only in 1865 were they permanently annexed to the Egyptian Sudan.

Nevertheless, Muhammad Ali's early operations in the Red Sea area brought about a complete revival of the pilgrimage and an even more striking revival of trade. The Red Sea route began to be used by the British for rapid communications with India; and Jidda, the Ottoman port in the Hijaz, became temporarily the most important commercial town between Bombay and Cairo. This in turn revived all the local trade-routes running inland on the African side of the Red Sea, especially those to the Ethiopian highlands. From this region the most highly valued female slaves were sent to the Hijaz, where they were bought as concubines by the more prosperous class of pilgrims. Also in great demand in the Hijaz and elsewhere in the Muslim world was the musk combed from the fur of the civet-cat, which was the speciality of the Sidama kingdoms. There was a similar revival in the gold trade from Enarya in the south-western highlands, and also in the splendid coffee grown all over the highland region. The political recovery of the Ethiopian state (in the northern provinces of Tigre and Amhara) and of its powerful daughter state of Shoa, which began in earnest in the 1830s and 1840s, was made possible very largely through the revenue from this commercial revival. The increased trade enabled the rulers of these states to start re-equipping their soldiers with fire-arms in place of spears.

## The Egyptian conquest of the Sudan

From the Red Sea, Muhammad Ali turned his eyes in 1820 towards the Sudan. The Arabian campaigns had been costly in troops, and he hoped to secure an inexhaustible supply of Negro slave recruits for his armies in the southern Sudan. The Funj sultanate was quite incapable of offering any resistance. It had already lost control of all the northern part of the Sudan; Dongola was in the hands of a group of Mamluk refugees who had escaped from Muhammad Ali's clutches in Egypt. With only 4,000 well-armed men, Muhammad Ali's son Ismail was able to make steady progress up the Nile, overcoming the Mamluks at Dongola, and entering the Funj capital at Sennar unopposed in June 1821. The Funj sultan was deposed, and he and his family received an Egyptian pension. There was one brief rising in 1822, in which Ismail lost his life. After this had been suppressed, the Egyptian colonial capital was founded in 1824 at Khartoum, at the junction of the White and Blue Niles, and the Sudan remained under Egyptian rule until the Mahdi's rebellion of 1881–4.

The economic benefits which Muhammad Ali's reign conferred upon Egypt and the Red Sea coasts did not generally extend to the Sudan. Attempts made by the Egyptian administration to widen the range of agricultural production, such as the settlement of Egyptian peasants in the Gezira around Sennar, were not very successful. The Arabic-speaking groups living in the Nile valley in the north were regularly taxed by the government, and

GREECE

*Black Sea*

Istanbul

Navarino Bay

Ibrahim Pasha

*Napoleon 1798*

CRETE (Egyptian 1823)

*Cyprus*

British Occupation 1882

Alexandria

Nile *Delta*

Port Said

*Suez Canal (1859-1869)*

Cairo   Suez

EGYPT

Battle of Tell al-Kabir 1882

Muhammad Ali

SYRIA

*Egyptian 1831-1840*

ARABIA

*Najd*

*Wahhabi*

Persian Gulf

Medina

*1811-1818*

Wadi Halfa

Jidda   Mecca

OMAN

Muscat

Dongola (Mamluks 1811-1820)

Suakim (Egyptian 1846-1865)

Nile

Beja

Red Sea

(Egyptian 1821)

El Obeid (Egyptian 1821)

Khartoum (founded 1830, Mahdi 1885)

Sennar

Massawa (Egyptian 1846-1865, Italian 1885)

Jabal Ghedi

Abba Island

*Tigre*

Axum

*Amhara*

Assab (Italian 1882)

Aden (British 1839)

*Socotra*

*Shilluk*

Lake Tana

Obok (French 1862)

Zeila (Egyptian 1874-1875, British 1884)

Alula

Bahr al-Ghazal

Fashoda

*Blue Nile*

*Shoa*

Addis Ababa

Berbera (Egyptian 1875-1884, British 1884)

Majerteyn Coast

To El Fasher (Egyptian 1874)

Sobat

*Galla*

Harar (Egyptian 1875-1884)

White Nile

*Enarya*

Obbia

Gondokoro

*Bari* (Evacuated by Egyptians 1889)

Lake Rudolf

*Galla*

Coast

Juba

Mogadishu

Benadir Coast

*Somalis*

Bunyoro Baker 1872

To Buganda

To Kismayu (Egyptian 1875-1876)

Egyptian expansion (Muhammad Ali Khedive Ismail)

Limits of Egyptian rule

12   North-East Africa: Egyptian expansion

some of them became quite prosperous through their involvement in the considerable shipping traffic that developed on the river; others became even more wealthy by partaking in the slave- and ivory-trades in the southern Sudan. The nomadic tribes in the deserts to the east and west of the river supplied the large numbers of camels and other domestic animals which, after slaves and ivory, formed the main exports of the Sudan. All the serious efforts of the Egyptian government were concentrated, however, on the region to the south of Khartoum. 'You are aware', Muhammad Ali wrote to his Treasurer in 1825, 'that the end of all our effort and of this expense is to procure negroes. Please show zeal in carrying out our wishes in this capital matter.' Every year the Khartoum government dispatched military expeditions southwards to Dar Fung and westwards to Kordofan and the Nuba mountains on official slave-raids, which returned with as many as 5,000 captives each. For a time the Shilluk with their centralised kingdom on the White Nile above Fashoda made an effective limit to the Egyptians' southward penetration. But Muhammad Ali, hoping for the discovery of gold, was always urging his governors to press farther south. In 1838 he even visited the Sudan himself to encourage these efforts. From 1839 to 1841 one of his Turkish sea-captains, called Salim, broke through the opposition of the Shilluk in a series of expeditions up the White Nile. He proved the river to be navigable for a thousand miles south of Khartoum, as far as Gondokoro in the land of the Bari near the modern Sudan–Uganda frontier. The dream of gold did not come true. In its place appeared the reality of hundreds of thousands of square miles of elephant country, the human inhabitants of which were still ignorant of the value of ivory. From then on the penetration of the traders developed fast, with European firms based on Khartoum in the forefront. Through their consuls these firms resisted the attempt by the Egyptian government to set up a monopoly over the ivory trade.

At first the forces at the disposal of the traders and of the local inhabitants were fairly evenly balanced. The traders with their armed sailing-boats were superior so long as they kept to the river, but on land the local people had the advantage. While these conditions lasted, the exchange of goods, though unequal in value, was peaceful enough. There came a time, however, when few elephants could be shot near the river banks and when the local demand for beads and cheap trinkets was satisfied. To get ivory it now became necessary to leave the river banks, and to try to find trade-goods which would arouse the interest of the peoples of the back-country, who were even less sophisticated than the groups alongside the rivers. The traders responsed to the new conditions by bringing up bands of armed Arab followers, recruited mainly from the Nile valley north of Khartoum. They placed these men in fortified encampments called *zeribas* spread over the whole back-country of the White Nile and the Bahr al-Ghazal. There was little surplus food available for them, and they were often forced to raid the villages in order to feed themselves. The local people, being mostly Nilotic pastoralists with the simplest material needs, wanted only cattle and ever more cattle. Armed raiding-parties therefore scoured the countryside for cattle, and exchanged them (often with the people from whom they had been captured) for ivory and slaves. Petherick, the British Consul in Khartoum, described the situation in 1863: 'Instead of the introduction of more valuable and civilising merchandise, such as cutlery, or cloth for wearing apparel, as articles for barter—when the value of glass and copper ornaments began to decline and lose their charm—the traders disgraced themselves by descending to enrich themselves by the plunder and destruction of tribe after tribe.'

### Muhammad Ali and the European powers

By the early 1820s Muhammad Ali was far stronger than his overlord, the Ottoman Sultan. He realised the importance of sea-power in the military forces of the European states, and at great expense built an Egyptian navy in the Mediterranean. In 1821 the first major revolt broke out in the Ottoman empire, when the Greeks rose to claim their independence. The Sultan was not strong enough to suppress the revolt, and called upon Muhammad Ali to help him. Egyptian forces rapidly overwhelmed the rebels on the island of Crete, and in 1824 a great military expedition under the Viceroy's eldest son, Ibrahim Pasha, set out for Greece from Alexandria. So successful was Ibrahim in the Morea (the southern part of Greece) that it seemed that the Greek revolt was doomed. At this point Russia threatened to intervene on the side of the Greek Christians. To prevent this a joint French and British naval force was sent to Greece, in an attempt to enforce an armistice between the rebels and the Egyptian army. Almost by accident hostilities broke out, and at the battle of Navarino Bay in 1827 the Egyptian fleet was destroyed. The following year Ibrahim Pasha had to evacuate his troops from the Morea, and Greece became independent.

This was the first serious reverse suffered by Muhammad Ali, and he naturally wanted recompense from the Sultan for the costly Greek campaigns. The Sultan went back on a promise to make him *pasha* (governor) of Palestine and Syria, and so, in 1831, Ibrahim's army took over these provinces from direct Ottoman control. By now the Sultan was thoroughly alarmed at the power of his over-mighty subject, but could do nothing to curb it. In 1833 Muhammad Ali was officially recognised as governor of Syria and Palestine. A further attempt by the Ottomans in 1839 to drive him out of these provinces ended in the defeat of the Sultan's forces by Ibrahim Pasha; the Egyptian forces seemed ready to march to Istanbul and dictate terms to a new Sultan, who was only a young boy. Again the European powers intervened (Britain and France were fearful lest Russia should take action by herself and thereby gain a foothold on the Mediterranean), and in 1840 forced Muhammad Ali to withdraw from Palestine and Syria. Yet he obtained one solid gain—the viceroyalty of Egypt was made hereditary in his family, and his authority over the Sudan was recognised by the Sultan.

To meet the shortage of recruits for the army after his Arabian and Sudanese campaigns, and because of the failure of his plan to obtain Negro slave soldiers, Muhammad Ali took in 1822 the new step of forcing into his army as conscripts the Egyptian *fellahin* (Arabic, peasants). Since the Arab conquests of the seventh century, all soldiers in Egypt had been foreigners. Now native Egyptians began to be recruited into the ranks, and later in the century they were even trained as officers. This was to have a great effect on the growth of nationalism in Egypt. Muhammad Ali also imported European—mostly French—military advisers and instructors to establish army medical, artillery and engineering schools. One result of this was that European text-books were translated into Turkish and Arabic, and some of the cleverest young Egyptian officers learned French and became familiar with western political as well as military ideas. Like every other successful African ruler of this time, Muhammad Ali was dependent on European arms and military equipment. It was in order to pay for these arms that he undertook most of the economic and administrative reforms in Egypt for which he is above all remembered. The amount of land under irrigation was greatly increased. Cotton and sugar were introduced as economic crops, and grain cultivation was expanded. The old Mamluk land-owning aristocracy was largely replaced by the family and favourites of the Viceroy. This did not put an end to corruption and exploitation, but it helped to spread new ideas. The main failing of Muhammad Ali's government was that all power remained so closely concentrated in his own hands. Weaker and less capable successors were unable to control the machine he had created.

### The Khedive Ismail (1863–79)

Muhammad Ali died in 1849, and was followed as viceroy by undistinguished successors—the brilliant Ibrahim Pasha had died the year before. Abbas I (1849–54), Muhammad Ali's conserva-tive grandson, was hostile to European ideas, and his son Muhammad Said (1854–63), the uncle of Abbas, a rather weak man, was by contrast too much under the influence of European favourites. During his reign, in 1859, the construction of the Suez Canal was begun. A new chapter, however, opened both for Egypt and for North-East Africa as a whole with the accession of another of Muhammad Ali's grandsons, Ismail. Ismail's ideas were large and enlightened, but they were not backed by good judgement or by any sense of financial prudence. At home Ismail lived the luxurious life of a mighty sovereign, and he was given the old Persian title of *Khedive* by the Ottoman Sultan. His public policies were undertaken in the same spirit. Egypt should be projected at one bound into the world of railways, telegraphs, factories, schools and town-planning. The Suez Canal, which Muhammad Ali had consistently refused to sanction, rightly foreseeing that it would place Egypt at the mercy of the much more powerful navies of the nations of Europe, was completed by Ismail (in 1869). A fleet of steamships was ordered, which were to ply between the Mediterranean and the Red Sea ports. In the year of Ismail's accession, the British explorers Speke and Grant passed through Cairo with the tale of the rich interlacustrine kingdoms at the head of the White Nile, and at once Ismail's imagination responded. He would pass round the Nile cataracts with a railway, and he would place steamers on the White Nile and the equatorial lakes. All the ivory flowing eastwards to Zanzibar would be diverted northwards to Cairo. In 1869 he commissioned Baker, the explorer of Lake Albert, at the huge salary of £10,000 a year, to put this immense scheme into effect. Baker in four years achieved little more than the assembling of some steamers on the White Nile, and was succeeded in 1873 by Gordon. Gordon insisted that the grand design could only work if Ismail occupied a base on the east coast of Africa. He noted in his diary on 21 January 1875:

I have proposed to the Khedive to send 150 men in a steamer to Mombaz Bay, 250 miles north of Zanzibar, and there to establish a station, and then to push towards M'tesa. If I can do that, I shall make my base at Mombaz, and give up Khartum and the bother of steamers, etc. The centre of Africa would be much more effectually opened out, as the only valuable parts of the country are the highlands near M'tesa, while south of Khartum is wretched marsh. I hope the Khedive will do it.

Ismail agreed, and later the same year sent another expensive expedition, this time to Kismayu at the mouth of the Juba river. This expedition, however, was recalled as the result of British pressure exercised on behalf of the Sultan of Zanzibar. At the same time Ismail's forces occupied Zeila and Harrar in northern Somaliland, but attacks on Tigre from Massawa resulted in heavy defeats at the hands of the Ethiopian emperor, John.

The only lasting achievement of Ismail's reign was the Suez Canal, and this was for many years of small benefit to Egypt. Ismail's vast ambitions for the modernisation of Egypt and the creation of an empire embracing the whole of North-East Africa only landed him in the clutches of European money-lenders. Already in 1875 he was forced to sell his own shares in the Suez Canal in order to meet his most pressing debts. By 1879 the Egyptian treasury was bankrupt, and later the same year Ismail himself was deposed by the Sultan at the suggestion of the European powers. A committee representing the European countries to whom Egypt owed money took over the direction of the Egyptian finances. European financial experts took seats in the cabinet of Ismail's son and successor, Tawfiq.

The economy measures introduced by the European advisers hit the army officers hardest. Many were put on half-pay, and a group of them, led by Colonel Urabi Pasha, rebelled in 1881 and set up military control over the Khedive's government. They threatened to repudiate the national debt. This military revolution led at last to the direct intervention of the European powers. Britain and France planned to act together to restore the weak authority of Tawfiq and to protect European financial interests.

In the end France was prevented from taking part by an internal political crisis and by events in Tunisia and Indo-China. Thus Britain invaded Egypt alone in 1882, and defeated the forces of Urabi Pasha at the battle of Tell al-Kabir. Britain's occupation of Egypt was to be a major factor in the partition of Africa that followed.

### The Sudan and the Mahdiyya (1881–98)

Only a year before the British occupation of Egypt the Sudan revolted against its Egyptian government. This was not a movement originating in the Negro south of the Sudan, where Egyptian rule had been most oppressive. The core of the rebels came rather from the nomadic groups to the west of the Nile, especially the Baqqara, Arabic-speaking cattle-owning people of Kordofan and the Nuba Mountains. The nomads were the first to rally to the standard of revolt. They resented the Egyptian government's attempts to tax and to control them more than did the settled agriculturists of the Nile valley north and south of Khartoum. These riverain Arabs, the descendants of the old population of the Funj kingdom, tended to 'sit on the fence', waiting until it was clear that the Mahdi was successful before joining him. Economically, their grievance was that the Egyptian government in the early days had conscripted many of their slaves, on whose labour they had depended for their livelihood. More recently, since the reign of Ismail, the government had prevented the importation of more slaves from the south, and had kept even the ivory trade in its own hands. Religious grievances were also important. The Egyptians had increasingly brought into the Sudan their own Muslim teachers and religious dignitaries, whereas Sudanese Islam had its own strongly established *shaikhs* (holy men) and religious brotherhoods, who resented the newcomers and their different ways. Ismail's appointment of Gordon, a Christian deeply committed to the anti-slavery campaign, as governor-general of the whole Sudan, upset the local Muslims still further. The nomads, at least, were ready to follow a religious leader who promised to overthrow Egyptian rule, which in their eyes was impious and heretical as well as being at times harsh.

Such a religious leader appeared in the person of Muhammad Ahmad, who was born in 1844, the son of a boat-builder near Khartoum. After an intensely religious upbringing, he became a teacher and was granted the title of *shaikh*. In 1881 he proclaimed himself the *mahdi*, the Saviour of the Muslims, who would re-establish Islam in its primitive purity. At first the British authorities in Egypt took little notice of what seemed to be a local religious movement. When, after the capture of El Obeid by the Mahdi's Baqqara horsemen in 1883, they realised its seriousness, it was already too late to restrain it except by a major military expedition far beyond the means of the bankrupt Egyptian state. The British government had at this time no wish to extend its responsibilities in Egypt and therefore decided that the reconquest must wait until Egypt's own finances were sufficiently restored to undertake it. Meanwhile it was clear that the Mahdi had the enthusiastic support of most sections of the Muslim Sudanese. Khartoum fell to him in 1885, and Gordon, who had been sent to evacuate the garrison, was killed in the fighting. The Mahdi himself died shortly after the capture of Khartoum, and was succeeded by his general, Abdallahi, who was known as the *khalifa* (Arabic, successor). Abdallahi established a strong secular administration in place of the Mahdi's dream of a society that would be organised on a religious basis similar to the Muslim state in the earliest days of Islam.

The Khalifa's rule lasted for thirteen years. It might have lasted longer if the European powers had not by then been partitioning Africa among themselves. As it was, the government of the Mahdiyya in the Sudan continued until almost the end of the nineteenth century. The reconquest of the Sudan by Anglo-Egyptian forces was almost the closing episode of the partition. It was one of the few cases in which a government that was still carrying out most of its functions had to be defeated and overthrown by an invading army in order to make way for colonial rule.

### The re-unification of Ethiopia (1855–89)

The most remarkable development in the whole of Africa during the later nineteenth century was perhaps the re-unification and development of Ethiopia into a state which could not merely survive the partition of Africa, but even in a sense take part in it. As we have seen, the opportunity for this revival had been created by the re-opening of the Ethiopian region to external trade during the second quarter of the century. This enabled the more enterprising local rulers to build up their power by buying fire-arms. So far there was nothing essentially different from what was happening in all the more powerful native states of tropical Africa. In Ethiopia, however, there was in addition the memory of

13. North-East Africa: Ethiopian expansion and the Mahdiyya

a great state which had existed in the past. The ancient Christian Church still existed as a single national organisation in Tigre, Amhara and Shoa and the other almost completely independent provinces of the old empire. It acted as a unifying influence. It marked off the Christian core of the country in the highlands from the Muslim states to the north and east, and from the pagan Galla lands to the south. Because of the education provided by the Church, there was still a small class of literate and sophisticated people. This educated class had some idea of how to enter into diplomatic relations with the outside world, and how to give foreigners the impression of a civilised power. All these factors were there to be used by a national leader, as soon as one arose. The first to do so was Ras Kassa, a successful robber chief from the north-western frontier, who in 1855 managed to have himself crowned as emperor by the leaders of the Church at the ancient capital of Axum in Tigre. Ras Kassa took the name of Theodore. Two consuls from the British Foreign Office visited Theodore soon after his coronation, and wrote their impressions of him in their official report:

King Theodorus is of a striking countenance, peculiarly polite and engaging when pleased, and mostly displaying great tact and delicacy. He is persuaded that he is destined to restore the glories of the Ethiopian Empire, and to achieve great conquests. Indefatigable in business, he takes little repose night or day; his ideas and language are clear and precise; hesitation is not known to him, and he has neither counsellors nor go-betweens. He is fond of splendour, and receives in state even on a campaign. He regards nothing with pleasure and desires but munitions of war for his soldiers.

(Plowden, *Travels in Abyssinia and the Galla Country*.)

Though fanatically pious and utterly ruthless, he undoubtedly believed that it was his mission to revive the Ethiopian nation, and in the twelve years after 1855 he did much to achieve this ambition. He was, however, already subject to fits of madness, when his career was cut short by a British military expedition, sent in 1867 in protest against the maltreatment by him of two British envoys. Surrounded by the British forces in his fortress at Magdala, he eventually shot himself.

His successor as emperor, John IV, fought his way to the throne with arms obtained from the British, who had encouraged him as a rival to Theodore. In the 1870s the main external enemy of the Empire of Ethiopia, which was still more a collection of semi-independent provinces than a unified kingdom, was Egypt.

The expansionist policies of the Khedive Ismail, directed towards the Red Sea and Somali coasts, threatened to revive the previous long isolation of the Christian lands in the interior mountains. As we have seen (page 80), Egypt took over control of Suakin and Massawa in 1865 from the Ottoman sultan, and occupied much of Eritrea. In 1875 Ismail extended an Egyptian protection over the Muslim rulers of Zeila and Harrar, and launched an Egyptian attack upon Ethiopia from both the north and the east. The Emperor John was successful in halting the Egyptian invasion, but the continued Egyptian occupation of the more important Red Sea and Somali ports severely curtailed the supply of arms and other goods to Ethiopia. This weakened John in his conflicts with Menelik, the powerful young ruler of Shoa, with whom he had to contend for the title of Emperor. Shoa, which lies to the south of Tigre and Amhara, had suffered greatly from the Galla invasions of the sixteenth to eighteenth centuries. The two rulers of Shoa before Menelik had been engaged during the previous fifty years on a similar course of re-armament and expansion (at the expense of the Galla and other pagan or Muslim peoples) to that undertaken by Theodore. In 1878 John had to make terms by which Menelik married his daughter and was recognised as his successor. Even so, concealed hostility and competition continued between the two, until John's death in battle against the Khalifa Abdallahi in 1889, when Menelik at last became emperor. In the early years of his rule over the state established by the Mahdi, Abdallahi had attempted to extend his control over all the Sudanese lands formerly occupied by the Egyptians. This inevitably brought him into conflict with Ethiopia, which conflict resulted in the fulfilment of Menelik's ambitions.

In a long reign, which lasted until 1913, Menelik completed the process which had been begun by Theodore. He united the provinces of Tigre and Amhara with Shoa, and extended Ethiopian rule over the Muslim and pagan states to the east and to the south. He fully understood the importance of modern weapons, and long before he became Emperor, he bought arms and ammunition from every available source, especially from the Italians. These changed places with the French (who operated from their Somali coast possession of Obok) in the 1880s as the principal external influence in Ethiopia. Italian consuls from Aden had made arrangements with Menelik in 1878–9 and after the establishment of a colony at the port of Assab in 1882, Italian envoys were in regular attendance at Menelik's court. As we shall see (Chapter 10), this Italian presence in Ethiopia led to the Wichale Treaty of 1889. Yet it was the Italians whom Menelik defeated in their attempted invasion of Ethiopia from their possessions in Eritrea, at the decisive battle of Adowa in 1896. To obtain money for his weapons, Menelik, like all his contempory rulers in North-East Africa, and in the interlacustrine lands, relied mainly on the profits of ivory, for which he raided deep into the pagan lands to the south-west and south-east of Shoa. He extended his political control behind the raiding armies. Ethiopian expansion at the expense of the Somalis of Harrar and the Ogaden caused the last great southward migration of the Somali peoples. By the turn of the century they were spilling over into the dry northern province of Kenya.

Long before direct European intervention in East and North-East Africa, the Muslim and Christian rulers of the more powerful and wealthy states in Africa itself were using fire-arms obtained from Europe to extend their trade with the peoples of the interior. They followed up these commercial activities with an extension of their political control. Egyptian expansion in the Sudan, and Shoan expansion in the lands to the south and east of the Ethiopian highlands, are examples of this process in North-East Africa. The Swahili-Arab penetration of East Africa, based on the sultanate of Zanzibar, is an example in East Africa. Only the Ethiopian rulers, however, were skilful enough to use the advantages of contact with the outside world while avoiding the financial and diplomatic entanglements which could lead to European intervention.

# 8

## NORTH-WEST AFRICA, 1800–1881

*North-West Africa and the European powers (1800–30)*

We have seen that at the beginning of the nineteenth century North Africa west of Egypt consisted of four Muslim states. Three of them—Tripoli, Tunis and Algiers—were nominally dependencies of the Ottoman empire. The fourth—Morocco—was an independent kingdom. Though all of them traded extensively with western Europe, all their religious and cultural connections, as well as a great part of their trade, lay with the eastern Mediterranean on the one hand and with the Muslim states of the western Sudan on the other. In particular, the steady flow of Negro slaves across the Sahara desert was directed mainly to the Balkans, Turkey, Syria and Egypt. During the first third of the nineteenth century this basic pattern changed very little. Thereafter, the growing power of western Europe made itself felt in a variety of ways which drastically changed the life of the people in North-West Africa. First there was the British campaign against the slave-trade, waged both in the Mediterranean and in the Atlantic. Next, there was the Greek war of independence (1820–9), fought with the support of the Christian powers. The success of the Greeks drove Muslim rule from a Christian country, and provided an example later to be followed by the other Balkan countries. Finally, with the invention of the steamship, and the consequent growth in the power and mobility of European navies, there came the concentration of the nations of western Europe on the Mediterranean Sea. For Britain and France the Mediterranean was a route to the rich lands of India and the East Indies. It was also the outlet (through the narrow straits at Istanbul) for the Russian fleet in the Black Sea. As we have mentioned in the previous chapter, Russia was a country greatly feared by the other European powers. It was to prevent the establishment of Russia as a Mediterranean power that Britain and France intervened against Muhammad Ali, in Greece in 1827 and in Syria in 1840. It was also because of these concerns, more than any interest in North Africa for its own sake, that led statesmen in France, Spain and later Italy to want to control the Mediterranean's southern shore.

At the beginning of the nineteenth century there was little awareness in the Maghrib countries that Christian Europe would prove the main threat to their continued independent existence. Certainly there was no idea among them of presenting a united front to European advances. In Tripoli, for example, the hereditary pasha, Yusuf Karamanli, who ruled the country from 1795 till 1830, had begun his reign by aiding the British against the French in Egypt, and thereafter enjoyed British support in maintaining his freedom from Ottoman control. This freedom he used to extend his authority over the Fezzan, the semi-desert country to the south of Tripoli, through which ran the caravan routes to the central Sudan. By 1811 Yusuf was master of the Fezzan, and by 1818 he had established treaty relations with Muhammad al-Kanemi in Bornu and with Muhammad Bello, the son of Dan Fodio, at Sokoto. Tripoli supplied Bornu with arms and ammunition for her wars against Bagirmi, and received a greatly increased supply of slaves in exchange. In spite of her friendly relations with Britain, the city of Tripoli became at this time the greatest slave-market of the Mediterranean. Of the 10,000 slaves brought annually across the Sahara, over half passed through Tripoli or else through Benghazi, the port of Cyrenaica.

The rulers of Tunis, like Yusuf Karamanli of Tripoli, based their country's almost complete independence from the Ottoman Sultan on their friendship with Britain. Algiers, in contrast, was linked more closely with France. During the wars which the Revolutionary government of France and the French Emperor Napoleon fought with most of the other European powers between 1792 and 1815, Algiers had supplied grain to the French forces, including those which had attacked Egypt. A large war-debt to the government of the Dey of Algiers had been incurred by France during these years. After the defeat of Napoleon in 1815 the new French government refused to pay this debt. This poisoned relations between the two countries, and led to the French invasion of Algeria in 1830.

Alone among the North African countries, Morocco did not have the Ottoman Sultan as a nominal master against whom it was necessary to seek an ally. Morocco therefore reacted to the increased European activity in the Mediterranean and the Atlantic by seeking to cut herself off from the outside world. Sultan Mawlai Sulaiman (1792–1832) forbade his subjects to leave the country, and restricted their dealings with Christians to the very minimum. The European consuls and merchants were made to stay in the ports of Tangier and Mogador. The efforts of the British consuls to interest the sultans in anti-slavery measures met with blank refusals even to consider the matter. In 1841 Sulaiman's successor, Abd ar-Rahman, declared firmly that he would not forbid a practice which had been sanctioned by the laws of every sect and nation 'from the times of the sons of Adam up to this day'.

### The French in Algeria (1830–79)

The French invasion of Algeria was one of the most unprincipled and ill-considered acts of policy in the whole of the nineteenth century. It was undertaken for no positive reason at all, but for the purely negative one of diverting the attention of the French people, by a spectacular military success abroad, from their resentment of the misgovernment of the kings Louis XVIII and Charles X. It did not even succeed in this object, for, within a few months of the attack on Algiers, Charles X had been overthrown by a popular revolution. But the French stayed in Algiers.

The excuse for the attack was a fit of anger by the Dey of Algiers, Husain, who in 1827, in the course of one of the endless discussions about the war-debt, struck the French consul in the face with his fly-wisk. Three years later the French government, announcing that it would put an end to the piracy of the Algerian corsairs, landed troops and defeated Husain's forces. Algiers and Oran fell almost at once, and Bone, the port of eastern Algeria, fell in 1832. There remained for the French the far more difficult task of ruling what they had conquered.

Like all previous conquerors of Algeria, the French imagined that they would be able to confine their occupation to the coastal plain. Indeed, the inhabitants of the coastal towns and those social groupings which had traditionally made up the *makhzan* (Arabic, allies) of the Dey proved friendly to the French and anxious to accept their protection. The reason was simply that the French were able to exploit the age-old rivalry between the townsfolk and the peasants of the coastal region on the one hand and the men of the hills and mountains on the other. The leader of the hill-folk was Abd al-Qadir, the son of a famous *marabout* (holy man) of the Atlas region, who in 1832 declared a great *jihad* against the French (and against the *makhzan*), saying:

We have assumed this important charge (the office of *amir*, commander), hoping that it may be the means of uniting the great body of Muslims and preventing dissensions among them, of affording general security to all dwellers in the land and of driving back the enemy who had invaded our country with a view to placing his yoke upon our necks.

With great skill and tact, Abd al-Qadir held together the quarrelsome tribes of western and central Algeria, organised an administration similar to that of the old Ottoman government, and built up a standing army with which he inflicted a number of defeats upon the French. His *jihad* made it quite impossible for the French to limit their occupation to the coastal plain: like all other conquerors of North Africa, they were drawn, whether they liked it or not, into the interior.

In 1841 General Bugeaud began the systematic conquest of Abd al-Qadir's territory. District after district was occupied by French military posts and patrolled by flying columns of mounted soldiers. This was no longer a war of armies which, while fighting one another, could spare the civil population. These small campaigns were brutal. One of the sons of the French king, serving with the French army, wrote: 'Our soldiers returning from the expedition were themselves ashamed. About 18,000 trees had been cut down; houses had been burnt; women, children and old men had been killed.' Similar ferocity was shown by the Arabs towards French soldiers and civilians, whenever the chance occurred. Resistance continued long after the capture of Abd al-Qadir himself in 1847, and great bitterness entered into the relations between conquerors and conquered.

In these circumstances, the settlement of French colonists, of whom there were by 1847 about 100,000, could not be a peaceful process. Bugeaud saw that the newcomers would have to be settled in concentrated areas, where they could be protected by the army. This meant the clearance (French, *refoulement*) of the more fertile regions in the coastal plains and movement of the former inhabitants into remoter, less fertile and already inhabited districts. This policy was carried out by force, and the fighting in Algeria contined until the 1870s. Once conquered, the Muslim areas were administered by a form of indirect rule. French officials governed the people through their territorial chiefs and councils. The system had much in common with the old Ottoman administration. Nevertheless, while the Deys had maintained their government with a force of 15,000 men, the French required

100,000, and in the interior regions military government only gave way to civil administration in 1879. Even then, Kabylia and other mountain districts remained unpacified.

The colonists, who in 1880 numbered some 350,000, did little to bring prosperity to Algeria. Nearly all of them were poor people. Most of those who settled on the land were small wine-growers from the south of France whose vineyards had been attacked by disease. In the towns most of the settlers were not even French, but Spaniards, Italians and Maltese from overcrowded home-lands, who came to seek paid employment and to engage in petty trade. As time went on, even the French agricultural settlers tended to drift into the towns, leaving the land which had been so expensively cleared for them to fall into the hands of a few wealthy individuals and companies who built up great estates. Unlike colonists in other parts of the world, the French settlers in Algeria, especially the wealthy ones, were able to keep close touch with their homeland across the Mediterranean. They came to have an influence on French politics out of all proportion to their numbers or real importance.

### Morocco (1830–94)

Morocco was much affected by the French occupation of Algeria. Abd al-Qadir's resistance was conducted mainly from western Algeria, and Sultan Abd ar-Rahman (1822–59) supported him with arms and, on occasion, provided him with refuge in Morocco. This brought French action against him in 1844, when Moroccan forces, fighting a European enemy for the first time since the sixteenth century, were badly defeated at the battle on the River Isly. Fortunately for Morocco, the French were too busy with Algerian affairs to follow up their victory. In 1859 Morocco also became involved with Spain, which claimed that the ports of Ceuta and Melilla on the northern coast, which she had held since the sixteenth century, were being constantly raided by the Sultan's subjects. A Spanish army invaded Morocco and inflicted a series of defeats on the Sultan's forces. The war was ended in 1860 by the Treaty of Tetuan, under which Morocco promised to pay Spain a huge indemnity. This indemnity opened Morocco to further European interference. To pay it, the Sultan had to raise a loan in London on the security of the Moroccan customs, and to accept control over these by foreign commissioners.

Within Morocco the government had the difficult task of

14  North-West Africa, 1800–1881

Key (left margin):
- settlement in Algeria
- Approx. area of Bilad al-Makhzan, Morocco
- Area of Sanusi Zawiyas
- Ottoman provinces of Tripoli and Cyrenaica

Labels on map:
SPAIN

Ceuta (Sp)
Tangier
Tetwan
Fez
Marrakesh
Mogador
Bilad al-Makhzan
Bilad as-Siba

Taghaza

Timbuktu
Niger
Sokoto
Muhammad Bello
FULANI

Agades
Ghat
Ghadames
Tuat

French conquests
Abd al-Qadir
Constantine
BEY
Bône
Bizerta
Tunis
Algiers
Fezzan

Italia

Ottomans
1835
Tripoli
Yusuf Karamanli
Benghazi
FEZZAN
1811
Murzuk
Bilma

Siwa (Sanusiyya)
Cairo
EGYPT
Muhammad Ali

Kufra (Sanusiyya)

Khartoum
SUDAN
(Egyptian)

DARFUR
(Egyptian
1874)

WADAI
KANEM
Muhammad al-Kanemi (d. 1837)
BORNU
Bagirmi

European trade-routes
to India and Far East 1811
Cyprus (British 1878)

Melilla (Sp)
Spain 1860

upholding the Sultan's authority against the religious movements of the *marabouts* and the hostility of the nomadic groups. Traditionally the country was divided into the *bilad al-makhzan* (the friendly country), which paid taxes into the Sultan's treasury, and the *bilad as-siba* (the unfriendly country), where the government could exert its influence only by threats and bribes. The relative size of these two areas was something that depended very much on the personality of each particular sultan. Mawlai al-Hasan (1873–94), the last great sultan before the French occupation, was continually on campaign reducing the area of the unfriendly country. For the first time since the seventeenth century the Sultan's authority was carried into the High Atlas region, and also deep into the Sahara in northern Mauretania. Mawlai al-Hasan was thus trying to make certain that no ungoverned groups existed which could cause frontier incidents of the kind which had led to the Spanish war. The fact that Morocco was able to keep its independence until 1912 is a tribute to Mawlai al-Hasan's enterprise and skill.

### *Tripoli under Ottoman rule (1835–1911): the Sanusiyya*

After the death of Yusuf Karamanli in 1830 two parties contended for the office of pasha, one supported by the British, the other by the French. After several years of confusion, during which the Bedouin of the Fezzan broke away from the control of any authority in Tripoli, the Ottoman government decided to reassert its authority over Tripoli, to counter Muhammad Ali's power in Egypt and the French presence in Algeria. In 1835 an Ottoman governor arrived in Tripoli and declared the Karamanli dynasty deposed. By 1842 this government had subdued most of the coastal tribes, but it could not control the Fezzan. The trans-Saharan trade suffered gravely, both from these events and from the wars which broke out all round the frontiers of Bornu after the death of al-Kanemi in 1837. During the 1830s and 1840s the central Sahara was so disturbed that traffic on the routes from Bornu and Wadai was restricted to a single annual caravan on each main route.

Peace returned to the central Sahara as a result of the rise of another Muslim brotherhood, that of the Sanusi. The founder of the order, Muhammad al-Sanusi, was born in Algeria about 1790 and studied in religious schools in Morocco before making the pilgrimage to Mecca. He established his first *zawiya* (Arabic, religious centre) among the Bedouin of Cyrenaica in 1843. His simple teaching of a return to the original practices of Islam, and his great tact and diplomacy, appealed to the feuding tribesmen, and held them together in a way in which neither the Karamanlis nor the Ottomans had been able to do. The order spread rapidly into the Sahara and the western Sudan, and its popularity was still increasing when Muhammad al-Mahdi (not to be confused with the Mahdi of the Egyptian Sudan) succeeded his father as *shaikh* in 1859. *Zawiyas* of the Sanusi order were set up all over Cyrenaica, the Fezzan, Wadai, Kanem-Bornu and as far west as Timbuktu. The followers of al-Sanusi were closely connected with trade, and paid regular dues out of their trading profits which went to enrich the *zawiyas*. These became the centres not only of religious propaganda but also of agricultural and commercial development. At the beginning of the nineteenth century the route from Benghazi to Wadai had been the least busy of the trans-Saharan routes. After the establishment of the Sanusi movement in Cyrenaica and in Wadai, at both ends of it, it became the most important. The Ottoman governors of Tripoli were forced to acknowledge the authority of the leaders (*ikhwan*) of the order over the desert peoples, and to keep on good terms with them, since they controlled the trade on which the prosperity of Tripoli and Benghazi depended. As a result of British pressure at Istanbul, the Ottoman government abolished the trade in slaves throughout the empire (except the Hijaz) in 1857. In Tripoli and Cyrenaica this law could not be enforced against the determination of the Sanusi traders to continue their operations. In this region the trans-Saharan slave-trade survived until the French occupation of Niger and Chad, and the Italian occupation of Cyrenaica, at the beginning of the twentieth century.

## *The Regency of Tunis (1830–81)*

All through the nineteenth century the *Beylikat* (Regency) of Tunis was the most progressive and westernised of the Maghrib states. As early as 1819 the Bey outlawed piracy. The beys were also the first Muslim rulers to abolish slavery and the first to adopt a constitutional form of government. The economy of Tunisia was varied enough to withstand the effects of the abolition of privateering and slavery. The plains of northern Tunisia provided rich harvests of grain and fruit, whilst Tunis and the other coastal cities produced many manufactured goods, such as cloth, leather-goods and metalware. The political situation, however, was by no means so secure, especially after the French invasion of Algeria and the restoration of Ottoman authority in Tripoli. The Tunisian government felt itself in a trap between two sources of likely attack, and turned to Britain for protection. In 1837, after the French occupation of Constantine, the Algerian fortress city near the Tunisian border, the British government promised to support the Bey not only against France but also against the Ottoman Sultan. It was this reliance on Britain that led Ahmad Bey to abolish slavery in a series of decrees issued between 1841 and 1846. The Bey's government had sufficient authority to enforce these laws throughout the country.

The constitutional decrees of 1857 and 1861 were passed, at the suggestion of the French and British consuls, in order to satisfy the ambitions of the wealthy, well-educated Tunisian middle-class, and of the influential French and Italian trading communities. The constitution granted equality of all men before the law and guaranteed freedom of trade. It also set up nominated councils to advise the Bey. In practice, the common people were not much helped by this constitution which gave political power to the wealthy few. The government largely ignored the constitution and it soon fell into disuse. However, the memory of it survived, and when nationalist political parties emerged in Tunisia during the twentieth century they took the name *Destour* (Arabic, constitution).

During the 1860s and 1870s British influence in Tunisia declined in relation to that of France, which was determined that no other European country should occupy a position of strength on the borders of Algeria. After a prolonged diplomatic and commercial struggle with Italy, which was by the 1870s united and was beginning to show interest in North Africa, France decided to take strong action. A dispute between the Bey's government and a French trading company, and the incursions of Tunisian hill-tribes across the Algerian frontier, provided the necessary excuse. In 1881 French forces captured Bizerta and Tunis. The Bey was forced to sign a treaty allowing France to occupy Tunisia and to take charge of her finances and foreign affairs. Unlike the Dey of Algiers fifty years earlier, the Bey and his government continued to function under French supervision.

The French occupation of Tunis, as much as the British occupation of Egypt which occurred in the following year, was one of the opening moves in the partition of Africa among the European powers. It was in fact the result of an informal agreement made in 1877 between Britain, France and Russia, by which each of these powers was to 'take one bite at the Ottoman cherry' with the tacit support of the others. Britain's bite was Cyprus, which was ceded to her under pressure by the Ottoman government in 1878. Russia's bite consisted of three formerly Ottoman provinces in the Caucasus mountains. Though viewed by Britain and Russia as a Mediterranean and Middle Eastern agreement, the French were conscious of its African implications. In occupying Tunis they were not merely protecting the borders of Algeria, but were extending a French North Africa which was ultimately to connect with the area of French conquests on the Senegal and the Niger.

# 9

## THE PARTITION OF AFRICA ON PAPER, 1879–1891

*European trading interests in Africa before partition*

During the last quarter of the nineteenth century events took place which changed the face of Africa, and which can only be understood by tracing their origin and development outside Africa. In 1879 more than 90 per cent of the continent was ruled by Africans. By 1900 all but a tiny fraction of it was being governed by European powers. By about 1914 the lives of almost all Africans were being deeply affected by the changes brought about by these foreign rulers. The European powers partitioned Africa among themselves with such haste, like players in a rough game, that the process has been called 'the Scramble for Africa'. The motives for this partition, the reason why the European powers acted as they did, and when they did, are a part of European history rather than African history, and it is to these European affairs that we must now turn our attention.

We have to remember, first of all, that throughout the first sixty-five years of the nineteenth century the only great powers in western Europe were Britain and France. Germany and Italy did not yet exist as separate and unified states. Of the lesser powers, Holland and Denmark actually abandoned their African

Main industrial areas

Dates of states in Balkans show partial and complete independence from Ottoman Empire

● Moscow

RUSSIAN EMPIRE

SWEDEN

NORWAY

DENMARK

Baltic Sea

GREAT BRITAIN

SCOTLAND

IRELAND

ENGLAND

WALES

London ●

HOLLAND

BELGIUM

Paris ●

GERMAN EMPIRE
Unified 1870

Berlin ●
(Conference 1884-1885)

Vienna ●

HAPSBURG EMPIRE

AUSTRIA

SWITZER-LAND

Franco-Prussian War 1870-1871

FRANCE

French provinces of Alsace-Lorraine lost to Germany 1871

ITALY
Unified 1860-1870

Rome ●

Marseilles ●

Black Sea

Caspian Sea

Caucasus Mts.

Russian advance

IRAQ

OTTOMAN EMPIRE

ANATOLIA

SYRIA

ROUMANIA
1829/1878

BULGARIA
1878

SERBIA
1817/1878

BOSNIA
1878-
Austrian
1908

Istanbul ●

Balkans

1878

GREECE
Independent
1829

Cyprus
(British 1878)

Suez
Canal

Cairo ●

EGYPT
British

CYRENAICA

Malta
(British 1798)

TUNIS
French
Protectorate
1882

TRIPOLITANIA

French

French

ALGERIA
French occupation
began 1830

GIBRALTAR
British 1704

SPAIN

PORTUGAL

MOROCCO

possessions (trading posts on the Gold Coast) during the nine-teenth century, leaving only Portugal as a minor competitor with France and Britain. We have also to remember that even France, despite her considerable military strength, was well behind Britain in the race for commercial and industrial development. Precisely because her manufactures were inferior or more expensive than those of Britain, France pursued a 'protectionist policy'—that is to say, she tried to reserve the trade of French colonies for her own merchants. In the Senegal from 1815, and from the 1840s in Guinea, the Ivory Coast, Dahomey, Gaboon and in Madagascar, there were, therefore, French naval and commercial bases from which non-French traders were kept out. These areas were, however, quite small. In the British possessions the same customs dues were charged to British and foreign traders alike. In fact, however, traders of all nations did the largest part of their business in Africa on stretches of the coast over which no European flag yet flew. So long as most of the trade was carried on near the coast, and so long as most of the coastline was free to all comers, Britain, at least, had no economic motive to annex large territories in Africa. Even France found that her protected settlements were more of a financial burden than they were worth.

## The development of Anglo-French rivalry in West Africa

By the 1870s, however, a new situation was beginning to develop in West Africa. The trade was no longer exclusively a coastal trade. At the few key points where railways or river steamships could be introduced, European trade was starting to penetrate the interior. The French were thrusting deep into the Senegal valley, and it was known that their objective was to connect the Senegal and the upper Niger by a railway, which would attract the trade of a great part of the West African interior into French hands. Here was a development which must affect the British trading posts on the Gambia, and which might in time affect the trade-routes leading to Sierra Leone and the Gold Coast. Again, on the lower Niger, the penetration of the interior markets by British firms trading up-river in their own steamers had reached a stage at which, to go further, it was necessary for them to come together and form a single company with a monopoly over the trade. Only by this means could the essential installations be afforded and a united front be maintained in dealing with the powerful Fula emirates of the interior. In 1879 George Goldie

16b Southern Africa on the eve of partition: African states and European settlements

Warsheikh

Coastal settlements of Sultan of Zanzibar

Buganda Missionary frontier 1880

Kilwa

Mozambique

Missionary frontier 1880

Quelimane

BUGANDA

BUNYORO

KARAGWE

ANKOLE

SULTAN OF ZANZIBAR'S CLAIMS

YAO CHIEFS

Beira

RUANDA

BURUNDI

Mirambo

Mloz.

Jumbe

BEMBA

Delagoa Bay

Msiri

AREA CLAIMED BY NDEBELE

ZULULAND

Kasongo

BAROTSE

SOUTH AFRICAN REPUBLIC (Transvaal)

ORANGE FREE STATE

NATAL

Durban

BASUTO

CHOKWE

BAMANGWATO

CAPE COLONY

GABOON

ANGOLA

Missionary frontier 1880

Libreville

European merchants

Missionary frontier 1880

Walvis Bay

Cape Town

MERINA

Missionary frontier

Mahdist State

British

Boer Republics

Portuguese

French

Ottoman Suzerainty

Frontier of Christian missionary activities about 1880

Main lines of missionary advance

Main African States and Chiefdoms

amalgamated the British firms trading up the Niger river, only to find himself facing competition from French traders. This he dealt with in a characteristically ruthless fashion, by undercutting their prices at a loss to himself and so forcing them to sell out their interests to his own company. Thus the French were left feeling that, for the future at least, their commercial companies must be given political support.

## The entry of new powers

Already, in the early 1870s, Britain and France had considered partitioning West Africa into 'spheres of influence', in each of which only the firms of one country would be allowed to trade. It had been suggested by the French that the Gambia should be given to France in exchange for British control over the coastline from Sierra Leone to the Cameroons. The scheme had fallen through in 1875, but, had it not been for the intervention of other European powers, it would probably have been revived in the 'eighties, so as to leave the French in control of the upper Niger and the waterways leading to the upper Guinea coast, and the British in control of the lower Niger and the coastlands of lower Guinea. In the early 1880s, however, the slow movement towards an Anglo-French partition of West Africa, arising from the commercial penetration of the interior, was both speeded up and complicated by the appearance on the African scene of two new European powers which had not previously shown any great interest in Africa. The result of these interventions was to force all the European powers, including France and Britain, to look far beyond their immediate economic needs. What each power feared was that its rivals would keep the trade of their new colonies to themselves by enclosing them within high tariff (or customs) barriers. Therefore each power felt compelled to enter the scramble for territory, in order to reserve the largest possible sphere for its own future activities.

## King Leopold and the Congo

The first of these newcomers was an individual rather than a nation state. It was Leopold II, King of Belgium, a little country situated uncomfortably between the European giants, France and Germany. The Belgian people did not share the expansionist dreams of their ruler. As early as 1861 Leopold had written: 'The sea bathes our coast, the world lies before us. Steam and electricity have annihilated distance. All the non-appropriated lands on the surface of the globe (mostly in Africa) can become the field of our operations and our success.' Leopold was a master diplomat, a man of boundless ambition, and in his younger days he had a genuine idealism—a belief in human progress and in the need to improve the conditions of less privileged peoples. As he grew older, his idealism was largely submerged by a growing love of wealth and power. As we have seen in Chapter 4, Leopold's opportunity came when Stanley's schemes for the opening up of the Congo basin, which the explorer had formed after his descent of the river in 1877, were rejected by the British government. In 1879 Leopold took Stanley into his service. During the next four years Stanley established road and river communications from the Congo estuary to Stanley Falls (Stanleyville, Kisingani). Leopold on the Congo, like Goldie on the Niger, was aiming at a commercial monopoly, which would attract all the trade of the Congo basin into his own river steamers and his own railway from Stanley Pool (Léopoldville, Kinshasa) to the coast.

Leopold did not at this stage attempt to obtain treaties of sovereignty or legal possession from the African rulers of the lower Congo area. He relied on his own mastery of the lines of communication. The immediate effect of his operations, however, was to stimulate the competition of a rival French group, whose agent, Savorgnan de Brazza, returned to Europe in the summer of 1882 with a treaty signed by Makoko, chief of the Bateke country on the northern shores of Stanley Pool. This treaty placed his territory under French sovereignty. De Brazza toured France, stirring up imperialist sentiment so successfully that he persuaded the French government both to ratify his treaty with Makoko and to set in motion a large programme of treaty-making and annexation along the Nigerian coast. This in turn led the British government to join in the race for Nigerian territory, and forced King Leopold to seek treaties granting sovereign rights in the lower Congo area. The scramble for West and West-Central Africa had thus begun in earnest.

Once he had started upon territorial annexation, King Leopold skilfully prepared the way for international recognition of his claim to rule the Congo basin. He persuaded the French government to support him by a secret promise that the Congo should revert to France if he himself should prove unable to govern it. He also gained the support of the German Chancellor, Bismarck, just at the moment when Germany herself was about to enter the colonial field. To English merchants he held out tempting hopes of valuable contracts, and with their help he broke down the British government's plan to bar his access to the Congo by recognising Portuguese claims of sovereignty over the river mouth. Finally, his American secretary, Sanford, persuaded the United States to join France and Germany in giving recognition to the Congo Free State.

### Germany enters the Scramble, 1883–5

During the 1850s and 1860s a great political and economic revolution had taken place in Germany, in which most of the independent states whose peoples spoke the German language became united around the North German state of Prussia, under the leadership of Bismarck. The basis of political unification was a customs union which enabled Germany to embark on industrialisation. This combination of political amalgamation or unification and modern industrial growth resulted in the emergence of a great new power in Europe. By the 1870s the new Germany was able to rival France militarily, and Britain industrially. The former rivalry led to the Franco-Prussian war of 1870–1, in which France was overwhelmed and lost the frontier provinces of Alsace and Lorraine to Germany. In both France and Germany some political groups turned from this war to thoughts of colonial expansion, the French as a form of compensation for the humiliation of defeat, the Germans out of the realisation of new-found strength. For a long time yet, Bismarck personally refused to take any outward interest in the colonial question. It was left to merchant groups in the North German ports to stir up a national demand for colonies. These groups succeeded so well, however, that from 1883 to 1885 Bismarck, suddenly changing his attitude, was able to take the diplomats of Europe by surprise in declaring German protectorates in four widely scattered parts of Africa— Togoland, the Cameroons (known to the Germans as Kamerun), East Africa and South-West Africa.

Germany's bid for colonies was not based on any substantial interest built up in Africa beforehand. It was a simple assertion of her new position among the world powers. There is much truth in the view that Bismarck himself took part in the Scramble mainly in order to dominate the international politics of the European powers which were connected with it. He wanted to turn French ambitions away from the recovery of her lost provinces, and the best way to do so was to involve her in rivalries with other powers for overseas territories. He therefore supported French claims in West Africa and the Congo, and made his own African annexations in places which would threaten British claims rather than French ones.

It was now that Britain's peculiar position in Egypt became of such vital significance in the diplomacy of partition. The British occupation of Egypt, it will be remembered (Chapter 7), had been planned as a joint Anglo-French operation, to crush Urabi Pasha's revolt and to restore the authority of Khedive Tawfiq. It was originally intended to be only a temporary intervention, and therefore nothing was done to alter the control of Egypt's finances by the International Debt Commission. British rule in Egypt was thus dependent at every turn on the good will of the Commission, on which, since French opposition to the continued British occupation was certain, the German vote was of the utmost importance. Bismarck, throughout the vital years of the partition, supported British rule in Egypt. His price was British acceptance of Germany's new annexations, and of his support of the claims of France and King Leopold to the north and south of the lower Congo.

It was Bismarck, therefore, who dominated the first round of the Scramble, which came to an end at the Berlin Conference (1884–5). The conference prepared the way for newcomers to the African scene by requiring that claims to colonies or protectorates on any part of the African coastline should be formally notified to the other powers taking part in the conference, and by insisting that such claims must be backed by the establishment of an effective degree of authority in the areas concerned. This put an end to the British idea of informal empire. The conference also decreed that there should be freedom of navigation on the Niger and the Congo, thus in theory frustrating British attempts to close the Niger against the French and the Congo against King Leopold. The years 1883–5, therefore, saw Britain checked, surprised or forestalled in one part of Africa after another. The former large sphere of British influence in lower Guinea was now broken up by a French protectorate in Dahomey and two German protectorates in Togoland and the Cameroons. The Congo and the Gaboon coast, where British trade had flourished for so long, was divided between France and King Leopold. The unity of the southern African coastal regions, so long dominated by Britain, was broken by a German protectorate in the south-west. The Merina kingdom on Madagascar had signed a treaty with France, despite the fact that British missionary influence had been an outstanding feature in the island since the 1830s. And the old area of informal empire exercised through the Sultan of Zanzibar in East Africa was shattered by the German annexations in the interior from Dar-es-Salaam. As bases from which Britain could build afresh, there remained only Egypt, the scattered possessions in West Africa, and the self-governing Cape Colony and Natal in the south.

*Lord Salisbury and the restoration of British initiative, 1885–91*
The revival of British fortunes in Africa, and their conversion to the new conditions of formal as opposed to informal empire, was very largely the work of Lord Salisbury. Salisbury was Prime Minister of Britain from 1885 to 1892, and rivalled even Bismarck as a master of diplomacy. His first act was to open a way for northward expansion from the Cape Colony by declaring a protect-orate over Bechuanaland (now Botswana)—the largely desert area lying between German South-West Africa and the independent Boer republic of the Transvaal (then known as the South African Republic). This action was to gain great significance from the discovery in the following year (1886) of the vast gold deposits of the Witwatersrand in the Transvaal. Although these were in Boer territory, the exploiters were nearly all English-speaking capitalists from the Cape Colony and from Britain itself. These British exploiters were led by Cecil Rhodes, who had already made a fortune in the diamonds of Kimberley. He shared the common belief that 'a second Rand' would be found in the highlands north of the Limpopo river, and was determined that Britain should control this apparently rich area. Bechuanaland was his 'Suez Canal to the North', up which in 1890 there travelled the 'pioneer column' of white settlers who occupied Southern Rhodesia (now Rhodesia). Salisbury disliked and dis-trusted Rhodes, but he was prepared to use his great wealth and energy to help carve out a belt of British territories in the high-lands between the Portuguese colonies of Angola and Mozam-bique.

Salisbury's second action was to rescue for Britain what re-mained of East Africa after the German annexations of 1884. In

1886 he negotiated with Bismarck a division of the area into two 'spheres of influence', following the present boundary between Kenya and Tanzania. In 1890, by ceding to Germany the North Sea island of Heligoland, he persuaded Bismarck to sign a comprehensive series of boundary agreements, by which Germany recognised British claims to Zanzibar, Kenya, Uganda, Northern Rhodesia (now Zambia), Bechuanaland and eastern Nigeria. In the same year Salisbury concluded a treaty with France in respect of the western boundary of Nigeria, in return for British recognition of the French protectorate over Madagascar (which the rulers of the island did not acknowledge), and in 1891 an agreement with Portugal in respect of Nyasaland (now Malawi) and the two Rhodesias.

Thus, by the end of Salisbury's period of office in 1892, though many interior boundaries remained to be drawn, the broad outlines of the European partition of Africa had been sketched out. The cornerstone of Salisbury's African policy was the continued British occupation of Egypt. As he himself recognised, the consequence was that Britain should give way to French claims for the predominant place in West Africa. German claims, too, had to be admitted in the four regions where these had been staked. The British West African possessions were confined to a modest extension from their pre-partition footholds. The main British share in the partition had to be found in a northward expansion of British South Africa through Bechuanaland to the Rhodesias and Nyasaland, and in a slice of East Africa, stretching from Mombasa to the upper Nile. Salisbury realised that Egypt, with British help, would soon be strong enough to undertake the reconquest of the Sudan from the Khalifa, and that the final extension of British power would take place in this direction. Salisbury admitted in a memorandum to the British Cabinet that the slogan 'all British from the Cape to Cairo' was a rough expression of his African policy as a whole.

It is important to remember that the outline partition accomplished by 1891 was in large measure a partition which existed only on paper. Despite the insistence of the Berlin Conference that claims to African coastlines must be supported by effective occupation, most of the claims recognised by the powers were in fact based on a few scraps of paper obtained by consuls and concession-hunters from African chiefs who had very little idea of what they were doing and whose authority usually extended only over a very small part of the areas claimed. There was not a single territory in Africa where anything like effective occupation existed at the time of the partition. The final division of territories reflected, not so much the strength of European interests on the ground as the political power of the claimants in Europe. The partition was nevertheless important. It represented the deliberate intention of powerful European states to carry their influence into the innermost parts of Africa, as they had already done in much of Asia, in the Americas and in Australasia. No one could doubt that they had the necessary power. The fact that they acted with so large a measure of mutual agreement that the partition did not cause an outbreak of war between them was probably of benefit to Africa as well as to themselves.

# 10

## THE PARTITION OF AFRICA
## ON THE GROUND, 1891–1901

### *European conflicts in Africa*

The first stages of the partition, when European states were laying claim to coastal regions and navigable rivers, and were defining on paper the boundaries running inland from these first footholds, were accomplished with surprisingly little bloodshed and conflict. The reason for this was that very small numbers of European forces were used in Africa during this time. The first occupying groups consisted of small, mobile expeditions of European officers or chartered-company officials, accompanied by a few dozen lightly armed porters, scarcely distinguishable from the expeditions of the first explorers. Africa itself was so immense that these first little groups of Europeans seldom came into contact with each other. Their attitude to the African peoples had necessarily to be that of negotiators rather than conquerors. They entered into the local politics of every region that they came to, supporting the groups and factions which had some reason to be friendly, and avoiding those which were hostile. In the later stages of the Scramble, however, towards the close of the nineteenth century, when forces were somewhat larger and when the final, interior frontiers were being claimed, meetings between rival

European expeditions became more frequent. Collisions occurred between the occupying forces and those of the larger and more organised African states, which often fought desperately for their survival. Numerically, the armies of these states often outnumbered the European expeditions by many hundreds to one, but the superiority of European weapons was overwhelming. A single machine-gun could put to flight a whole army of undisciplined men armed only with ancient guns and spears. As it raced towards its conclusion, therefore, the Scramble produced increasing bloodshed. At first there were small incidents in West Africa, in the Congo, and in East Africa. Then came the French 'pacifications' of Madagascar and Morocco, the war between Ethiopia and Italy, and the reconquest of the Sudan. Finally came the deadly struggle in South Africa, in which white fought white.

### The French advance down the Niger

After the Berlin Conference, the French took steps to consolidate their possessions on the West African Coast. By 1893 the colonies of the Ivory Coast and French Guinea had been officially established. In the same year French troops entered Dahomey and deposed Behanzin, the last independent king of Dahomey. Dahomey became a French colony in 1900. The main French expansion in West Africa, however, took place from the basin of the Senegal river. Here, by 1879, the French advance up the river had brought them into contact with the empire of Ahmadu Sefu, the son of al-Hajj Umar (Chapter 3). Indecisive clashes between General Gallieni's Senegalese troops and Ahmadu's forces continued for many years, but Ahmadu's empire broke up once its military power had been destroyed. The French entered the upper Niger valley and captured Bamako in 1883. A more determined opposition to French penetration was put up by Samori, a Muslim Mandingo. This leader had, in a series of conquests begun in the early 1870s, succeeded in uniting under his rule most of the peoples in the vast area between the sources of the Niger and the Upper Volta basin. Samori became the hero of the fiercely independent southern Mande peoples in his relentless opposition to the French. Although his homelands around Bissandugu were occupied in 1891, he was not finally defeated and exiled by the French until 1898.

Samori's resistance delayed but could not halt French penetration down the Niger. Timbuktu was taken in 1894, and Say

17  European partition: North-West Africa

18  European partition: West Africa

**Penetration by**

- - - → Anglo-Egyptians
⟶ British
⟹ French
⟹ Italians
⋰ African States

**Benghazi**
CYRENAICA
Sanusi
resistance to
Italian
occupation
Cairo
British 1882

Slaves

EGYPT

1876   European financial control
1882   British occupation

Kufra
(Sanusi Zawiyas)

Wadi Halfa

Sanusi trade routes

WADAI

1887
-1900

Rabih

Chari

DARFUR
El Fasher
1916

El Obeid
Omdurman
1898   Khartoum

Sennar

Fashoda

ERITREA
It 1889

Massawa
(It 1885)   FR. SOM.

Adowa 1896

Assab
It 1883   Obok
Jibuti   Fr 1862
Fr 1884   Zeila

BRITISH
SOMALILAND
(Brit Prot
1884-1885)

Aden
Br 1839

Alula

Berbera
Br 1884

Marchand
1898

BAHR
AL-GHAZAL

ETHIOPIA

Territory ceded by France
to Germany in 1912 in
return for German
recognition of French
Protectorate over
Morocco

Gondokoro

LADO

Congo Free State
1891

Stanley Falls

Congo

1890

ITALIAN SOMALILAND
(It Prot 1889-1892)

Majerteyn Coast

Obbia
(It Prot
1889)

Mijjertein Coast

Mogadishu
(ceded by Zanzibar
to Italy 1892)

Benadir

19   European partition: East Africa

in 1896. Beyond Say, the French advance was blocked by the
British in Hausaland. Once in control of the upper and middle
Niger, therefore, they turned their attention to filling in the gaps
between the Niger valley and their possessions on the coast. This
task was completed by the turn of the century. It was at this

stage that frontier incidents with rival British expeditions in the Nigerian and Gold Coast interiors became frequent.

### British expansion in the Gold Coast and Nigeria

We have seen (Chapter 9) that Britain was prevented by the wider pattern of the diplomatic partition of Africa from pressing claims to a large consolidated area of West Africa. All she could do was to extend, by effective occupation on the ground, her existing footholds in Sierra Leone, the Gold Coast and Nigeria. In the Gold Coast the local situation depended upon relations between the coastal 'colony' and the Ashanti empire, whose outlying dependencies were detached from their allegiance by treaty-making expeditions as a preliminary to the military occupation of Ashanti itself in 1896. In 1898 the Northern Territories, part of which had been tributary to Samori, were declared a Protectorate, in order to forestall expansion by the French from the north.

Britain's occupation of Nigeria was more complicated, and took place from three different spheres. The first was from Lagos, where the small island colony expanded into a Protectorate covering most of Yorubaland. The second was from the Oil Rivers, where British consuls supported the Liverpool firms in breaking the power of the African middleman chiefs like Jaja of Opobo, as soon as these tried to make treaties with other European nations. The third was from Nupe and Southern Hausaland. Here, Sir George Goldie's National African Company, which in 1886 became the Royal Niger Company, had powers under its Royal Charter to administer justice and maintain order. Goldie secured the friendship of much of Hausaland by a treaty made with the Sultan of Sokoto in 1885. Nupe and the Emirate of Ilorin, however, had to be conquered by the Royal Niger Company's army, the West African Frontier Force. Goldie's officers, notably Captain Lugard, were involved in incidents with the French, who were advancing down the Niger and up from the coast into Dahomey. Borgu was occupied only after a French expedition there had been forced to withdraw. These military operations against a rival European colonial power soon proved too expensive and too dangerous for a private Company. In 1898 the British government brought the charter to an end, and two years later (1900) took over the control of northern Nigeria. British expansion continued in the direction of Bornu and Lake Chad. Kano was occupied in 1902.

### The French in the central Sudan: Rabih

The French moved into the central Sudan from three directions—from the Niger valley, from the Gaboon and from Algeria. By about 1900 expeditions from all three were converging on Lake Chad. Goldie's Royal Niger Company prevented the French from occupying any but the northern desert fringe of Hausaland, as they moved eastwards from Say on the Niger. In the Gaboon the French government had begun to occupy the interior after the Berlin Conference, and by the late 1890s was in a position to start pushing northwards towards the Shari river basin. Finally, in the wake of Captain Lamy's pioneer trans-Saharan expedition of 1898–9, the French began to occupy the principal oases—Tuat, Tamanrasset, Air and Zinder. The nomadic Tuareg of the surrounding deserts, however, remained practically unaffected by the French presence until after the Second World War.

The final resistance to the French occupation of the central Sudan was put up by the Sanusi order from its fortified *zawiyas* in the Bilma region, and above all by Rabih, an Arab soldier from Sennar. He had earlier served the Egyptian government in the Bahr al-Ghazal. After refusing to submit to the Mahdi, he had set off westwards with his armed followers. He failed in an attack against the Sultanate of Wadai in 1887, but by 1892 he had conquered Bagirmi and much of eastern Bornu. Here he set up a slave-raiding state, which disposed of its booty along the Sanusi trade-routes leading to Tripoli and Benghazi. As the French closed in on him from all sides, he fiercely resisted their advance. He was finally defeated and killed in 1900.

### The reconquest of the Sudan: Fashoda

Before the French had defeated Rabih, the British in Egypt had reconquered the Mahdist state, which appeared to be threatened both by the Italians in Eritrea and by the French advance from the Congo. To forestall such moves, an Anglo-Egyptian military force, trained by the British commander Kitchener, moved into the Sudan in 1896. In 1898 this force defeated the Mahdist armies at the battle of Omdurman, in which 20,000 Sudanese were killed. Khartoum then fell to Kitchener. A week later news reached him that a French force of African soldiers led by Commandant Marchand had installed itself at Fashoda, some 200 miles further south, after an incredible march from the Gaboon, which had lasted nearly two years. Kitchener hastened up the White Nile with a much larger force. The hostile camps faced one another for several months, while telegraphic messages flashed to and fro between the Sudan and Europe. In the end the French gave way, and Marchand hauled down his flag; but not before France and Britain had been brought to the brink of a major war.

A brief mention can be made here of the last two territories in northern Africa to be seized by the European powers. In 1911 Italy launched an unprovoked, but not unexpected, invasion of the Ottoman province of Tripoli, and the next year pushed from there into Cyrenaica. Here the Italian armies met bitter opposition from the Bedouin tribesmen who belonged to the Sanusi order. Their resistance continued until the 1930s (see Chapter 14). At the western end of North Africa, Morocco escaped European control until 1912, not because of the Sultan's ability to oppose it, but because the European powers quarrelled among themselves over which of them should occupy his kingdom. Their disagreements twice brought Europe within reach of war. Finally, the two powers most concerned, France and Spain, partitioned Morocco, Spain taking the smaller northern portion. Germany was bought off by being given extra territory in the Cameroons. A French protectorate was declared over the main portion of the kingdom, the Sultan remaining as the nominal head of his country.

### East Africa and the Congo

In East Africa and the Congo the Arabs put up the main opposition to the occupation forces of the Germans, the British and the Belgians. This opposition did not come openly from the Sultan of Zanzibar. His capital would have been an easy target for the guns of European warships, and he therefore had to submit gracefully to the declaration of a British protectorate over the islands of Zanzibar and Pemba in 1890, and to the partition of his mainland territories. These were divided between the British and the German chartered companies, which were beginning to occupy what is now Kenya, the mainland of Tanzania and Uganda. In 1886 these mainland territories of the Sultan were declared by an international commission to extend only ten miles into the interior. The Germans then bought the coastal strip adjoining their treaty areas for a lump sum, while the British company leased the coastal strip of Kenya for an annual payment. That is why, throughout the colonial period, the red flag of the Sultan continued to fly over

Mombasa, Malindi, Lamu and other Kenya ports. It may also be the reason why there was no Arab revolt in the British coastal sphere. The active opposition from the Swahili-Arabs came from two directions. The first was from the German part of the coast. The second was from the former slave and ivory traders scattered over the interior from Lake Nyasa in the south, around both sides of Lake Tanganyika, and up into Uganda in the north. The movement probably stemmed from the attempt of Sultan Barghash to consolidate his mainland dominions on the eve of European partition. With its central leadership withdrawn, however, it exploded in a series of local risings, which the Europeans dealt with one by one. The sharpest of these struggles, though also the shortest, was that in 1888–9 between the Germans and the east-coast Arabs under their leader, Abushiri. Longer and more intermittent was that between the British and the Arabs of northern Nyasaland, which began in 1887 and was finally settled ten years later. King Leopold's officials fought their campaigns against the Arabs of the eastern Congo between 1891 and 1894. In Uganda, as in Nyasaland, Arab opposition to European penetration, though strongly influenced by the German occupation of the Coast, began while the only Europeans in the area were missionaries. This opposition was an aspect of the local political situation. The local Christians supported the entry of European influence; the local Muslims opposed it. In the kingdom of Buganda the Christian factions prevailed, and made Buganda the principal ally of the British in their occupation of the region as a whole. The Arabs and the local Muslim faction retreated into the neighbouring kingdom of Bunyoro, which remained the centre of resistance to British rule. It was finally conquered by the British with the help of Buganda levies in a series of campaigns which lasted from 1894 till 1899 (see Chapter 12).

The one country in East Africa which successfully resisted European attempts at occupation was Ethiopia. The European nation involved in this attempt was Italy, which had entered late into the Scramble. Italy had occupied a part of the Eritrean coast of the Red Sea in 1883, and in 1886 had participated in the division of the Sultan of Zanzibar's mainland possessions by staking a claim to the eastern Somali coast. In 1889, immediately after becoming emperor, Menelik signed with the Italians the Treaty of Wichale. This treaty defined the boundary between Ethiopia and Italian Eritrea. It also stated in its Amharic version that Menelik's government might, if it wished, use Italian diplomatic channels for its contacts with the outside world. The Italian version of the treaty used a slightly more definite expression, implying that Menelik had agreed always to conduct his external affairs through Italian channels. It does not seem that the Italian negotiators deliberately intended to deceive Menelik—certainly they never intended to create a Protectorate. Nevertheless it was on the basis of this phrase that the Italian Foreign Office two years later notified the powers which had taken part in the Berlin Conference of Italy's claim to a Protectorate over Ethiopia. Italy now attempted to enforce this invalid Protectorate upon Menelik, and disputes between the two sides resulted in the war of 1896. The Italian army was decisively defeated at Adowa, one of the first battles of modern times in which a non-European army beat one officered by, and partly consisting of, Europeans. Menelik turned from his victory over the Italians back to his lifelong interest, which was the extension of his kingdom to the south. Some of this country had paid tribute to the Ethiopian kings of the late medieval period, and had been lost since the Galla invasions of the sixteenth century. Menelik's conquests, however, reaching to Lake Rudolf in the south and to the ancient kingdom of Kaffa in the south-west, more than doubled the dominions which had come to him by inheritance and marriage. They made Ethiopia almost a participant in the Scramble for Africa.

## The French conquest of Madagascar

In the late 1880s the Merina kingdom began to break up under the pressure of French commercial and diplomatic influence. The Prime Minister, Rainilaiarivony, would not admit that the 1885 treaty gave France protectorate rights over the island. The French considered it did. Acting under what they understood were the terms of the treaty, the French in 1894 sent a large military expedition to Madagascar. This expedition entered Tananarive the following year and removed the Prime Minister. A definite treaty of protection was forced upon the Queen. This foreign interference was the signal for one rebellion after another throughout Madagascar. Pagans turned upon Christians. The new religion was blamed for the troubles which had come upon the island. The people of the old Betsileo kingdom rid themselves of the hated Hova domination. French military actions against these rebellions only made matters worse. At one time Tananarive was the only place the French could hold. In 1895 General Gallieni came from his campaigns in West Africa to conquer (or 'pacify', as this action used to be called) Madagascar, which was declared to be a French colony. Nine years of bitter fighting passed before all the peoples of Madagascar had been forced by Gallieni and his second-in-command, Lyautey, to accept French rule. The Merina monarchy was overthrown, the last queen, Ranavalona III, being exiled in 1897. The French administered the island as a unit, thus completing the work of unification begun by Nampoina more than a century before.

### Rhodes and central Africa

The occupation of central Africa was left by the British government very largely to Rhodes and his British South Africa Company. This was incorporated by Royal Charter in 1889 and was empowered to develop the region between Bechuanaland and the Zambezi which was later to bear Rhodes's name. In 1891 the company was allowed to extend into the lands north of the Zambezi which became Northern Rhodesia (Zambia). South of the Zambezi, Rhodes's agents had extracted concessions from Mzilikazi's successor, Lobengula, on the strength of which a body of farming and mining settlers was sent in 1890 into Mashonaland, where they founded the Southern Rhodesian capital at Fort Salisbury. Further north Rhodes's agents raced those of King Leopold to secure possession of the Katanga. The result of this 'scramble' had in fact been decided beforehand by the international agreement of 1885 which fixed the Congo–Zambezi watershed as the limit of King Leopold's territory. Most of Msiri's kingdom (see Chapter 4) therefore passed to Leopold. Msiri himself was shot by a Belgian officer in a brawl arising from the treaty-making. The lands on the Zambezi side of the watershed became British and later proved to include a substantial part of the rich copper-belt. The only part of central Africa excluded from the company's sphere was Nyasaland (Malawi), where British missionaries and traders, who were hostile to the British South Africa Company, had been active since the later 1870s. This part of the country became a Protectorate under the direct control of the British government in 1891.

The early years of the colonists' settlement in Southern Rhodesia were a time of constant fighting. There were unofficial wars between the settlers and the Portuguese on the Mozambique

20 *a*    Southern Africa: the European partition,
Britain, France and Germany.

border. The settlers had to conquer the Ndebele, who soon
became thoroughly resentful of their presence in neighbouring
Mashonaland. It is not pleasant to read how the colonists
deliberately provoked the conflict with the Ndebele, but the war

20*b*   Southern Africa: the European partition, Leopold and Portugal.

was probably an inevitable consequence of the European settlement. Lobengula died shortly after his regiments had been
defeated in 1893. The seizure of land and cattle by the victorious
settlers provoked both the Ndebele and the Mashona to make a
last attempt to drive them out in 1896, when the Africans' will to
resist the white man was finally broken by the machine-gun.

## The Anglo-Boer War

Rhodes was prime minister of the Cape Colony from 1890 to 1896. In addition he directed the activities of the British South Africa Company in the territories to the north. Rhodes had visions of uniting the whole of southern Africa, including the Boer republics, as a self-governing dominion under the British flag. He talked of 'equal rights for all civilised men south of the Zambezi'. It would seem that what he meant by this was primarily an alliance between Boer and Briton to develop the wealth of the country and to promote more white immigration. The Boer leader, Paul Kruger, President of the Transvaal, had very different ideas. He wanted a South Africa dominated by the Boers, who would retain their own language, Afrikaans (which had grown out of the Dutch of the original settlers), their old-fashioned pastoral way of life, and their refusal of political rights to the Bantu or other coloured peoples. Although glad of the wealth from the Witwatersrand gold-mines, Kruger was well aware that these were being developed mainly by British immigrants into the Transvaal, who might soon become a majority of the white population. While taxing them heavily, therefore, he denied them the vote. On the other hand he used the wealth with which they provided him to build up his defences and his railway links with the outside world.

Rhodes tried to persuade the disgruntled immigrants (Afri-kaans, *Uitlanders*) to stage a revolution and topple Kruger's government. A raid on the Transvaal from Bechuanaland in 1895, led by Rhodes's henchman Jameson, was a total failure, and no rising occurred. The raid ended Rhodes's political career, but elements in the British government which had been implicated in the plot were now determined on a decision with the Transvaal. The British High Commissioner in South Africa, Sir Alfred Milner, deliberately incited the Transvaal to war. This broke out in 1899, and the Orange Free State stood beside its sister republic. The Boer armies—and after they were beaten, the irregular commandos—fought the whole might of Britain with tenacity and courage for more than two years. Destruction was widespread, and casualties on both sides were very high. Before peace finally came, the Boers had been inspired with an even greater bitterness against Britain and British institutions than they had had before. For the time being, however, the whole of South Africa was in British hands.

SPANISH
MOROCCO

IFNI (Sp)

MOROCCO

RIO DE ORO

ALGERIA

TUNISIA

LIBYA

EGYPT
(British occupation)

FRENCH
SOMALILAND

BRITISH
SOMALILAND

ITALIAN

FRENCH WEST AFRICA

GAMBIA

RT
INEA

SIERRA
LEONE

LIBERIA

GOLD
COAST

TOGO

NIGERIA

EQUATORIAL AFRICA

ANGLO-
EGYPTIAN
SUDAN
(Condominium)

ERITREA

ETHIOPIA
(Italian 1936-1941)

KAMERUN

SPANISH
GUINEA

FRENCH
CONGO

CABINDA(P)

BELGIAN
CONGO

UGANDA

BRITISH
EAST
AFRICA
(KENYA)

GERMAN
EAST
AFRICA

ZANZIBAR (Br)

ANGOLA

NORTHERN
RHODESIA

NYASALAND

MOZAMBIQUE

SOUTH
WEST
AFRICA

SOUTHERN
RHODESIA

BECHUANA-
LAND

UNION OF
SOUTH
AFRICA

B?

MADAGASCAR

| | British |
| | French |
| | Belgian |
| | German |
| | Spanish |
| | Portuguese |
| | Italian |

21   Africa: the final stage of partition, 1914

## 11

# COLONIAL RULE IN TROPICAL AFRICA (1)

### POLITICAL AND ECONOMIC DEVELOPMENTS, 1885-1914

The colonial period in tropical Africa lasted for about seventy years. The first thirty years of this period may be called the years of establishment, the next thirty may be called the years of active development, and the last ten may be called the years of retreat. In this chapter we shall deal with the years of establishment mainly from the point of view of the colonial governments. In the next chapter we shall try to look at the same years mainly from the point of view of the African peoples, and to consider the changes which the colonial period introduced into everyday life.

### The policies of the colonial powers

Once Africa had been divided between them, the European governments lost much of their earlier interest in the continent. There were few parts of Africa which were expected to produce immediate wealth. The European nations had partitioned Africa mainly in order to ensure that they would not be excluded from regions which might prove valuable in the future. Possession was what mattered to them, not development.

At the end of the nineteenth century European states took a much narrower view of the functions of government, even within their own frontiers, than they do today. European states of those days had, for example, no public health services or old-age pensions, and no public housing other than the workhouse. In most European countries state education was still a recent introduction, and it was not yet provided for all children. Taxation was very much lower than it is today. Government spending was jealously controlled by the elected representatives of the voters who were still, for the most part, the wealthy members of each community.

It is not surprising therefore that it was felt in Europe that the main duty of governments in the new African colonies was to maintain law and order, and to do so without expense to the European taxpayer. Education on the one hand, and economic development on the other, were left almost entirely to the private enter-prise of Christian missions and commercial companies. Even the work of government was sometimes delegated to chartered companies, which were empowered to recruit their own officials and police forces, to collect taxes and administer justice. Where European governments assumed direct responsibility for the government of their new colonies, the most strict economy was practised. Officials were few in number; military and police forces consisted of ill-trained and poorly armed local recruits commanded by a few European officers.

Such governments were at first obliged to seek allies among their new subjects by entering into the web of inter-tribal politics, and by aiding the friendly groups in their struggles with their traditional enemies. Unfriendly groups were often left severely alone for as long as possible. If action against such groups proved necessary, the small colonial forces, aided by their native allies, often burnt the villages of the resisters and seized their cattle. Such raids were continued until the authority of the colonial government was recognised. Only as local revenues were slowly built up from customs duties and head-taxes could colonial governments afford to employ regular civil services and police forces which could effectively occupy and administer the whole of the territories under their rule. In most African colonies this position had barely been reached by the time of the outbreak of the First World War in 1914.

Nevertheless, in most African colonies a surprising amount was achieved during this period, and this laid the foundation for the period of active development which was to follow. By 1914 the construction of railways and feeder roads had opened most of tropical Africa to some kind of wheeled traffic, with the result that cash crops could be grown and marketed profitably. The great number of small, tribal sovereignties which had been such a barrier to almost every kind of progress had been amalgamated into approximately forty separate territories, most of which were capable of growing into modern states with sufficient resources to stand on their own feet. The greatest benefit and that which impressed itself vividly on the memories of most Africans who had experienced the pre-colonial period was the relative peace and security imposed by all the colonial governments, even the harshest and most arbitrary ones. It was above all 'the colonial peace' which freed energies for new activities, and which made possible, not only economic developments but also the spread of the universal religions of Christianity and Islam, and the beginnings of modern education and learning. It is against this general background that we must now consider the various types of colonial government which emerged in different parts of tropical Africa during the period between partition and the First World War.

### West Africa: the realm of the peasant producer

The distinguishing feature of this region was that the peoples of the coast had been trading for more than three centuries with the peoples of Europe. Among them the demand for European goods had become so deeply ingrained that, after the abolition of the slave-trade, they had made the most strenuous efforts to develop for themselves cash crops which could be exchanged for the imports which they had come to regard as necessities. This meant that colonial governments in West Africa had one supreme advantage over governments in other parts of the continent. They could begin to build up their revenues by taxing an established trade. Even a light customs duty on imported spirits and fire-arms could yield them the revenue out of which to pay their first small bodies of officials and military forces. It could provide them with a basis on which they could borrow money. It was this fact, far more than any climatic differences from other parts of Africa, which caused colonial governments to seek to establish their revenues by building up peasant production rather than by trying to attract concessionaire companies or private settlers with gifts of land. They had inherited an economic system on which they could build. Most colonial administrations in Africa would have liked to build their economies on peasant production. In West Africa conditions enabled them to do so. At the beginning of the colonial period, even in West Africa, it was only a small part of the region that was affected by the growth of a cash economy. The basic economic activities of the majority of people still consisted in producing food crops, housing materials, fuel and clothing, mostly for their own consumption. Although this involved a considerable amount of local trade and even some long-distance trade, the way of life was still of the kind called by economists a 'subsistence economy' as opposed to a 'cash economy'. It has been estimated that in 1900 such activities accounted for about 90 per cent of Nigerian production and 75 per cent of that of the Gold Coast. Yet in spite of the predominance of the 'subsistence economy', the beginnings of a cash economy were in existence and provided a growing-point for the future.

## French West Africa

The most consistent pattern of colonial rule was that developed by the French in their West African possessions. This was not the result of any imperial plan thought out beforehand. It was due to the fact that the seven younger colonies of Soudan, Mauretania, Upper Volta, Niger, Guinea, Ivory Coast and Dahomey were all in a sense extensions or offshoots of the old colony of Senegal. Access to the first four of these was at first mainly through the Senegal. In all of them the occupation was carried out by military forces, of which the backbone was the Senegalese army trained by Faidherbe and Gallieni in the course of their struggles with al-Hajj Umar, Ahmadu Sefu and Samory in the region between the upper Senegal and the Niger rivers (see Chapters 3 and 10). The fighting with Samory continued until 1898. Because the French had become so accustomed to fighting for the occupation of their territories they were less willing than the British to negotiate with those African rulers who might have been open to such an approach. The kingdom of Dahomey, the Mossi states of Wagadugu and Yatenga, and other important states, were broken up. The French administrative units (called *cercles*) which replaced them were more uniform in size and more directly controlled, first by military officers and later by civilian officials, than their counterparts in British territories.

The economic policy of the new French West African colonies was likwise based on the example of the Senegal, where Faidherbe and his successors had made the colonial administration self-supporting by encouraging the African population to grow ground-nuts on their own farms. This meant that the Senegalese peasants had a crop which they could sell for cash, with some of which they could pay the head-tax imposed by the government. As the French armies advanced into the interior, the civilian administration set up in the newly conquered districts at once sought to introduce similar cash crops. Particularly high hopes were set on the development of cotton-growing in the Niger basin. As in all other parts of the African interior, however, the great obstacle was the lack of transport. The first railway, built by the military as a strategic link between the upper Senegal and the upper Niger, though adequate for the movement of troops and supplies, proved useless for commercial cargoes. The railway terminals could only be reached by small steamers of shallow draught, and even they could only make the journey at certain seasons of the year. The difficulty of navigation on the Senegal was only overcome with the completion of the line from Dakar to Kayès in 1924. The uncertainties of navigation on the upper Niger remain to this day. In the coastal parts of Guinea, the Ivory Coast and Dahomey there was some early development in palm-oil, cocoa and other forest produce. Here again the opening-up of the interior had to await the building of railways, and this was not begun until the early years of the twentieth century. Indeed the railways were only starting to make significant progress by about 1914. The earliest cash earnings of the people of Soudan and Upper Volta were in fact those of migrant labourers who went to seek work in the ground-nut areas of Senegal and the palm-oil and cocoa districts of the Gold and Ivory Coasts.

It was the problem of economic self-support which led the French to federate their West African territories in a single unit, in which the richer and more accessible regions could help to support the poorer and more remote. In 1895, the Governor of Senegal had been given supervisory powers over his colleagues. This had been mainly in order to secure military co-ordination at a time when French armies were fighting with Samory around the interior frontiers of Soudan, Guinea and the Ivory Coast. Under French laws passed in 1902 and 1904, at the beginning of the great period of railway building, all the West African territories were grouped under a Government-General situated at Dakar. This Government-General consisted of the governor-general, his officials and advisory councils. It took an important share of the customs duties levied in all the coastal colonies. With this revenue the Government-General negotiated loans for railways leading to the interior. This meant, in the early days, that Senegal and Dahomey were between them contributing three-quarters of the federal budget of French West Africa, although to the great benefit of the region as a whole.

## British West Africa

The British West African territories presented, at the beginning of the period, a rather confused appearance. Not only were they geographically separated from one another, but their longer and more divided history had left them under three different kinds of

government. As explained in the previous chapter, there were the four Crown Colonies of the Gambia, Sierra Leone, the Gold Coast Colony and Lagos. In eastern Nigeria there was the Oil Rivers Protectorate, administered by the Foreign Office. And, finally, in northern Nigeria, there was the territory administered under charter by the Royal Niger Company. These differences, however, were not as important as they appeared. The Royal Niger Company, as we have seen, surrendered its charter in 1898. In 1900 Northern Nigeria became a British Protectorate, the same year as eastern Nigeria was taken over by the Colonial Office. Thereafter the British West African colonies came to resemble more closely than any others in Africa their French neighbours. They resembled them above all in the fact that they were economically based on the production of cash crops by African peasants. They resembled them further in that the prosperity of the coastal regions was used to build up administration in, and communications with, the interior. Moreover, though geographically much smaller, the British West African territories had more than double the population, and perhaps three or four times the wealth of the whole of French West Africa. And so, despite the lack of a federation between them, they went ahead faster than the French territories.

The Gold Coast moved quickest. Here the great political problem was the continued unity and strength of the Ashanti nation, which had largely recovered from its defeat of 1874. Two more serious military campaigns in 1896 and 1900 were fought before Ashanti would submit to the authority of the British colonial government. Even before the final defeat of the Ashanti, deep mining for gold by British companies had begun in Adansi, and in parts of southern Ashanti which had been annexed by Britain after the war of 1874. Mining provided the impulse for the construction of the first railway in the colony, which reached the gold-mining district of Tarkwa from Sekondi by 1901. At the end of the nineteenth century gold exports from the Gold Coast were actually falling, from a value of some £80,000 in 1897 to £22,000 in 1901. After the railway reached Tarkwa, the value rose rapidly: £97,000 in 1902, £255,000 in 1903, £1,165,000 in 1907 and £1,687,000 in 1914. Within a few years of its extension to Kumasi in 1903, to ensure military and political control over Ashanti, the second great significance of the railway proved to be its opening-up of the forest region, first to rubber-tapping and then to cocoa-farming. In 1901 the value of cocoa exported from the colony was £43,000; it was £95,000 in 1902, £515,000 in 1907 and £2,194,000 in 1914. By that year cocoa amounted to 49 per cent of all exports, and cocoa alone was already paying for all the Gold Coast's imports. The exportation of timber, worth £169,000 in 1907, also resulted from the building of the railway. Cocoa, gold and timber made the Gold Coast, by 1914, the most prosperous of all the African colonies.

In Nigeria, as in the rest of West Africa, it was the peasant producers of the coastal regions who, by the customs duties levied on their imports even more than by their direct taxes, provided the revenues out of which colonial administration and a modern system of communications was gradually extended over the interior. The Lagos Protectorate in the south-west and the Protectorate of Southern Nigeria (the old Oil Rivers) in the south-east were amalgamated in 1906 as the self-supporting colony of Southern Nigeria. The North, meanwhile, with its vast population, remained cut off from access to world markets save by the long and difficult link of river communications on the Niger and the Benue. The colonial administration there, despite continuing grants-in-aid from the British Treasury, was able to maintain itself only by making the utmost use of the existing Fulani system of government. Under British overrule the Fulani emirs continued to police, tax and administer justice to their Hausa subjects, while accepting advice from British Residents posted at their courts. The system worked, but it was scarcely progressive. Even Lugard, the first Governor of the North (1900–6), who was responsible for the system, realised that Northern Nigeria could only be modernised when it had been politically amalgamated with the South, and linked by railways with the coast. Lugard returned to Nigeria in 1912, and two years later (1914) became Governor-General of the whole territory. By this time the differences between north and south had hardened too much to be easily eliminated. Nevertheless, the administrative unification of the country marked a great step forward.

*The realm of the concessionaire company:*
*France and King Leopold in the Congo basin*

The region of Africa drained by the Congo and its tributaries was, as we have already seen, a very different one from West Africa. At its heart was the equatorial rain-forest, inhabited sparsely by

Africa's most isolated and therefore most backward peoples. The denser and more civilised populations of the area lived around the rim of the river basin. Their former trading links had been in some cases northwards to Libya and Egypt, in some cases eastward to the Zanzibar coast, in some cases westwards to Portuguese Luanda. Before the coming of the river steamer in the 1880s very little trade had passed by water through the forest centre to the Congo mouth. Along the West-Central African coast from the Cameroons to Luanda the trade established in the nineteenth century had been disrupted by the activities of the Free State officers on the lower Congo, and of the French in Gaboon. There was no worth-while exchange of European manufactures against African produce on which the colonisers could build, as they had been able to do in West Africa. No government could support itself by levying customs on the trade passing through Boma or Libreville, still less raise a loan for the building of railways round the Congo cataracts, or south from the upper Kasai to the Katanga. The finance required for such projects was 'risk capital', which had to be attracted by the possibility of large long-term gains in order to offset the lack of immediate returns. In these circumstances the time-honoured solution was that followed in railway development in North and South America—private capital was attracted by grants of land and mineral rights in the area to be opened up.

Such was in fact the origin of the system of concessionaire companies which was to become the distinguishing feature of the colonial history of this region. In 1886 King Leopold made the first contract of this kind with the *Compagnie du Congo pour le Commerce et l'Industrie* (C.C.C.I.), under which the company agreed to build a railway round the lower Congo rapids from Matadi to Leopoldville, in exchange for which it could claim 1,500 hectares (about $5\frac{1}{2}$ square miles) for every kilometre of line constructed. Thus, the lower Congo railway alone involved the alienation of more than 3,000 square miles. No sooner was it completed in 1898 than similar contracts were made with two other companies. These organisations undertook to build railways from the upper Congo to Lake Tanganyika, and from the limit of navigation of the Kasai to the heart of the Katanga. A variation on the railway concession was that given in 1891 to the *Compagnie du Katanga*. This was at the time when Rhodes was threatening to overrun the Katanga from the south and when King Leopold could not himself afford to undertake the effective occupation of the region. He therefore chartered the Katanga Company to do so, in exchange for one-third of the vacant lands and mineral rights in the area.

All the land conceded in this way was in theory 'waste land', the villages of the Congolese and the land actually under cultivation by them being excluded. But since land was useless without labour, every form of pressure was put upon the local inhabitants to work for the concessionaire company. The worst abuses occurred during the period from about 1895 to 1905, when the invention of pneumatic rubber tyres for bicycles and motor-cars was causing a great demand for rubber. In the long term this demand was met by the development of rubber plantations in South-East Asia. While the boom in wild rubber lasted, however, very large profits indeed were made by the concessionaire companies in the Congo. In theory these companies employed, but in practice compelled, their Congolese neighbours to tap rubber in the forests, usually for very small rewards. The profits secured in this way aroused the greed of King Leopold who took over and managed himself large areas of Crown land. Other areas he leased to private companies on a profit-sharing basis. The system proved so attractive that it spread into French Equatorial Africa. Here the French government saw in it a means of reducing the large annual deficits which had been accumulating since the beginning of colonial rule. In both territories the worst abuses of the system were brought to an end between 1906 and 1910, when the end of the wild rubber boom coincided with an outcry by international public opinion. In 1908 King Leopold was forced to cede the Congo to Belgium. In an effort to provide a more direct administration, and to cut down expenses, France in 1910 joined the four territories of Gaboon, Middle Congo, Ubangi-Shari and Chad into the federation of French Equatorial Africa. This was modelled upon the Government-General of French West Africa. Its capital was at Brazzaville. Both the French and Belgian governments, however, had contracts with the concessionaire companies, which they could fulfil only by leaving the companies in possession of large areas of land and with commercial monopolies over still larger regions. The Belgian Congo was further burdened with an enormous debt which King Leopold had incurred by borrowing money on the Congo's account and spending it on his palaces and on other public building in Belgium.

The interest on this debt at one time absorbed nearly a fifth of the country's revenue.

Certainly the foundation of colonies in the Congo basin presented a very different problem from that faced in West Africa. The region was a very poor one, and the people who lived in it had practically no sources of income that could be taxed to pay for the expenses of government and of modern communications. The only possible way to create such wealth was to reorganise the labour of the people. In a very crude manner the concessionaire companies did achieve this end.

### *The realm of the European settler: Britain, Germany and Portugal in East and Central Africa*

Like the Congo basin, and unlike West Africa, the new colonies of East and Central Africa had at the time of their occupation no trade, other than the declining trade in ivory, on which colonial revenues could be built. Unlike the Congo territories, however, these colonies in East and Central Africa were mostly crossed by the chain of highland country running from the Kenya highlands south-westwards towards the Cape. Here were lands, sparsely occupied by Africans, on which Europeans could settle as farmers. To colonial governments in search of revenue, a policy of limited white settlement by Europeans who would act as employers and organisers of African labour appeared as an attractive solution.

The German government was committed in principle to promoting settlement for its own sake. Germany at the end of the nineteenth century had a large and growing rural population, and German peasants had been emigrating in hundreds of thousands to the United States for many years. One of the main aims of the promoters of the colonial movement had been to enable such emigrants to settle in German lands overseas. In Tanganyika and South-West Africa, therefore, and even to some extent in the West African colonies of Cameroon and Togoland, settlers were encouraged to make claims. Land was set aside for them, particularly in the areas destined to be opened-up by railways.

The British government in London had no such fixed inclination to favour European settlement. In Southern and Northern Rhodesia settlement was promoted by the British South Africa Company. This was done for two reasons. Firstly the idea agreed with the ideals of Cecil Rhodes, that the highlands of Central Africa would make an excellent home for English-speaking farmers. The second was that land grants were a means of rewarding the occupiers, who would otherwise have had to be paid out of company funds. But in Nyasaland, where a Protectorate government was established in 1891, and in Uganda and Kenya, when these countries were taken over from the Imperial British East Africa Company in 1894–5, governors were left by the British government to solve their own problems in their own way. It is remarkable that the Uganda Railway, completed from Mombasa to Kisumu on Lake Victoria by 1901, was paid for by the imperial government out of an interest-free loan, which was later written off as a gift. In Uganda, after five years of mainly military activity the colonial government settled its account with its Baganda allies by signing a special agreement with them. This turned the Baganda chiefs into a land-owning aristocracy and gave the Buganda state a degree of recognition which would have made a policy of European settlement almost impossible to carry out. The Baganda responded to the situation by taking up the cultivation of cotton on a scale which soon made the country independent of grants-in-aid. Kenya, on the other hand, and also Nyasaland, were thought to present revenue problems which could only be solved by encouraging settler plantations.

The Scramble for Africa among the more powerful European nations put new life into the ancient Portuguese colonies of Angola and Mozambique. New settlers were encouraged to leave Portugal, to become farmers in the interior of these colonies. The Portuguese looked upon this colonisation by settlers more as a means of controlling their huge African possessions than as a means of developing them. In many parts of Angola and Mozambique the settler landowner was more like a one-man concessionaire company than was his British or German opposite number. On his estate he collected taxes and administered summary justice to his African tenants, from among whom he recruited both his labour and his private police force. This was feudal Europe of the Middle Ages surviving in twentieth-century Africa.

The Europeans who settled in East and Central Africa during the period up to 1914 were very few in number—some ten thousand in what is now Rhodesia, some three thousand each in what are now Zambia, Kenya, Tanzania and South-West Africa, probably not many more in Mozambique and Angola, and only a few hundreds in Malawi and Uganda. Several thousand Frenchmen settled in the highlands of Madagascar, and formed the largest group of French *colons* in Africa outside the Maghiib. Numerically the European settlers were much less significant than the Indians, who settled in the wake of the colonial occupation as artisans and petty traders all over East Africa, and in parts of Central Africa also. The Indians settled in the towns and villages, and lived by their own labour. The Europeans, on the other hand, settled in competition with the Africans, on the land, and lived as employers of African labour. Even so, only small areas were directly affected, and most of the areas of dense African population—for example, those around Lake Victoria and Lake Nyasa—were untouched. Indeed, throughout the greater part of all these countries African communities lived their lives and were ruled by the colonial administrators on much the same lines as in West Africa. Unlike West Africa, however, instead of being encouraged to add cash crops to the subsistence crops grown on their own land, the Africans were encouraged to earn the money they needed to pay their taxes by working, usually as migrant labourers, on European farms. Like the concessionaire company in the Congo basin, the European farmer settler of East and Central Africa was at this time chiefly important for the part he played in reorganising African labour by bringing some of it into the market economy. Politically and socially, as we shall see in the next two chapters, the European settler introduced much more confusion into tropical Africa than the concessionaire company. Whereas the company thought mainly of its profits, the settler was apt to think mainly of his children and grandchildren and of the position they would occupy in society. This posed a problem which grew steadily more important during the years after the First World War. It had then to be decided whether these parts of tropical Africa were to be developed in the interests of the settlers or of the indigenous inhabitants. The result was a series of uneasy compromises, which we shall examine in Chapter 13.

# 12

# COLONIAL RULE IN TROPICAL AFRICA (2)

### SOCIAL AND RELIGIOUS DEVELOPMENTS

## *The impact of colonial rule*

The impact of colonial rule on African societies varied greatly, not only from one territory to another but also from one part of a territory to another. To some extent the reasons for this sprang from their social organisation or the way in which they made their living. For example, specialised pastoralists, like the Masai in Kenya or the Herero in South-West Africa, found it much more difficult to adapt themselves to the wishes of colonial governments than most of the peoples who lived by agriculture. Or again, warrior groups, like the Ndebele of Southern Rhodesia or the Ngoni of Northern Rhodesia and Nyasaland, themselves the colonialists of an earlier period, found it more difficult to work and pay taxes than their former subjects, the Mashona and the Chewa. Much more important than the sociological reasons, however, were the sheerly accidental circumstances under which each group in a particular territory made its first contacts with the colonial government.

(*a*) *The people who gained from colonial rule.* In nearly every territory there were 'favourite peoples', who by good luck or good judgement made common cause with the colonial power and received privileged treatment as a result. To such peoples the colonial period brought at first no shame, but on the contrary extended frontiers, enhanced prestige and a sense of prosperity and achievement. In Northern Rhodesia, for example, the Barotse, who under the influence of the missionary Coillard had written to ask for British protection, received quite special treatment from the British South Africa Company. Because of their readiness to sign treaties and concessions, they were recognised as the over-lords of a wide surrounding region. By signing away the land and mineral rights of the peoples supposedly subject to them, they were able to protect their own country from most kinds of European interference.

In German East Africa it was the Swahili people of the coastal belt who were the most favoured by the German colonial government.

Sayyid Muhammad: v. British, Italians and Ethiopia: 1891–1920: OGADEN

Adowa: 1896: Italians defeated by Ethiopia

Alula

Berbera

Majertein

Obbia

Mogadishu

Guardafui Coast

Benadir Coast

Map labels:

Coptic Christians

Adowa: 1896: Italians defeated by Ethiopia

Massawa

Ethiopian Coptic Church

Harar

Kenya Highlands

Egyptian revolt against Britain 1919–1920

CYRENAICA:

TRIPOLITANIA:

Sanusi: Bedouin War v. Italians 1912–1931

RABIH: 1900: resistance to French

Conquered by Royal Niger Co. 1897

IBO

IJAW EFIK

FULANI EMIRS

NUPE

ILORIN

YORUBA

BENIN conquered by British 1897

DAHOMEY

FANTE

ASHANTI 1898–1900 resistance to British

SIERRA LEONE

RIF: Abd al-Qrim's war against Spain and France 1921–1926

Lyautey's pacification of the Blad as-Siba 1912–1925

SAMORI 1884–1898 Resistance to French

SENEGAL

SENEGALESE

Kenya L.
Kenya Highlands

MASAI
Displacement of Masai from Kenya Highlands

BUGANDA

BUNY...

1890-1898 Bunyoro resistance to British penetration

SWAHILI

Abushiri revolt against Germans— 1888-1889

HEHE
Maji-Maji revolt against Germans 1905-1906

Chilembwe uprising against British in Nyasaland 1915

NGONI
CHEWA
NYASA
YAO

TIPPU TIB
Arab resistance to Congo Free State 1891-1894

LUNDA
(Mwata Yamvo)

BAROTSE

MASHONA
Mashona revolt against S. Rhodesian settlers 1896

NDEBELE
Ndebele—Settler war 1893
Ndebele Revolt 1896

ZULU
Zulu Revolt 1906

Anglo-Boer War 1899-1902

Pro-German Boer Revolt 1913

Bondelswartz—South Africa bomb village 1922

Series of uprisings by Malagasy people against French and Hova domination, 1885-1905-

BAKONGO
Uprising against Portuguese 1913

OVIMBUNDU
Bailundo revolt against Portuguese 1913

HERERO
Herero-German War 1904

NAMA
Hottentot resistance to Germans 1904-1906

:::::::: Islamic regions

BUNYORO Peoples or rulers overthrown by colonial rule

_YORUBA_ Peoples or rulers benefiting from colonial ru e

23b Southern Africa: resistance to European rule

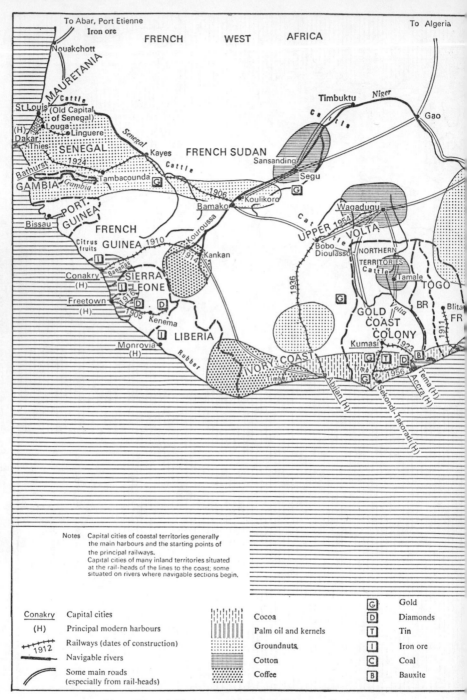

24a   West Africa: economic development during the
Colonial period, Western half

To In-Salah, Algiers

Agades

Cattle

NIGER

Cattle    Zinder

CHAD

Niamey

Nguru

Fort Lamy

Kaura

Kano

Gaya

NORTHERN

NIGERIA

Zaria

Fort Archambault

Kaduna

TOGO

DAHOMEY

Paraku

Minna

BAUCHI

Jos

Benue

Jebba  1911

Niger

Baro

1916

Ilorin

Makurdi

FR

Saven

Oshogbo

1901

Ibadan

1926

Enugu

BR

CAMEROONS

UBANGI-SHARI

Bangui

Abeokuta

Porto Novo

Lagos (H)

SOUTHERN

NIGERIA

Cotonou (H)

Grand Popo

Tome (H)

Calabar

Bananas

Port Harcourt (H)

Victoria (H)

Douala (Old German capital)

Yaounde

1927

Fernando Po (Sp)

Principe (P)

RIO MUNI

FRENCH  EQUATORIAL  AFRICA

Companies

Congo

Sao Tome (P)

Libreville (H)

Timber

Rubber

Concessionaire

Port Gentil

Ogowe

Timber

GABOON

Region  of

MIDDLE  CONGO

Kasai

Rubber

Brazzaville

Leopoldville

1934

1898

Pointe Noire (H)

Boma

Matadi (H)

24b   West Africa: economic development during the
Colonial period, Eastern half

25a   West-Central Africa: economic development during the
Colonial period, mineral deposits

SUDAN

ETHIOPIA

BELGIAN CONGO

UGANDA

KENYA

ITALIAN SOMALILAND

G

Kasese

Co

Entebbe

Kismayu

Kigali

RUANDA

Mwanza

URUNDI

T

G

Usumbura

G

Shinyanga

D

Mombasa

Ujiji

Tabora

Tanga

Kabalo

Albertville

Luluaborg

D

C

Tanga

Kabongo

L

Mpanda

TANGANYIKA

(GERMAN EAST AFRICA)

Dar es-Salaam

D

Kamina

Kilwa Kivinje

Bukama

T

Mikindani

Mtwara

Kolwezi

M

KATANGA

Cu

U

Elizabethville

RHODESIA

COPPER BELT

Co

Ndola

NORTHERN

NYASALAND

L

Z

Broken Hill

Lusaka

Mozambique

MOZAMBIQUE

Salisbury

Livingstone

C

Wankie

Que Que

G

Quelimane

Southern Rhodesia.
Steelworks at Que Que.
Secondary industries and
engineering works at
Salisbury, Bulawayo and
other towns

SOUTHERN

U

RHODESIA

G

Bulawayo

CH

Fort Victoria

Beira

Tu

G

Shabani

Francistown

West Nicholson

BECHUANALAND

Messina

Co

UNION OF

TRANSVAAL

SOUTH AFRICA

Pretoria

Lourenco Marques

Johannesburg

G

SWAZILAND

25b  East-Central Africa: economic development during the
Colonial period, mineral deposits

Douala
Bangui
Libenge
Banzyville
Bangassou
Bondo
Buta
Aketi
Lisala
Libreville
Stanleyville
Rubber
Ponthierville
Coquilhatville
Timber
Brazzaville
Leopoldville
Port Francqui
Pointe Noire
Timber
Lusambo
Matadi
Kabongo
Luanda
Kamina
Malange
Bukama
Maize
Cattle
Kolwezi
Lobito Bay
Benguela
Nova Lisboa
Maize
Cattle
Mossamedes
Sa da Bandeira
Villa Serpa Pinto
Zambezi
Timber
Livingstone

Approx. areas of land
occupied by European
settlers or estates

Cotton
Coffee
Sisal
Tea
Tobacco
Sugar
Palm products
Cocoa
Groundnuts

Cattle
Sheep
Walvis Bay
Windhoek
Gobabis

Gaberones
Mafeking

26*a*   West-Central Africa: economic development during the
Colonial period, agricultural products

26*b*   East-Central Africa: economic development during the
Colonial period, agricultural products

Douala

Libreville

Bangui
Libenge    Banzyville
                            Bondo
        Mongala      Aketi   Duta
            Lisala   Congo.  Itimbiri
Ubangi      Lulonga
                Stanleyville
Coquilhatville      Pouthierville
            Tshuapa

        Lukenje
            Kasai   Port
1934  Brazzaville    Kwilu    Francqui  Sankuru
Pointe Noire  Leopoldville              Lusambo
(H)     1898
(H)Matadi       Kwango   Luluaborg
                        Lulua   1928
                                    Kabo

Luanda      1899              Kamina
(H)         Malange           Bukama
                        1931
                              Kolwez
                1928
(H)Lobito Bay
Benguela    Nova Lisboa

Sa da Bandeira
Mossamedes      Villa Serpa
                Pinto
                        Zambezi

                        Livingstone

                    Tsumeb
                        Grootfontein

Gaberones  Capital cities

(H)     Principal modern harbours
                        1906
        Navigable rivers
                    1902
        Main railways with dates  Walvis Bay  Windhoek  1929
            of construction    (H)                Gobabis
        Some main roads
                        1912        Gaberones

                                    Mafeking

27a    West-Central Africa: economic development during the Colonial period,
       railways and waterways (bolder lines indicate navigable portions of rivers)

27b  East-Central Africa: economic development during the Colonial period, railways and waterways (bolder lines indicate navigable portions of rivers)

The coastal Swahili were the first people in East Africa to experience the rule of the German East Africa Company. As Hemedi bin Abdullah, a poet from Tanga put it:

> At Kilwa and Dar es Salaam
> There was a plague of Europeans;
> There was no free speech:
> They had throttled the country.

Under their leader Abushiri, the Swahili rebelled against the Germans, and after their defeat early in 1889 theirs was the first part of the country in which the Germans worked out a system of district administration. In this administration the Swahili played an important part. As the Germans later moved into the interior, they took with them a highly privileged class of Swahili soldiers and policemen, clerks and interpreters. These people understood their system of government and were able to turn it to their own advantage in a variety of ways.

In Uganda it was the Baganda who filled this intermediate role between the British and the other peoples of the Protectorate. Baganda armies fought alongside the British in many early campaigns, and received their reward in the extension of Buganda's boundaries at the expense of her neighbours. Far beyond even these extended boundaries, Baganda accompanied the expanding Protectorate administration and were employed for a time as chiefs in nearly every district in the country. Buganda got in first with every colonial improvement. The new roads radiated from Buganda; the first schools and hospitals were built there; it was there that the first cash crops, coffee and cotton, were grown.

In Nigeria, to take one more example, there were two privileged groups: the Fulani ruling class in the north, and the already educated townsmen of the coast—Yoruba from Lagos, Efiks and Ijaws from the city-states of the Delta, Ibos from the river-ports of the lower Niger. The Fulani were early resisters, who swiftly came to terms with their conquerors, and in consequence found their system of government supported, extended, and made more profitable than it had been before. The success of the coastmen was more like that of the Swahili. They were the clerks, the merchants, the schoolmasters, who accompanied the British administrators as they moved inland, and who helped to transform the institutions of the Yoruba city-states and the Ibo village communities into a pattern acceptable to the colonial government.

(*b*) *The people who suffered from colonial rule.* These then were
the people who gained from colonial rule. The losers were those
who, through ill-luck or ill-judgement, or simply from an excess
of patriotism, challenged the colonial power and found themselves disastrously overthrown. In Madagascar many of the people
who had long been hostile to the Hova ruling group seized the
opportunity of its decline in power at the time of the French
invasion. They rose against the Hova and the French. But the
rebellions were put down with a heavy hand by the French. The
condition of many of these groups was no better under colonial
rule than it had been under Hova domination. In Southern
Rhodesia first the Ndebele and then the Mashona very understandably rose in the attempt to drive out the white colonists,
who were visibly settling down in their land and taking it over for
their own use. The result of the war of 1893 and revolts of 1896–7
was that most Ndebele and Mashona found themselves driven
off the land they had previously grazed or farmed, and herded
roughly into 'reserves'. Here they had to start life afresh, often
without their cattle, often without even the support of their old
social groupings, which had been broken up as a result of warfare
and flight. A still worse fate befell the Herero of South-West
Africa, who in 1904 rose against the German settlers who had
been infiltrating into their land. Two-thirds of the Herero were
exterminated in the course of the German counter-measures. The
Herero country was declared the property of the state, and the
survivors were forbidden to keep cattle, since they no longer
possessed any land on which to graze them. A handful of refugees
escaped into Bechuanaland. The remainder passed into European
employment.

Nowhere else in tropical Africa was settlement and resistance
quite so unfortunately combined. North of the Zambezi, the
areas required for European settlement were very small, and the
earlier inhabitants of those areas were either left where they were
or, at worst, moved only a few miles. The largest displacement
was that of the northern Masai from the central part of the Kenya
highlands, and this was brought about by agreement, not by
force. The groups which suffered most by the colonial occupation
were not those who lost a small part of their land to settlers. They
were those who, for one reason or another, found themselves
opposing rather than supporting the spread of colonial power.
Of this the Banyoro of Uganda are a particularly unhappy

example. These people opposed the British mainly because the British were supported by their traditional enemies, the Baganda. Between 1890 and 1897 Bunyoro became a place of retreat for Arab and Swahili traders, for Muslim Baganda, and for all those who opposed the pro-British, Christian parties dominating the Buganda scene. These refugees included the rebellious Kabaka of Buganda, Mwanga. Advised by their Baganda allies, the British came to regard Bunyoro as ready for conquest. When this had been carried out with the assistance of Baganda levies, the British deposed the ruler in 1899, carved off the outlying districts of his kingdom and gave them to Buganda. For ten years or so the British even forced the Bunyoro government to employ a number of Baganda chiefs in key positions. The result of all this was a feeling of helplessness and frustration, which lasted right through the colonial period, and which made Bunyoro the last district in Uganda to adopt any of the useful innovations that came with British rule. Bunyoro had its Tanganyikan counterpart in the kingdom of Uhehe, its Congolese counterpart in the Lunda kingdom of Mwata Yamvo, its Nigerian counterpart in the kingdom of Benin, its French West African counterpart in the kingdom of Dahomey, its Ghanaian counterpart in the kingdom of Ashanti. And so on.

The basic question in the social and religious history of any particular African people at the beginning of the colonial period was whether it was swimming with the tide of advancing colonialism or against it. Eventually, no doubt, *all* African societies suffered a great blow through the loss of sovereignty, as the colonial governments progressively established the effectiveness of their overrule. In African societies, as in all others, the ultimate sanction behind authority was that of religion. The religious sanction began to be undermined as soon as the authority ceased to be absolute. Though the ordinary man in the ordinary village might continue to live his life much as before, and to be ruled for all practical purposes by the same village headman, it could only be a matter of time before he realised that there had been a change in the ultimate authority which controlled his life. Sooner or later a murder would be committed, and the accused and the witnesses would be taken, not to the chief's court as of old, but to the court of the colonial power, with its strange procedures and punishments. Sooner or later the European District Officer would appear on tour, with the local chief very much a subordinate in his train. There would be demands for labour to build roads, for porters to carry luggage or building materials or trade-goods. There would be talk of taxes to come, payable at first in kind, but later only in the unfamiliar pieces of minted coinage. It might be necessary to obtain this money by working for others or by trading in markets far outside the tribal area. Against these demands the tribal authority offered no protection, and therefore its divine sanction was slowly undermined.

### Christian missions and western education

At this point in time the Christian missionary, or, in some parts of tropical Africa, the Muslim missionary, was fortunately available to help build up again what had been broken down. As we have seen, the missionary had entered most parts of tropical Africa ahead of the colonial governments. At any time up till 1914, and in most places long after, he would have been a much more familiar figure, in the rural areas at least, than the government official. With the coming of the colonial period his activities took on, almost everywhere, a new lease of life. It is a remarkable and often overlooked fact that the colonial expansion of the nine-teenth century provoked among the young men and women of Europe a response not only from those who wished to rule, but even more from those who wished to serve, in the backward places of the world. Missionary societies of every denomination experienced a boom in recruitment and in financial support, with the result that missions all over tropical Africa were able to be strengthened very greatly during the years between 1890 and 1914.

The object of all missionaries was to bring African people into membership of the Churches to which they themselves belonged. At this period they at last began to be outstandingly successful in doing so. All over the previously pagan parts of tropical Africa, from about the seventh parallel of north latitude southwards, Africans flocked to join the Churches—and not only to join them, but also to serve them actively as evangelists and catechists and ordained ministers. Only where Islam was already well estab-lished—in Senegal and Guinea, in Soudan and Niger, in Northern Nigeria and the Chad territories, in the northern Sudan and in Somaliland, and in the coastal belt of East Africa—did Christian propaganda encounter any serious resistance. Only in these areas did Islam itself carry out a comparable expansion, spreading from its town bases into the surrounding countryside, and consolidating itself through the development of Quranic schools and religious brotherhoods. In southern Nigeria, Yorubaland, poised between the Muslim north and the Christian coastlands, experienced both movements simultaneously.

The main means used by all the Christian missions in their evangelism was to found networks of village schools in which children of all ages could be given a very simple education in reading, writing and arithmetic alongside the religious instruction leading to baptism and Church membership. These 'bush-schools' as they were called, were not impressive places architecturally. This description, written in N. Rhodesia in 1912, would have been typical of many other territories. 'The school consisted of a fence of grass, 6 feet high, surrounding a big tree, a few poles laid across short, forkey sticks for seats, and a mass of wriggling, youthful humanity.' A little later on a school like this would probably have developed into a building of the kind so well described by Bishop Kitching in northern Uganda, which served as a school on weekdays and a church on Sundays. Kitching wrote:

Imagine a rough shed, built of mud and wattle and thatched with grass. Very likely it is leaning sideways and is propped up with extra poles at varied angles. A few gaps left in the mud serve for windows and doorways. At one end the floor is raised a few inches by way of a chancel, and a pole or bamboo runs across as a Communion rail. At each side a mud-walled enclosure does duty as reading-desk and pulpit. On the inside of the roof hang innumerable hornet's nests, and possibly a few bats. On the walls, suspended from little pegs, are sheets displaying the alphabet, or rows of syllables, some of them nibbled by intrusive goats or fretted by the ubiquitous termites. Look in at about 8.30 in the morning, and you will see groups of readers of mixed ages and sexes, seated on the floor in front of the sheets, saying over the letters or syllables in a sing-song voice. Somehow they get the syllables memorised, and are promoted to reading consecutive print.

Such were the beginnings of western education in tropical Africa. The first instructors were, of course, European missionaries, but the brighter pupils who emerged from the system were given further training as catechists and teachers. As a result, education soon developed into a popular movement, in which foreign missionaries occupied only the supervisory positions, and in which most of the teaching and evangelistic posts were held by Africans. These educated men constituted a new and very real kind of leadership rivalling that of the traditional chiefs. In the

Africa of 1900–14 these mission teachers were the men and women who understood and felt at ease in the new world of the colonial period. To the tribal beliefs of their parents they had added a faith which they knew to be shared by people of all colours and all climates. Their religion taught them that all men had the same capacity for improvement in this life and salvation in the next. They were not therefore cast down by the changes which confronted them, but regarded them as opportunities to be seized. The development of the colonial administrations, of commercial and mining companies and of European plantations all increased the demand for clerks and skilled craftsmen, especially for those who knew a European language. The mission school soon emerged as a clear avenue for advancement, along which the ambitious could escape from the narrow discipline of village life into a wider world of well-paid urban employment.

## The birth of nationalism

Part of the significance of the Christian missions was that, in their religious as well as in their educational work, they were introducing Africans to the modern world into which they were now entering. They were showing them how they could succeed in that world. They were helping to make them into good colonial citizens. At the same time, however unconsciously, the missionaries were teaching the Africans to weigh up and criticise the influences of Europe *from within*. During the earliest years of the colonial period opposition to colonialism had been the opposition of the least westernised groups, whose leaders simply wanted to drive out the Europeans and restore the situation which had previously existed. From the mission schools, however, there was beginning to emerge, even before 1914, a new kind of opposition to colonialism. This opposition did not aim to restore the pre-colonial situation. On the contrary, the aim of the mission-educated Africans was to capture the political and religious institutions introduced into Africa from the West. This they meant to do either by taking over these institutions from the inside, and gradually replacing their European masters, or by imitating them from the outside, and establishing similar alternatives to the colonial institutions.

These mission-educated Christians were, in fact, the first real African nationalists. Some of them believed that the way forward lay in joining the Churches planted by the missions, and in seeking the best employment they could get in the service of colonial governments and commercial companies. They hoped that one day their children or grandchildren would rise naturally into the controlling positions. Others already believed that this hope was vain, and that it would be necessary for Africans to found their own independent Churches, and to prepare for an ultimate and revolutionary challenge to the colonial authorities. Either way, these new nationalists were thinking in modern terms—not in terms of a reversion to tribal beliefs and tribal organisations, but in terms of Christian Churches under African leadership, and of African successor states based on the existing colonial territories and governed along western rather than along traditional African lines.

There is a pamphlet written in 1911 by a Nyasaland African called Charles Domingo which gives a very good picture of the outlook of the more radical of these early nationalists. Domingo wrote:

There is too much failure among all Europeans in Nyasaland. The three combined bodies—Missionaries, Government and Companies or gainers of money—do form the same rule to look upon the native with mockery eyes. It sometimes startles us to see that the three combined bodies are from Europe, and along with them there is a title Christendom. And to compare and make a comparison between the Master of the title and his servants, it provokes any African away from believing in the Master of the title. If we had power enough to communicate ourselves to Europe, we would advise them not to call themselves Christendom, but Europeandom. Therefore the life of the three combined bodies is altogether too cheaty, too thefty, too mockery. Instead of 'Give', they say 'Take away from'. There is too much breakage of God's pure law as seen in James's Epistle, chapter five, verse four.

As you can see, Charles Domingo was not a very highly educated man. His ideas were simple ideas. His use of English was far from perfect. But what is interesting about him is that he was judging the Europeans he had met according to their own professed standard of moral judgement, namely the New Testament. He evidently did not doubt that the Epistle of James represented 'God's pure law', and nor did the people for whom he was writing. The conclusion he drew from the failure of Europeans to practise their Christianity was not that Africans should abandon it, though he realised that that was a danger, but that they could and should practise it better under their own leadership. Charles Domingo and those like him all over tropical Africa at this time represented the *most* westernised element in the colonial societies. Even on the Equator, most of them dressed in all the elaborate finery of early twentieth-century Europe. In every aspect of their lives they were the pioneers of European taste and customs. The independent Churches founded at this period were mostly even more European in their ritual and procedure than the mission Churches. Yet, for all their imitativeness, these early African nationalists had learned one thing above all others from their mission education: they wanted to run their own lives for themselves.

Although historians now know that opinions such as these were forming under the surface, they were not, in the years before 1914, much in evidence to Europeans who lived or worked in Africa at the time. Outwardly, the colonial governments, the missionaries, the settlers and the commercial companies appeared to be in complete control of their several spheres. Almost everywhere the first, military stage of colonial occupation had been succeeded by civil administration. Modern communications had penetrated to most districts. Cash crops were being widely grown. Migrant labourers were moving freely over long distances to various kinds of European employment. Taxes were being paid. Finally grants-in-aid from the governments of the European countries were being steadily eliminated. Most Europeans imagined that the foundations of empire were being laid down for a thousand years to come. To the extent that they were aware of the mission-educated Africans—the slowly developing intelligentsia—they wrote them off as an unrepresentative and unimportant minority. Even so great an administrator as Lugard referred to them contemptuously as 'trousered blacks', from whose exploitation the uneducated majority must be protected for a long time to come. The eyes of the colonial administrations were fixed upon the traditional chiefs and the old social hierarchy, whose influence they were unconsciously doing so much to destroy by their patronage. They ignored the new men, on whom the future of Africa was really to depend.

## 13

## THE INTER-WAR PERIOD, 1918–1938

*The war and the mandates system*

The First World War, fought between 1914 and 1918, marked an important turning-point in the history of the tropical African territories. Before the war these colonies had been backwaters, each connected with the main-stream of world events only through the single channel linking it to one or other of the colonial powers. There had been little overall policy. Each colony had been thought of as a separate problem, and mainly as a problem of economic self-support. After the war things moved faster. Most African colonies were by now sufficiently established to be able to think of more than mere survival. Their revenues were beginning to show modest surpluses over the bare cost of law and order. Colonial governments were able for the first time to contemplate expenditure on education, on health, on agricultural and veterinary services, and on economic development of various kinds. After the war, too, colonial powers started to take their colonial responsibilities more seriously. They tried to work out consistent policies for the African colonies. They developed within their colonial ministries important specialist departments and advisory services designed to assist all the colonial governments under their control. This increasing centralisation did much to break down the previous isolation of individual territories.

The war also made the colonial powers somewhat responsible to international opinion. The former German colonies were divided among the victor nations. Britain took most of the former German East Africa as Tanganyika Territory, and Belgium the remainder as Ruanda-Urundi. South Africa took the former German South-West Africa, and France and Britain each took parts of the Cameroons and Togoland. The changes were not outright annexations in the manner of the original partition. In the hope of avoiding further conflicts, the victorious powers had set up an international authority, the League of Nations. Largely on the initiative of the American President, Woodrow Wilson, it was agreed that those powers taking over German colonies should do so as 'mandatories' of the League. Those undertaking the task were required to recognize that the interests of the population concerned must have equal weight with those of the administering power. In spite of the lead taken by Wilson, the United States Congress would not agree to America joining the League. This gravely weakened the organisation from the very start of its life. Nevertheless, with strong British support, the establishment of a Mandates Commission of the League went forward. The Mandatories agreed to govern their territories as 'a sacred trust of Civilisation' until such time as they were 'able to stand on their own feet in the strenuous conditions of the modern world'. Annual reports on each of the Mandated Territories had to be sent to the League at its headquarters at Geneva in Switzerland, and in the Mandates Commission of the League it was possible for international opinion to have some influence on the policy of the mandatory powers.

## The dual policy in British Africa

In practice it turned out to be the mandatory powers themselves who made most of the running at the commission's meetings. This was significant because it showed that these powers were not merely concerned to defend their actions in the mandated territories but were also seeking a defensible policy of colonialism which could be applied to all their overseas possessions. Foremost among these practical thinkers about colonialism was Lord Lugard, who had ended his career as colonial administrator and had become the principal British representative on the Mandates Commission. In 1922 he published a book called *The Dual Mandate in British Tropical Africa*, which inspired a whole generation of colonial administrators and was accepted as a guide by politicians and civil servants in Britain. Lugard started from the doctrine that a colonial power had a double responsibility, on the one hand to the colonial peoples under its rule, and on the other hand to the outside world. To the colonial peoples it owed material and moral advancement leading ultimately to self-government. To the outside world it had the obligation to see that the natural resources of its colonies were developed, and that they found their way on to the world market. Lugard argued that, properly balanced, these two obligations need not conflict with one another. To secure a proper balance, it was necessary to ensure that in the economic field as well as in that of government, the colonial peoples were encouraged to do as much as possible for themselves.

In the field of government Lugard prescribed a general adoption of the system of indirect rule, which he had first evolved in Northern Nigeria and later adapted to the differing circumstances of the South. Indirect rule meant government through the traditional chiefs. In Lugard's words, a colonial official 'would consider it as irregular to issue direct orders to an individual native ...as a General commanding a division would to a private soldier, except through his commanding officers'. At the same time indirect rule was not just a system for concealing the exercise of power by the colonial government. It was basic to Lugard's thinking, though not always to that of his followers, that the traditional local government of the chiefs should be progressively modernised. The aim was that it should be able to take more and more responsibility, especially financial responsibility for the raising and spending of public funds. Under indirect rule taxes were collected by the chiefs, who passed on most of the money to the colonial government for national use. The chiefs were, however, allowed to keep a proportion of the taxes for their own 'Native Treasuries' and to spend the money on local needs and largely at their own discretion. This expenditure included the salaries of local government employees, such as clerks, messengers and policemen, and also local public works, such as offices, court-houses, dispensaries, markets, country roads and footpaths. Lugard looked forward to a time when the smaller traditional chiefdoms would federate with their neighbours to form larger units. In this way he imagined that a class of people would eventually emerge with the experience necessary to take responsibility at a national level.

In economic development Lugard was once again insistent that the largest possible place should be left free for the enterprise of Africans in their own countries. He recognised, of course, that large-scale and long-term economic investment, such as that required for railways and harbours, was clearly beyond the scope of local communities. Equally he thought that projects of this kind were too important to be left to outside private enterprise, and therefore in these matters he was a strong and early advocate of state ownership. In other kinds of large enterprise, such as mining, he saw a legitimate field for outside enterprise, though he stressed that, not only colonial governments, but also local 'Native' governments, should receive an interest in the profits. In the field of agricultural production, however, he was a firm opponent of the outside enterprise that was seeking to establish plantations for tropical produce in the West African countries. These European companies used arguments such as those put forward in 1924 by Lord Leverhulme when he said, 'The African native will be happier, produce the best, and live under the larger conditions of prosperity, when his labour is directed and organised by his white brother who has all these million years start ahead of him.' Lugard in the 1920s regretted the policy of white settlement in East Africa, which he had himself advocated in the 1890s. He saw that it had the effect of obstructing African enterprise of the kind which had flourished so successfully under the West African system of peasant production. That Lord Leverhulme's United Africa Company was refused permission to acquire plantations in any of the British West African colonies was due very largely to Lugard's influence.

### The dual policy in East and Central Africa

Obviously the part of tropical Africa where the dual policy was hardest to apply was in East and Central Africa, from Kenya south to Rhodesia. Here Europeans had been encouraged to settle, and here they were now claiming the right to take an increasing share in government. In Rhodesia this process had indeed gone too far to be stopped. When, in 1923, the British South Africa Company asked to be relieved of its governmental responsibilities, effective power was transferred to the 33,000 white settlers. North of the Zambezi, however, the British government was already by this time showing signs of its change of heart. The policy adopted in 1918 of encouraging demobilised army officers to settle in Kenya had led, within three years, to an acute labour crisis. During this crisis the colonial government had instructed its administrative officers to put pressure on the chiefs to direct their subjects into European employment. This led to such an agitation by missionaries and by the administrative officers themselves that public opinion in England was aroused. When the settlers pressed for further political powers in 1922–3 they were resisted. In July 1923 the British government issued a White Paper stating that:

Primarily Kenya is an African territory, and His Majesty's Government think it necessary definitely to record their considered opinion that the interests of the African natives must be paramount, and that if and when these interests and the interests of the immigrant races should conflict, the former should prevail. As in the Uganda Protectorate, so in the Kenya Colony, the principle of Trusteeship for the Natives, no less than in the Mandated Territory of Tanganyika, is unassailable.

The following year (1924) the British government sent an all-party parliamentary commission under the chairmanship of one of Lugard's greatest admirers, William Ormsby-Gore (later Lord Harlech) to investigate the guiding principles of British policy in East Africa. In its report the commission reaffirmed that there need be no conflict between the interests of the settlers and those of the native inhabitants. White settlement should not be allowed to hold back the education of Africans, or their training in economic skills, especially training in the best use of their own land. Though it did nothing to attack settlement, the Ormsby-Gore commission envisaged a great expansion in the functions of colonial governments, in the building up of health services, education services, agricultural and veterinary services. All these measures were directed towards the African population of the territories. It was this report which helped to set British policy in East Africa in line with that pursued in the West.

### Education in the British colonies

In 1925 Ormsby-Gore, now Under-Secretary of State for the Colonies, summoned the governors of the West and East African colonies to London. He ordered them to pursue a much more active policy of education, by entering into partnership with the Christian missions of all denominations and by subsidising the mission schools on condition that they conformed to the proper standards of efficiency. This did not result in a great increase in the total number of African children attending school, which remained at about one-third of those of school age. But, of those who did attend, the great majority now stayed at school for at least four years. And from this time onwards there were government inspectorates in every colony. Subsidies were only given on condition that teachers were trained and that the prescribed syllabuses were followed. In Muslim areas, like Northern Nigeria, local-authority schools were set up and staffed by government-trained teachers. As a result, during the fourteen years from 1925 to 1939 the standard of primary education was very much improved, and the effects were felt over the whole field of employment. The higher standards were noticed in government, and especially in local government, in the Churches, in commerce, industry and in every walk of life where a little clerical skill and a little knowledge of the world was needed.

More revolutionary still, however, was the progress made in secondary education. Here the numbers involved were very small indeed. Nigeria was probably the only country in British Africa which in 1939 had more than a dozen secondary schools. In most countries the output was between a hundred and two hundred students a year. Nevertheless it was these few hundreds of secondary school students who demonstrated that tropical Africans were capable of filling a wide range of posts of skill and responsibility, for which it had previously been thought necessary to import Europeans. With the exception of a few West Africans from well-to-do families who had been educated abroad, it was from this generation that there emerged the first professional men. There were doctors and veterinary surgeons, the first agricultural and forest officers, the first managers of retail stores, the first secondary schoolmasters, and, above all, the first educated chiefs and local government officials. Not all of these secondary-school students, however, consented to fill the occupations intended for them by the colonial authorities. It was in this generation that most of the leaders of the nationalist revolution received their secondary education: Kenyatta, Banda, Azikiwe towards the beginning of it, Nkrumah, Tafawa Balewa and Oginga Odinga towards the end of it. It is probably true that had the colonial governments and the Christian missions not provided the means of secondary education during this inter-war period, there could have been no successful nationalist revolution until long after the Second World War.

## *The French policy of association*

If it was Lugard and Ormsby-Gore who laid the foundations of British colonial policy between the wars, their French equivalent was Albert Sarraut, Minister of Colonies in 1920–4 and 1932–3. Sarraut's outlook was very different from that of the Englishmen. It was less respectful of the African personality and yet more fraternal towards the African. Sarraut never talked of 'allowing the African to develop along his own lines'. His dominant thought was rather that France and her African colonies must be kept as united in peace as they had been in war. The key to his plan was the rapid economic development of the colonies, to provide France with raw materials and with markets for French manufactured goods. 'Our colonies', he wrote, 'must be centres of production, and no longer museums for specimens.' Assimilation of Africans into French culture remained the ultimate objective, but no special effort was made to hurry it on. In 1936, apart from the four coastal *communes* of the Senegal with their 80,000 black *citoyens* (citizens with full political rights), only about 2,000 out of 14,000,000 French West Africans had received French citizenship. The immediate emphasis was on 'association' meaning the collective association of the French colonies with France. Economically the French empire was to become as centralised as it already was administratively. There was no thought that any of the colonies would ever become independent. African chiefs were merely the 'agents' of the French administration, and there was no intention at all of allowing their powers to grow. Indeed the top-grade chiefs, the *chefs de canton*, were really officials of the French administration. They were normally chosen from among the more efficient clerks and interpreters in the government service rather than on any hereditary principle.

It was above all in education that French policy differed from British. Although a few mission schools received government subsidies for exceptional efficiency, nine-tenths of the formal education given in French Africa between the wars was given by the state. Moreover, all teaching was in French. The aim of education was neatly defined by one governor-general of French West Africa as 'instruire la masse et dégager l'élite' (give primary education to the masses and win over the *élite*). Primary education was given in 'regional schools', of which there were by 1937 about eighty scattered over French West Africa. There were a very much smaller number in French Equatorial Africa. Secondary education was limited to filling the needs of the government service. Nearly all of it was given in three first-class institutions in Dakar. The best known of these institutions, both academically and for its output of later nationalist leaders, was the teacher training college called the École William Ponty.

In the Congo the Belgians pursued between the wars a policy which resembled the French policy in so far that rule was direct rather than indirect. In 1919 the Congo was being administered in no less than 6,000 separate chiefdoms (*chefferies*). By 1934 this had been reduced by amalgamations to some 2,500, but even at this figure the African chief in the Belgian Congo was scarcely even the equivalent of the French *chef de canton*. Like his opposite

GREAT BRITAIN

GERMANY

FRANCE

African soldiers, especially Senegalese, fighting in Europe

Moroccan and Algerian soldiers

Tangier
1923: Recognition
of international status

O T T O M A N

Istanbul

E M P I R E

Damascus

Sanusi revolt against
Italians received some
Ottoman support

Sanusi
attacks
on British
in Egypt

Egypt.
British
Protectorate
1914-1922

Suez Canal

Arab revolt against
Ottoman rule Hijaz

Saharan frontiers settled by
**Colonial Powers**   and Egypt by mid-1920s

Tuareg and Sanusi resistance
to French encouraged by
Germans and Ottomans

SENEGAL

CAMEROONS

TOGOLAND
TOGO

NIGERIA

GOLD
COAST

DAHOMEY

1914 Lome

1916

CAMEROUN

Duala

GABON

Territory ceded to Germany
in 1912, returned to French
colonies of Gabon and Congo

BELGIAN
CONGO
Belgian-African
forces

RUANDA

URUNDI

UGANDA

KENYA
British
-African
forces

JUBALAND
ceded by
Britian to
Italy 1920

TANGANYIKA
(GERMAN
EAST
AFRICA)

Dar-es-Salaam

Smuts

South African forces

German General
von Lettow-Vorbeck
still fighting in
Portuguese territory
at end of War in 1918

MOZAMBIQUE

African labour corps for service in France

SOUTH
WEST
AFRICA

Walvis Bay

Windhoek
1915
Smuts

and Botha

Boer pro-German
rebellion 1914

UNION OF S.
AFRICA   1910

British Mandates under
League of Nations

French  Mandates under
League of Nations

Belgian Mandates under
League of Nations

Union of South Africa
Mandate under League of Nations

British (South African)
French and Belgian forces

African troops sent to Europe

28   Africa and the First World War

number in French West Africa, he was strictly the agent of the colonial government. In the Belgian colonial service, as in the French, administrative districts were much smaller than in most British territories, and the administrative staff was larger. Control, therefore, was correspondingly closer. In education the Belgians, like the British, preferred to subsidise mission schools rather than to organise a state education service. Unlike the British, however, they subsidised only 'national', that is to say Roman Catholic, missions. Even more severely than the French, the Belgians limited schooling to primary education only. Their stated aim was to bring forward the inhabitants of the Congo at a uniform pace, and so to prevent the exploitation of the many by the few. Actually, as it turned out, the result was to leave the country with few effective leaders at independence, and with not nearly enough educated people to operate the machinery of government.

### Colonialism and nationalism

Although by the 1920s the tropical African colonies of all the European powers were being run at least partly in the interests of their African inhabitants, developments were still dominated by European governors, administrators and commissions of inquiry. No important decisions were made by Africans, and in a sense there were fewer Africans of importance in this period than there had been in the period before 1914, when a few of the old leaders still survived from the pre-colonial period. By the 1920s most of these older men were either dead or in retirement. Their places had been taken by men who owed their promotion to Europeans, and who tended to be the 'trusties' of the colonial administrations. A small but important number of educated men and women were leaving the secondary schools, but these were still young and inexperienced, and they held as yet only minor jobs in government and commerce. A very few were able to study in Europe and America, and became doctors and lawyers, but on their return to Africa they were often not given the status merited by their qualifications. Most such people considered that their attainments deserved greater rewards. Out of these individual grudges emerged a more general dissatisfaction with the way their countries were being governed.

The earliest political associations were formed, naturally, in West Africa, where the coastal people had been in contact with Europeans for centuries, and where a tiny minority had enjoyed western education for several generations. In Sierra Leone the leading freed-slave families, and in Senegal the Creoles (descendants of marriages between Frenchmen and African women), had taken part in local politics since the middle of the nineteenth century. In the Gold Coast and in Lagos small associations had sprung up during the early twentieth century among the lawyers, doctors and businessmen. As early as 1918 a Gold Coast lawyer, J. E. Casely Hayford, founded the National Congress of British West Africa, which spread to Nigeria in 1920. The Congress demanded that Africans should participate in the government. For the most part, however, the activities of these early politicians were confined to local affairs, and they had little influence upon the colonial governments. In French West Africa political consciousness centred upon the four coastal *communes* of Senegal, where the 80,000 *citoyens* had as early as 1914 elected a black Senegalese, Blaise Diagne, to the Chamber of Deputies in Paris. In 1917 Diagne became the Under-Secretary of State for the Colonies of metropolitan France, and this helped to set the fashion that politically conscious Senegalese should join the political parties of France. From about 1936 onwards, increasingly left-wing governments were elected in France. Socialists and Communists were now able to obtain appointments in the colonies, especially in the Education Service. As a result, considerable numbers of French West Africans joined the French Socialist and Communist parties.

In the field of pan-African politics, student organisations in Britain and France were the chief means of turning local and individual grievances into a true spirit of nationalism. Much of the inspiration of these organisations came from the writings and activities of American and West Indian Negroes, such as Edward Blyden, W. E. DuBois and Marcus Garvey, who stressed the similarities in the conditions of black people on both sides of the Atlantic. Under their influence, Africans began to think in terms of taking over control of the political units which the colonial powers had created, and of uniting them after the manner of the United States of America or the Union of Soviet Socialist Republics. Foremost among the student organisations was the West African Students' Union, founded in 1925 in London by the Nigerian Ladipo Solanke. The Italian invasion of Ethiopia in 1935 added fuel to the growing fire of nationalist feelings. The decisive event in the history of nationalism in British West Africa was undoubtedly the return in 1935 of Nnamdi Azikiwe from his studies in America, and his launching, first in the Gold Coast, and then in his native Nigeria, of a popular press. This was the most essential step in getting the political ideas of pan-Africanism accepted by a mass audience. Soon after his return Azikiwe helped to send to America eight Nigerians and four Gold Coasters, all of whom grew into key figures of the post-war nationalist revolution. The most prominent of this group was a young Gold Coast teacher named Kwame Nkrumah.

Most of the West African politicians were men who had broken away from their tribal backgrounds. They organised their activities in a European way, using newspapers and popular agitation. These caused riots at times, but were essentially non-violent. In East Africa discontent with European rule still assumed a mainly tribal form. The history of nationalism in Kenya, for example, is largely the history of Kikuyu dissatisfaction and resistance. The numbers of the Kikuyu were increasing rapidly. Their natural path of expansion out of the forests around Mount Kenya was blocked by the European settlers. Many became squatters and farm labourers on European estates, whilst others left the land and joined the growing numbers of unemployed in Nairobi. In 1922 a clerk in government service, Harry Thuku, started a political association which drew attention to these problems. He was sacked from his job and arrested, whereupon a large crowd assembled in Nairobi and was fired upon by the police. Thuku was banished to the remote Northern Frontier District, but political groups spread widely among the Kikuyu. When in the late 1920s some missionary societies attempted to interfere with Kikuyu initiation customs, many teachers left the mission schools and formed an Independent Schools Association. Jomo Kenyatta first came to prominence as secretary of the main Kikuyu party, the Kikuyu Central Association, before he left to study and work in Britain in the 1930s. When Thuku was released from detention in 1931, he formed a moderate party which quarrelled bitterly with the Kikuyu Central Association. The Kikuyu were thus unable to present a united front to the government and the settlers, and this of course suited the Europeans very well.

Kenya was by far the most troubled territory in British Africa between the wars, though the calm and slow pace of political and economic change in much of the rest of the continent was deceptive. Under the surface, African society was changing rapidly, and not in the way Lugard had hoped it would. The 'trousered blacks' rather than the long-robed chieftains were setting the pace. Africa was seething with new ideas and new ambitions, making ready to exert its will in opposition to the rule of European governments. Still, without the added ferment of of the Second World War it is very doubtful if the authority of the colonial governments would have been challenged until very much later than in fact it was.

## 14

## NORTH AND NORTH-EAST AFRICA, 1900–1939

### *The pan-Islamic movement*

By 1914 North Africa and the Muslim lands of the Horn of Africa were all in European hands. Only Ethiopia clung to a precarious independence. The variety of political and social conditions in this region was staggering. The contrast between Somali pastoralists on one hand and the wealthy citizens of Cairo on the other was extreme. Yet they possessed a common faith and a single cultural tradition which set them apart from most of the people of tropical Africa. The European powers had to adapt their policies and their methods of administration to the institutions of Muslim society. These were too deeply rooted to be set aside. Warfare and political conflict loomed larger over these countries throughout the colonial period than in any other part of Africa. Resistance to the loss of independence was inflamed by the intense religious hostility long felt by Muslims for the Christian peoples of Europe. As a result, revolts led by *shaikhs* and holy men continued until the 1930s, by which time nationalist opposition, organised on modern political lines had developed. Nationalism, here as elsewhere, was influenced by European political ideas absorbed in colonial schools and metropolitan universities. Throughout this region it was influenced also by the pan-Islamic reform movement.

The pan-Islamic movement was a reaction against the relentless encroachment of Christian Europe upon the lands of Islam. It began among groups of educated Turks in the Ottoman empire

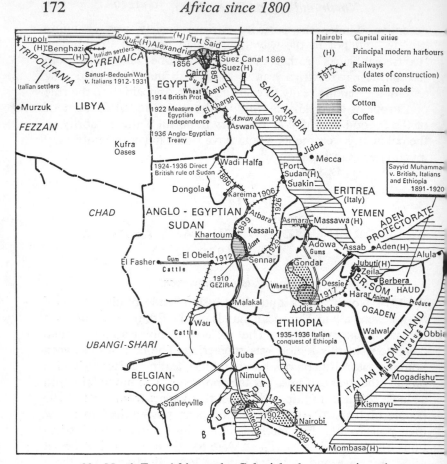

29  North-East Africa under Colonial rule: economic and
political development

in the 1860s and the 1870s. The movement owed something to the
example of the unification of Italy and Germany which was taking
place about that time. The ideas spread to Cairo, Damascus and
other Arabic-speaking cities of the Middle East. The central
argument of the pan-Islamists was that the only way the Muslim
world could survive in the face of European aggression was for
all Muslims to sink their political and local differences, and to
unite against the common foe. Political unification could only be
brought about through a thorough re-thinking of the principles
and practices of the Muslim religion. Al-Azhar University in
Cairo became the main centre for the teaching of pan-Islamic

ideas, in spite of the British occupation of Egypt after 1882. To Al-Azhar came students from all over the Muslim world, including the Maghrib and the Sudanic lands. These students returned to their homes inspired by the reforming movement.

### French rule in the Maghrib

By the beginning of the twentieth century Algeria had already been governed for many years as if it were a part of France. In Tunisia and Morocco, however, the governments of the Bey and the Sultan survived the establishment of the Protectorates. They were, however, increasingly staffed with French officials. All three countries were poor, suffering from perennial droughts, poor soils, and, above all, from difficulties of communication caused by the mountainous interior. The French now tackled these problems with determination, especially that of communications. By the 1930s it was possible to travel from Marrakesh to Tunis by train, and Maghribi roads were the best in Africa. The growth of Casablanca offers an outstanding example of development under French rule. In 1900 it was a tiny fishing village. Even before the establishment of the Protectorate in 1912 the French had constructed an artificial harbour, with rail links to the iron and phosphate mines of the interior. By 1936 it had a population of a quarter of a million. Moroccans flocked to Casablanca (as Algerians did to Algiers and Oran) to work in the factories and port installations, the more poorly paid among them living in shanty towns on the outskirts of the city.

In all three countries Frenchmen were encouraged to settle as *colons*. In Algeria by the turn of the century there were more than half a million, and by 1936 they had grown to nearly one million. In the same year there were more than two hundred thousand *colons* in Morocco, and nearly as many in Tunisia. Undoubtedly, most of the economic development which took place under French rule was attributable to these immigrants, though their presence in such numbers caused grave political and social difficulties. Not only did they occupy much of the land, but in every town they competed for jobs with the indigenous Muslim population. The Muslim population was also growing rapidly: in Algeria alone it doubled itself, rising from four and a half millions to more than nine millions during the first half of the century. With the best land and the highest paid jobs in European hands, the Muslims tended to become poorer as their numbers increased. By the 1930s many thousands of Maghribis had migrated to France in order to earn a better livelihood.

The *colons* of Algeria remained, in the fullest sense, citizens of France. They elected their own Deputies to the National Assembly in Paris, and exercised a steady pressure on French politics. Theoretically, the same rights of citizenship could be granted to educated Muslims, but only if they abandoned Muslim for Christian law, which few of them cared to do. The *colons*, needless to say, did nothing to encourage them. In 1913 a French writer summed up the settler point of view as follows: 'In a conquered country almost the only kind of co-operation that can occur between the two races is one in which the conquered work for the conquerors.'

### Morocco: Lyautey and Abd al-Qrim

The territory which differed most from Algeria was Morocco. This was partly because French rule there did not begin until 1912. It was mainly because of the outstanding character of its first Resident-General, Marshal Lyautey, who held the office for thirteen years, from 1912 till 1925. Lyautey was a colonial ruler of the highest order. He understood and respected the traditional institutions of North African Islam, and was determined that they should be preserved with dignity. At the same time he had a sure grasp of economic affairs, and the rapid modernisation of the Moroccan economy was largely his work. When he came to Morocco he found it 'submerged in a wave of anarchy'. In particular he had to take on the task of pacifying the tribes of the *Bilad as-Siba* (see Chapter 8). For centuries no sultan of Morocco had been able to subdue these tribes. Perhaps Lyautey's greatest achievement was the bringing of law and order to areas that had never previously been controlled by the central government of Morocco, and by means more humane than forceful conquest. His principle was 'to display force in order to avoid using it'. His policy of combining French interests with those of the Sultan and the tribal *kaids* (chiefs) was similar to Lugard's work in Hausaland, and suffered from the same defects.

In the early 1920s Lyautey's pacification was rudely interrupted by the Rif War. The Berbers of the Rif mountains in the northern zone of Morocco rose against the inefficient and often unjust Spanish military government. Brilliantly led by a former *Qadi* (Muslim judge) called Abd al-Qrim, they defeated a Spanish force in 1921 and followed this up by pushing the Spaniards into the coastal towns. Abd al-Qrim proclaimed a 'Republic of the Rif'. The term was modern, but he had a thoroughly old-fashioned ambition—to become Sultan and found a new dynasty in Morocco. His military successes made him the hero of the Muslim world. This gave him the false confidence to extend his operations into the French zone. By doing so he brought the whole might of the French army against him. France and Spain, in the words of an American observer, 'had enveloped the Rif in a wall of steel, employing every device of scientific warfare against the embattled tribesmen'. Once this had happened, further resistance was futile. In May 1926 Abd al-Qrim

came riding astride a mule into the French lines. At one point he was crossing a stream in which French soldiers were bathing. As soon as they saw who he was, they came rushing towards him. Though naked, they saluted him in correct military fashion, and expressed their great admiration for his qualities as a soldier and a leader.

(Rom Landau, *Moroccan Drama*.)

The French exiled him to the island of Réunion, but years later he returned to play a part in the Moroccan nationalist movement.

In 1925 Lyautey sent in his resignation to the French government in protest against the delays in sending him the reinforcements which he had asked for during the crisis of the Rif War. To his surprise and grief, his resignation was accepted. It is said that he boarded his ship at Casablanca with tears streaming down his face. His successors, who were lesser men than he, soon pushed the old ruling classes into the background, giving them no further opportunity to modernise the traditional institutions. In 1927, when the old Sultan died, the French arranged for a young prince, Sidi Muhammad, to accede to the throne of Morocco. The French imagined that they could educate the young Sultan to rule entirely according to their wishes. They could not have been more mistaken, for after the Second World War Sidi Muhammad became the leader of the Moroccan nationalist movement. The French also attempted to play off the Berbers against the Arabs: the result was to unite them in opposition to French rule.

### The beginnings of nationalism in the Maghrib

Nationalism in the Maghrib was a reaction against the realities of French rule, which were at variance both with the theory of

assimilation in Algeria and with the terms of the Protectorate treaties in Tunisia and Morocco. As early as 1920 Lyautey had forecast that 'a young generation is coming along which is full of life, and which needs activity. Lacking the outlets, which our administration offers them so sparingly, they will find another way out, and will seek to form themselves into groups in order to voice their demand.' In Morocco and Tunisia it was possible to foresee the emergence of free, reformed, Muslim states. Moroccans looked back with pride over a long and glorious past. Their Sultan claimed descent from the Prophet Muhammad, and was the spiritual as well as the temporal leader of the country. The young Sidi Muhammad did not abandon his outward show of subservience to the French until after the Second World War, but his sympathies were known long before. The foundations of the nationalist movement, however, were laid by others. One summer's evening in 1926 ten young men met in a garden in Rabat, sipping mint tea under the boughs of a mulberry tree. They were addressed by an eighteen-year-old student, Ahmad Balafrej, who was one day to be Prime Minister of Morocco. 'Without freedom,' he said, 'the darkness of the grave is more comforting to the spirit than the light of the sun.' The ten agreed to form a secret association to oppose French rule by any and every means. Nearly twenty years of preparation by journalism and political organisation were to be necessary before early movements like this one were able to combine in 1944 as the *Istiqlal*, or Party of Independence. The Istiqlal Party had the support of the Sultan and of a large section of the Moroccan people.

In Tunisia the beginnings of democratic political organisation went far back behind the colonial period to the middle of the nineteenth century, when, as we have seen in Chapter 8, the *Destour* (Constitution) Party was formed to curb the power of the Ottoman Bey. The Destour Party remained active during the early years of French rule, but represented mainly the wealthy citizens of the capital. In 1934, however, Habib Bourgiba broke away from the old party to found the *Néo-Destour*, composed of younger, more radical groups, with a modern secular policy. Bourgiba proclaimed that: 'The Tunisia we mean to liberate will not be a Tunisia for Muslim, for Jew, or for Christian. It will be a Tunisia for all, without distinction of religion or race, who wish to have it as their country and to live in it under the protection of just laws.' But in 1934 Bourgiba and his supporters had still a long struggle ahead of them. Being generally sympathetic to France and French culture, they wanted to negotiate Tunisia's independence in a friendly way. The French and Italian settlers in Tunisia were opposed to such an independence, as were the French civil service who staffed the Tunisian administration in large numbers. Above all, the French military chiefs were determined that Tunisia should remain French. They saw Tunis and the naval station of Bizerta as a necessary base for the coming war against Fascist Italy. Until after the Second World War therefore the French dealt with the *Néo-Destour* by imprisoning its leaders, by banning its newspapers, and finally by outlawing the party and closing its offices.

In Algeria, nationalism had to deal with an even more difficult situation. The political structure of the country had been entirely refashioned by the French. Most educated Muslims had been to French schools. and spoke French better than they spoke Arabic. Yet the privilege of French citizenship was in practice denied to them. There was little surviving from the past on which they could build. In 1934 Ferhat Abbas wrote despairingly: 'Men who die for a patriotic ideal are honoured and respected. But I would not die for an Algerian fatherland, because no such fatherland exists. I search the history books and I cannot find it. You cannot build on air.' The sense of an Algerian nationhood was born only during the bitter war fought with France between 1954 and 1962, in which the more moderate nationalists of the 1920s and 1930s, like Ferhat Abbas, were swept aside by younger, more extreme leaders. Nationalism in Algeria could hardly make a beginning until nationalism in Tunisia and Morocco had all but gained the victory.

### The British in Egypt and the Sudan

After the British occupation of 1882, Lord Dufferin, who had been ambassador in Istanbul, was sent to Egypt to report on a possible system of government. He advised that the country could not be administered from London with any prospect of success. 'Any attempt on our part to do so would at once render us objects of hatred and suspicion to its inhabitants.' Unfortunately for both countries, this warning went largely unheeded. As allies of the Ottoman Sultan, who was still the nominal sovereign of Egypt, Britain could not annex the country outright. The Khedive and his ministers continued outwardly to govern the country. In reality, the British Consul-General in Cairo held absolute power in Egypt. Lord Granville, the British Foreign Minister, wrote: 'It is essential that in important questions affecting the administration and safety of Egypt, the advice of Her Majesty's Government should be followed, as long as the provisional occupation continues. Ministers and Governors must carry out this advice or forfeit their offices.' Compared with other African countries Egypt was highly developed, both socially and economically. Nevertheless, the British carried out many improvements, especially in irrigation. The Aswan dam was completed in 1902. It stored sufficient water to irrigate the Nile valley all the year round, and for the first time in five thousand years Egyptian agriculture became independent of variations in the annual Nile floods. In other fields, however, the problem was not the lack of modernisation but the fact that modernisation had outrun the financial resources of the country. Indeed the foremost aim of Lord Cromer, who as Consul-General from 1883 until 1907 held the position of supreme power, was to simplify the elaborate government of the khedives, and so to lighten the burden of taxation upon the peasant *fellahin*.

Material benefits, however, did not endear the British to the Egyptians, and discontent soon developed into nationalist demands for their withdrawal. Already by the 1890s most Egyptian politicians were nationalists, and from then on Anglo-Egyptian relations ran round in a vicious circle. The nationalists had only one demand; that the British should quit Egypt. The British replied that they could not do so until a really strong and financially stable government had been established. This was impossible because the nationalists would not co-operate with the Khedive and the British to form one. Thus a growing gulf of misunderstanding and hostility separated the rulers from the ruled. In 1914, when Turkey sided with Germany in the First World War, and when Britain as a countermeasure declared a Protectorate over Egypt, this gulf grew wider. Egypt became the base for all British military operations in the Middle East. Egyptians suffered real hardship from the foreign troops who were quartered among them. These troops requisitioned their labour, their animals and their produce for military purposes. They voiced their resentment against Wingate, the High Commissioner for the Protectorate, in a popular song:

Woe on us Wingate,
Who has carried off our corn,
Carried off our cotton,
Carried off our camels,
Carried off our children,
Leaving only our lives,
For love of Allah, now leave us alone.

(John Marlowe: *Anglo-Egyptian Relations*.)

Egyptian resentment boiled over into open revolt in 1919, when Britain and France failed to keep their promises to grant independence to the Arab provinces of the old Ottoman empire. Britain, now realising that she could only hold the country by force, decided to give way to Egyptian demands. But so suspicious had Egyptians become of British intentions that no politician was prepared to risk his reputation by signing a treaty with the occupying power. In 1922, therefore, Britain issued a one-sided declaration, granting Egypt a modified form of independence. British forces still remained in the country, but under a new constitution the Khedive was recognised as king, and parliament was to be elected under a universal male franchise.

One of the immediate results of self-government in Egypt was to show how unreal was the joint rule of Britain and Egypt over the Sudan under the so-called Condominium arrangement. The Sudan had been 'reconquered' in 1898 by the Egyptian army with the aid of British troops. The annual deficit in the Sudan's budget, which had persisted from then until 1913, had been met from the Egyptian, and not from the British Treasury. For twenty-five years after the reconquest Egyptians had held all but a hundred or two of the most senior posts in the army and the civil service. Nevertheless, all real power in the Sudan was exercised by the British Governor-General and by the senior British administrators and military officers. British power was exercised on the assumption that the Sudan was a separate country from Egypt, with interests of its own which were more important than those of Egypt. For example, education in the Sudan was launched along English lines, very distinct from the largely French tradition prevailing in Egypt. More sinister still from the Egyptian point of view, the British were planning to use the Nile waters for a great irrigation project in the cotton-growing district of the Gezira, south of Khartoum. This scheme was undoubtedly beneficial to the Sudan, but it emphasized to every

Egyptian that the waters of the Nile, the life-line of Egypt, was in the control of another power. In fact, Egypt, which had ruled the Sudan in the nineteenth century, had been squeezed out of it by Britain in the twentieth.

This resentment over the Sudan led, in 1924, to the assassination by an Egyptian nationalist of the Governor-General of the Sudan, Sir Lee Stack, when he was passing through Cairo on leave. The British reaction to the incident was severe. King Fuad was given 24 hours in which to order the withdrawal of all Egyptian officers and army units from the Sudan, and there followed a replacement of nearly all the Egyptian civil officials by British or Sudanese. From this time the Sudan took on more and more the appearance of an ordinary British colony. 'Indirect rule' became the order of the day, and with it there grew up a new concern for the non-Muslim population of the southern Sudan. The British came to distrust the educated Sudanese emerging from the northern schools. They were felt to be disloyal to the government and sympathetic to Egypt. Just as the Egyptians had been excluded from the government of the north, so the northern Sudanese were now excluded from the government of the south, with the result that the two halves of the country grew further apart instead of closer together. The north was accessible to the outside world, and most of the economic development took place there. The south, though protected from northern and Islamic influences, remained equally isolated from the economic and social developments which might have enabled it to stand on its own feet. The results of this policy were to be disastrous when, on Sudanese independence, a mainly northern government had to undertake the administration of the south.

Meanwhile, in Egypt, political power was alternating between the *Wafd* party and the court party of the King. The *Wafd* party was led by Zaghlul Pasha, a moderate nationalist, who had been forced by the circumstances of the 1919 rebellion to take up a hostile attitude to the British. By the 1930s disillusionment with the intrigue and corruption of the professional politicans had become general. Rich Egyptians—many of them of the old Mamluk, Turkish class—seemed to get richer, whilst the lot of the urban workers and the *fellahin* grew harder. The mood of the country in 1935 was expressed by the young Gamul Nasser, then still a pupil at secondary school who wrote in a school essay: 'The nation is in danger, and the disputes among the Parties are being fomented by Imperialism, the Palace, and the Party leaders themselves. Thus they hope to keep the country divided and busy with the race for lucrative posts, so that the Egyptians shall forget that they have a right to freedom.' In their frustration many young people turned to political groups actively hostile to parliamentary democracy. The most influential of these was the fiercely nationalistic Muslim Brotherhood. This body aimed at re-establishing a truly Muslim state, in which the great extremes of riches and poverty would disappear.

In 1936, after years of fruitless negotiations, Britain and Egypt signed a treaty, the fundamental provision of which was that British troops were to be confined to the Canal Zone. Although an attempt was made to solve some of the problems of the Sudan, no real understanding on this territory was possible. Britain and Egypt agreed to administer the Sudan in the interests of the Sudanese. Egyptian army units rejoined the Sudan garrison, and the virtual exclusion of Egyptian civilians from the Sudan was brought to an end. The Egyptians had to face the fact that, as a result of the Anglo-Egyptian estrangement, the sense of Sudanese separateness from Egypt had gone too far to be undone. This, no less than the temporary return of British military government to Egypt during the Second World War, and the emergence of a western-supported Jewish state in Israel, determined that in the long term Egyptian nationalism would continue to grow in hostility towards the West.

### The Italian spheres of influence: Libya

The remaining parts of Arabic-speaking Muslim Africa were those subject to Italian domination, of which the most turbulent throughout this period was Libya. We have already seen (Chapter 10) how in 1911–12 Italy conquered the Ottoman provinces of Tripolitania and Cyrenaica. The elimination of the Turks, however, merely gave the Italians possession of the coastal towns. They soon came up against the real rulers of the interior, the *shaikhs* of the Sanusi *zawiyas* described in Chapter 8 (p. 100). These *zawiyas* were by now established in all the tribal territories of the nomadic Bedouin of Cyrenaica and the Fezzan. The *shaikhs*, though still primarily religious leaders, had come to be regarded by the Bedouin Arabs as their natural representatives in all their dealings with the outside world. The *shaikhs* had usually co-operated with the Turkish officials, who had been their fellow Muslims. When the Christian Italians conquered Tripoli and Benghazi they moved into solid opposition. What had been mainly a religious movement now became a nationalist and political one. In 1912 the head of the Sanusi brotherhood, Sayyid Ahmad, moved his headquarters from the Kufra Oasis into southern Cyrenaica, and during the next six years concentrated all his energies on organising armed resistance to the Italians. His efforts were supported by Muslims throughout the Middle East. Gifts of money and arms flowed in from unofficial committees in Egypt, Turkey, Syria and the Hijaz. When Italy in 1915 entered the First World War on the side of the Allied Powers, Turkey, which was fighting on the side of Germany and Austria, began to give him official support. When the Allied Powers emerged victorious from the world struggle, Sayyid Ahmad retreated to Istanbul, retaining his position as head of the Sanusi brotherhood, but relinquishing his temporal power in Cyrenaica to his nephew, Sayyid Idris, who was to become, twenty-five years later, the first King of Libya.

Idris, between 1918 and 1922, entered into a series of only half-sincere agreements with the Italians, in which he undertook to recognise Italian sovereignty in exchange for a large measure of autonomy in the Bedouin areas. In 1922 the Fascist Party of Benito Mussolini seized power in Italy and denounced these agreements. The Arab leaders of Tripolitania and Cyrenaica thereupon met in conference and recognised Idris as *Amir* of all Libya, and Idris, having accepted, withdrew to Egypt in anticipation of the expected military action of the Italians. This was launched at the end of the year. From then onwards for nine years, the Libyan Bedouin fought a war which, on a smaller scale, can only be likened to the Algerian War of 1954–62. There were never more than 1,000 Bedouin under arms, but with the secret support of the entire civil population they engaged the continuous attention of an Italian army of 20,000. They forced the Fascists to adopt methods, such as aerial bombardment and the isolation of the civilian population in concentration camps, which sickened the whole of the civilised world. The main organiser of this phase of Libyan resistance was a Sanusi *shaikh*, Sidi Umar al-Mukhtar, whose capture and public execution by the Italians in 1931 brought military operations to an end. Italy had thus only eight years of undisputed rule before her North African empire was submerged in the Second World War, from which the Libyans under Idris emerged with their right to independence recognised.

*Somalia and Ethiopia*

We saw in Chapter 10 how the first round of Italian imperialist expansion in North-East Africa was brought to a halt in 1896 by the decisive victory of the Emperor Menelik at Adowa. In the peace treaty that followed this battle Italy managed to retain her foothold on the Red Sea coast in Eritrea. She also had her protectorate treaties signed in 1889 with the Majerteyn Somali sultans of Alula and Obbia, and her lease from the Sultan of Zanzibar of the Benadir ports of Brava, Merka, Mogadishu and Warsheikh. This lease was changed in 1905 into an outright purchase. Until 1905 the Italian government did little to build upon these earlier foundations. Eritrea centred around the declining port of Massawa, from which the Ethiopian trade was being increasingly diverted to the new harbour of Jibouti in French Somaliland. A railway from Jibouti to Addis Ababa was begun in 1896 and completed in 1918. In Somaliland the Alula and Obia Protectorates were left alone except for occasional visits by Italian gunboats. The Benadir ports were ineffectively administered by two Italian commercial companies, the first of which went bankrupt in 1896, the second in 1904.

In these circumstances the first outburst of Muslim Somali resentment against Christian imperialist domination fell, not upon the Italians but upon the British. The small British Protectorate on the southern shores of the Gulf of Aden was the home of a great religious leader of the nomadic Somali, Sayyid Muhammad Abdile Hassan. He was known to his British opponents as 'the mad mullah'. Born in 1864 in the region inland from Berbera, Sayyid Muhammad gained an early reputation for piety and learning. During his early travels as a wandering *shaikh* he visited Mogadishu, Nairobi and parts of the Sudan. In all these places he became aware of the threat to Islam of the expanding forces of western Christendom. When Sayyid Muhammad returned home in 1891 he began to preach resistance to the British, and was declared by them to be an outlaw. He retreated with his followers into the Haud and the Ogaden, the unadministered 'no-man's land' between Ethiopia on the one hand and British and Italian Somaliland on the other. From the Haud and the Ogaden Sayyid Muhammad lauched attacks on the three neighbouring governments. British, Italian and Ethiopian troops were continuously and expensively engaged in expeditions against him until his death in 1920. Sayyid Muhammad wrote a great number of letters to friends and enemies. His letters to the British were frequently most expressive in their defiance. In one of them he wrote:

If the country were cultivated or if it contained houses or property, it would be worth your while to fight for it. But the country is all jungle [he meant that it was uncultivated], and that is no use to you. If you want bush and stones you can get these in plenty. There are also many ant-heaps, and the sun is very hot. All you can get from me is war and nothing else.

It was from Sayyid Muhammad that the three or four million nomadic Somali, till then conscious only of their clan loyalties, derived their first sense of a wider national unity. Today he is rightly regarded in Somalia as the father of Somali nationalism. However, unlike the founder of the Sanusi movement, whom he so much resembled, Sayyid Muhammad left no successor. On his death Somali resistance to the British and Italians ceased. Normal colonial governments were developed in British and Italian Somaliland. The centre of political interest in North-East Africa now switched to the renewed plans of the Fascist government of Italy to conquer the kingdom of Ethiopia. This conquest had been long prepared, but it could not be put into operation until Italian troops were freed from the long war against the Sanusi in Libya. The excuse for the attack was found in the disputed frontier between Somalia and Ethiopia in the Ogaden. Here the Italians intrigued with the Somali clans who lived within Ethiopian territory and gradually advanced their military posts far across the undemarcated border. At last in December 1934 the expected clash occurred between an Ethiopian escort patrol accompanying a Boundary Commission and the garrison of an Italian military post at a place called Walwal. The Emperor Haile Selassie appealed to the League of Nations. Haile Selassie had been crowned in 1930, although he had been the real ruler of Ethiopia since 1916, under his old name of Ras Tafari. In the League of Nations, Britain and France supported his cause, but did not show sufficient determination to prevent the Italian aggression. In 1935, therefore, Mussolini's armies marched up the already prepared military roads from Massawa in the north and Mogadishu in the south-east. With their vastly superior weapons they completed their conquest by May 1936. The Emperor was forced to become a refugee in England. The Italian East African Empire, made up of Eritrea, Ethiopia and Somaliland, had become a reality, after being the dream of many Italians since the time of the partition of Africa. It was, however, to last only five years.

The effects of Mussolini's militaristic colonialism of the 1920s and 1930s were very wide. Though it has been argued that Italy was only doing in a more ruthless way what other European countries had done in the rest of Africa twenty or thirty years earlier, both the place and the time in fact made a vast difference. By the 1920s and 1930s the other colonial powers had gone far in reforming their colonial policies in the interests of the governed. Britain, especially, had recognised the ultimate right of colonial subjects to govern themselves. In Libya and in Somalia, Italy had put the clock back. In Ethiopia she had committed naked aggression against an internationally recognised state which had shown considerable ability in modernising itself without any outside interference. This was the first occasion on which the peace-keeping activities of the League of Nations had been tested, and had been found wanting. Adolf Hitler who had recently come to power at the head of another Fascist movement, in Germany, was not slow to read the lesson. In the year of Mussolini's victory over Ethiopia, Hitler set out on the path of aggression which was to lead directly to the Second World War. German troops invaded the Rhineland, the zone between France and Germany which had been demilitarised after the First World War. In the introduction to his history of the Second World War, Winston Churchill drew attention to the influence of Mussolini's action in Ethiopia. He wrote: 'If ever there was an opportunity of striking a decisive blow for a generous cause it was then. The fact that the nerve of the British government was not equal to the occasion, played a part in leading to a more terrible war.'

# 15

## SOUTH AFRICA, 1902–1939

South Africa was the first African country to experience the social stresses resulting from the transformation of an agricultural into an industrial economy. The pace of change between 1900 and the outbreak of the Second World War was faster, and on a larger scale, than in any other part of the continent. By 1939 the concentration of mines and factories on the Witwaterstrand was comparable to the industrial regions of Europe and North America. In the centre of the Rand was Johannesburg, the largest city in Africa except for Cairo. From Johannesburg gold flowed to the banking houses of the world, binding South Africa into the web of international finance and commerce. Yet the fruits of this material prosperity were unevenly distributed. Only gradually did even all the white people reach a high standard of living. Africans, because of their colour, were excluded from all but a meagre share. Political change in no way kept pace with economic advance. The white rulers were restricted by attitudes and policies which had taken root in the nineteenth century and earlier. They seemed incapable of any fresh approach to the racial tensions which became sharper as more and more Africans were integrated into the expanding economy.

### South Africa after the Boer War

After defeating the South African Republic (Transvaal) and the Orange Free State in the Anglo-Boer War, the British felt guilty at the way in which they had bullied the two small Boer republics. They tried to conciliate the defeated enemy by yielding, amongst other things, to their demands on the political status of the Africans. Concession to the Boers was considered to be more urgent than protection of African interests. One of the clauses of the Peace of Vereeniging (1902) gave the white people in the conquered Transvaal and the Orange Free State the right to decide whether or not to extend the parliamentary franchise to Africans. When Britain granted self-government to the two territories in 1906 and 1907, political power passed once again into Boer hands, and non-whites were permanently excluded from the vote.

The debate on African rights now shifted from Britain to the four colonies themselves. The political leaders of these colonies wanted to set up a Union. They hoped by this means to put an end to the disputes which had caused the war, and to promote the economic and political development of South Africa as a whole. At the heart of the whole idea of union was the necessity evident to every white politician of developing a single policy towards the Africans. As the future Boer leader and statesman Jan Smuts had written in 1892:

The race struggle is destined to assume a magnitude on the African continent such as the world has never seen, and the imagination shrinks from contemplating; and in that appalling struggle for existence the unity of the white camp will not be the least necessary condition—we will not say of obtaining victory, but of warding off (or, at worst, postponing) annihilation.

If Union was to be achieved, three traditional white attitudes towards Africans had somehow to be reconciled. The first was the 'Liberal' tradition of the Cape. The second was *baaskap*, the uncompromising inequality practised in the Transvaal and the Orange Free State, The third was the policy of protective segregation which British governors had tried to adopt in parts of Natal and the Cape, and also in the three Protectorates of Basutoland, Bechuanaland and Swaziland.

Cape Liberalism was the tradition inherited from the British colonial government of the Cape Colony, which accepted as citizens those Africans and other coloured people who conformed to white standards. Under this system educated Africans who owned or leased property to a certain value could register as parliamentary voters. In 1909 Africans formed 4·7 per cent of the Cape electorate. Cape leaders defended this system not only on grounds of idealism, but also on grounds of expediency. Merriman, a distinguished liberal politician, argued that the colour-blind franchise was a 'safety valve', for 'to allow no African vote at all would be building on a volcano'. Sauer, another Cape leader, in 1904 expressed more genuinely liberal beliefs when he said: 'I do not believe that where representative institutions exist a class that is not represented will ever receive political justice, because after all it is material interests that will eventually prevail, and therefore the class having no political power will suffer.' The Cape Liberals were supported by many educated Africans, who were anxious to preserve their hard-won privileges (such as exemption from the pass laws). They felt they could no longer identify themselves with the mass of tribal Africans, from whom they had grown apart. For nearly thirty years John Tengo Jabavu was the mouthpiece of these enfranchised Africans. As early as 1884 he had launched, with white financial backing, the newspaper *Imvo Zabantsundu* (African Opinion), stating that 'the time is ripe for the establishment of a journal in English and Xhosa, to give untrammelled expression to the feelings of the native population'. But *Imvo's* criticism of white rule was very mild, and Jabavu's faith in the political future of the white Liberals became towards the end of his life (he died in 1921) rather pathetic.

*Baaskap* was the simple exercise of white domination, which had been evident from the earliest days of Dutch settlement on the Cape frontier. The Boers had taken this attitude with them when they trekked northwards, in the 1830s, and had written it into the constitution of the South African Republic (Transvaal), which proclaimed, 'There shall be no equality in State or Church between white and black.' The miners from England and elsewhere who flocked to South Africa after the discovery of diamonds and gold quickly adopted the *baaskap* attitude. They protected their high wages by an industrial 'colour bar' which prevented Africans from performing skilled work. *Baaskap* led to the intermingling of the races of South Africa, not to their separation. The Boers wanted as much African land as they could get. Like the miners, they thought of the Africans only as cheap labour which had no need of land of its own.

The physical separation of whites and Africans had been attempted in the Cape, first by the Dutch, and later by the British colonial government. It had broken down because of the impossibility of controlling the frontier. By the end of the nineteenth century the frontier problem had been replaced by that of the various pockets of land or 'reserves' into which Africans had retreated before the white advance. Separation found a new wave of support among missionaries and administrators. This led to the demarcation of the Transkeian Territories by the Cape government. In addition the British Protectorates of Basutoland, Bechuanaland and Swaziland were established. A commission set up after the Boer War by the British High Commissioner, Lord Milner, reported in 1905 in favour of the widespread application of separation throughout South Africa. The Cape politician Merriman remarked that such a policy was at least a century too late to be practicable. The advocates of *baaskap* on the other hand, who opposed separation in 1905, were to adopt it some thirty years later. By then there was proportionately less land available on which Africans could lead a separate existence, because the African population had greatly increased.

### 1910: Union

In the negotiations which led up to Union the white people of the two northern colonies and Natal proved themselves more determined to prevent the spread of Liberalism than the Cape delegates

31a  Western South Africa from 1900: minerals; communications; industrial area

BECHUANALAND

*Limpopo*

Messina
Co

Pietersburg

Gaberones

I

T

MOZAMBIQUE

CH

Mafeking

TRANSVAAL

First railway
on Rand 1890

1894

Pretoria

C

1894

D

Johannesburg

G U

Witbank

G

A

Mbabane

Lourenco
Marques (H)

II

SWAZILAND

Vereeniging
(Peace Treaty 1902)

C

1895

1906

Vaal

Welkom

G U

Kroonstad

ORANGE

Newcastle

C

FREE

C
I

Kimberley

D

Bloemfontein

STATE

1906

1886

Tugela

NATAL

ZULULAND

Orange

1884

Maseru

BASUTOLAND

Pietermaritz-
burg

First railway in
Durban 1860

De Aar

1890

1895

Durban (H)

1892

C

Umtata

1898

1883

1883

CAPE

PROVINCE

TRANSKEI

CISKEI

1878

1879

Grahamstown

East London (H)

Port Elizabeth (H)

Anglo-Boer War 1899–1902, fought over
Transvaal, Orange Free State, northern Natal
and parts of Cape Colony.
  After the war the defeated Boer Republics,
the South African Republic and the Orange
Free State, became British Crown Colonies of
the Transvaal and the Orange River Colony.
  At Union, 1910, the four British colonies
became provinces of the Union:  the Cape
Province, Natal, the Transvaal — the Orange
Free State reverted to its republican name.
  The mandated territory of South West
Africa is administered as if it were a fifth province of the Union.
  In 1960 South Africa became a Republic,
and broke away from the Commonwealth in
1961. The word 'Union' was dropped from the
title of the state.

31*b*   Eastern South Africa from 1900: minerals; communications; industrial areas

Walvis Bay

Windhoek

Cattle

BECHUANALAND

Kalahari    Desert

S O U T H

W E S T

A F R I C A

Luderitz Bay

Sheep

Keetmansdorp

Bondelswartz
1922

Orange

Okiep

Sheep
De Aar

C A P E

P R O V I N C E

Karroo

Sheep    Sheep

|||||||| Approx. areas of land
held by Africans in South Africa.
Africans, over ⅔ of total population
of South Africa, possess 13% of land

:::::::::  African land in British
:::::::::  Protectorates

Cape Town

Wheat
Wine Fruit

Worcester

Wheat

Simonstown

Fruit

32*a*  Western South Africa from 1900: agricultural products;
areas of African settlement

32b  Eastern South Africa from 1900: agricultural products;
areas of African settlement

were to promote it. At the National Convention of 1908–9 a compromise was reached, by which the first Union Parliament was to be elected on the existing colonial franchises. This meant that qualified Africans in the Cape would retain the vote, whereas Africans in Natal, the Transvaal and the Orange Free State would have no political rights. It was further agreed that not even in the Cape should any African be able to stand as a parliamentary candidate. The Cape delegates did succeed in entrenching the franchise provisions in the constitution, so that they could only be amended by a two-thirds majority of both Houses of the Union Parliament sitting together, This, however, was not a very secure safeguard, and the compromise as a whole was certainly felt as a bitter blow by the educated Africans. For once even Jabavu joined forces with his more militant compatriots in trying to resist the form of Union decided upon by the National Convention. One of the many meetings called by Africans at this time 'noted with regret that the contemplated Union is to be a Union of two races, namely the British and the Afrikaners—the African is to be excluded.' Only one white Liberal, W. P. Schreiner, supported these African protests. Alone in his community, he felt that human rights were more important than Union:

To embody in the South African constitution a vertical line or barrier separating its people upon the ground of colour into a privileged class or caste and an unprivileged inferior proletariat is as imprudent as it would be to build a grand building upon unsound and sinking foundations. In our South African nation there must be room for many free peoples, but no room for any that are not free, and free to rise.

A delegation which included both Schreiner and Jabavu went to London, but failed to persuade the British government to change the proposed Union constitution in any way. The Union of South Africa was established on 31st May 1910. The British government maintained that it could not interfere with the decisions of the National Convention. It declared, however, that the three Protectorates of Basutoland, Bechuanaland and Swaziland would not be transferred to the new South African state until it had become clear how the racial provisions of the constitution would work in practice.

Though Jabavu soon reverted to his alliance with the white politicians of the Cape, other more politically conscious Africans launched in 1912 the (South) African National Congress, as a Union-wide body to protect African interests. Soloman Plaatje a highly cultured Tswana journalist and writer, became the Secretary-General of the Congress. The first legislation denounced by the Congress was the Natives Land Act of 1913, which prevented Africans from acquiring land outside their own areas. Of this Act Plaatje wrote: 'Awakening on Friday morning, June 20th 1913, the South African Native found himself a pariah [outcast] in the land of his birth,' Javabu wrote in favour of the Act, because it had been introduced by Sauer, one of the Cape Liberals in the government. This proved the end of the old man's influence among his fellow Africans. His failure was but one sad facet of the failure of the Liberal cause in general. Liberalism became hopelessly compromised by the discriminatory legislation of the Union government. The attitudes that prevailed in South Africa were summed up by an Afrikaner historian fifty years later, when he said:

Particularly significant was the fact that the act and 'compromise' of Union enabled the ex-Republics of the Transvaal and the Free State to indoctrinate the rest of the Union with their traditions and ideals. This was eminently true of the two great principles which counted as cornerstones of the national existence of the Afrikaner people: republicanism, and the practice and theory of the inequality between white men and black men.

(D. W. Kruger, *The Age of the Generals.*)

## Smuts and Hertzog

Smuts, who served under General Botha until 1919 and then became Prime Minister of the Union, was a man of great learning, with profound insights in the fields of religion, philosophy and science. In 1917 he became a member of the British War Cabinet in the war against Germany, and from then until his death in 1950 he was looked upon as a statesman of world renown. He was a close friend of Sir Winston Churchill during the Second World War, and was one of the founders of the United Nations Organisation. Yet on the racial problem, which surely would have benefited from the application of such a penetrating mind, he lacked any constructive ideas. In 1906 he had written to Merriman:

I sympathise profoundly with the native races of South Africa, whose land it was long before we came here to force a policy of dispossession on them. And it ought to be the policy of all parties to do justice to the natives and to take all wise and prudent measures for their civilisation and improvement. But I don't believe in politics for them...When I consider the political future of the natives in South Africa, I must say I look into shadows and darkness; and then I feel inclined to shift the intolerable burden of solving the problem to the ampler shoulders and stronger brains of the future. Sufficient unto the day is the evil thereof.

This timidity pervaded the first ten years of the Union's history. Meanwhile the racial problems were becoming more difficult, and the younger generation of white people seemed no more capable of solving them. The African policy of Botha and Smuts was muddled and indecisive. It consisted of a further dose of *baaskap*, of colour bar and pass laws, coupled with a half-hearted attempt to put into practice some of the recommendations of Milner's commission on the subject of separation.

In 1922 white mine-workers struck, and seized control of the Rand, because the mine-owners threatened to employ Africans as skilled workers at lower wages than the whites enjoyed. Smuts had to use soldiers to put down this 'rebellion'. Consequently he was defeated in the 1924 election by a combination of the Labour Party, which represented the views of the rebellious white miners, and the Afrikaner National Party. This party had been formed by General Hertzog in 1913. Although he was one of the main architects of *Apartheid*, Hertzog was one of the most honest of the white politicians. He rightly said that it was the fear of being overwhelmed and swept aside by the vastly superior number of Africans that was at the root of the white attitude: 'The European is severe and hard on the Native because he is afraid of him. It is the old instinct of self-preservation. And the immediate outcome of this is that so little has been done in the direction of helping the Native to advance.' His policy was to remove this fear by physically separating the races, so as to create two South Africas, one White, the other African. He believed that when Africans were deprived of political and other rights in the Union as a whole, they should be given compensation in the form of more land, and of some measure of local self-government.

Hertzog never abandoned his Afrikaner principles. He stood for the primacy of the Afrikaans language in South Africa and for the abandonment of any deference to British policy in international affairs. Nevertheless he welcomed a reconciliation of the Dutch and British elements in the white population. When the world economic crisis of 1929–33 produced a demand among the white electorate for a 'National' government, composed of the leaders of the two main parties, Hertzog was prepared to enter a coalition with Smuts. In 1934 most of Hertzog's Afrikaner National Party

joined with most of Smuts's South African Party to form the
United Party, which was to remain in power till 1948. Smuts's
side of the compromise was to support the Natives Representation Act, introduced in 1936, which brought to an end the
registration of qualified Africans as voters on the common roll
with whites in the Cape Province. Hertzog's side of the compromise was to modify his anti-British line, both inside South Africa
and in relation to the Commonwealth. Among Smuts's followers
there was one, the brilliantly clever and deeply religious Jan
Hofmeyr, who spoke against the 1936 Act. Hofmeyr said:

By this Bill we are sowing the seeds of a far greater potential conflict than
is being done by anything in existence today. We have many educated and
semi-educated Natives in South Africa. Many of them have attained to,
and many more of them are advancing towards, European standards.
They have been trained on European lines. They have been taught to think
and act as Europeans. We may not like it, but those are the plain facts.
Now what is the political future for those people? This Bill says to these
Natives 'There is no room for you. You must be driven back on your own
people.' But we drive them back in hostility and disgruntlement, and do not
let us forget this, that all this Bill is doing for these educated Natives is to
make them the leaders of their own people, in disaffection and revolt.

Although Hofmeyr was a cabinet minister in the governments of
Hertzog and Smuts, his words were received in stony silence.
Much more significant than Hofmeyr in South African electoral
terms were the nineteen 'Purified Nationalists', led by D. F.
Malan, who refused to follow Hertzog into the coalition. These
followers of Malan advocated still sterner measures to ensure the
survival of the white man in South Africa. In 1934 they were not
very important politically. But in racially divided communities,
where a minority race holds power, 'the enemy is always on the
Right', that is, the racial extremists. The future in South Africa
lay with those nineteen members, whose successors, in 1948, were
to sweep the United Party from power and introduce yet another
round of racialistic legislation.

### The African predicament

By 1939 the economic and political grievances of the African
population in South Africa were already so great that a revolution
would not have been surprising. The material prosperity of the
country depended on the gold mines; the gold mines depended on
African labour. Yet African workers in the mines, as also in the

growing number of industrial jobs, received about one-eighth of the wages paid to white men. They were supposed to have their homes in the 'reserves', and to come and work in the white towns as migrant labourers without their families. The social and moral harm caused by this frequent disruption of family life was generally ignored by the white employers. Yet the land left to the Africans was totally inadequate to support them. In 1913 Africans, who formed nearly three-quarters of the population, possessed only 7 per cent of the land of South Africa, and this amount was only with great difficulty increased to 11 per cent by the late 1960s, through government purchase under Hertzog's legislation of 1936. Many Africans had long before this abandoned the impoverished reserves, to live permanently in slums on the outskirts of the white towns. By 1936 more than a million (22 per cent) of Africans had become urban dwellers. Another two million were working on white farms, completely subject to their masters. They received wages that were so low that it was only just possible for them to pay their taxes. The prices of most things that Africans bought went up 50 per cent between the two world wars, yet African wages were nearly stationary. Africans had no means of increasing their wages or improving their conditions of work. The colour-bar laws prevented them from performing skilled work. Their wages were fixed by law. It was a criminal offence for them to combine in strike action. Their every movement was controlled by Pass Laws, which required that all Africans outside the reserves must carry a variety of permits. As early as 1919 a Johannesburg newspaper, *The Star*, had commented that 'the Native is crowded off the land, denied a permanent foothold in urban areas, exploited at every point, badgered from pillar to post, and under disabilities of all kinds, whether he stays at home or seeks work away from it.'

Nevertheless African reactions to these conditions of discrimination and restriction were still very far from revolutionary. During the inter-war years the African National Congress had little influence or authority even among Africans. It continued to hold its conventions year by year on the outskirts of Bloemfontein, but in 1938 it still had less than 4,000 members. Much more significant through most of this period was the Industrial and Commerical Union, founded in 1919 by Clements Kadalie, an ambitious clerk from Nyasaland. At one time the I.C.U. could boast a membership of 200,000. But the I.C.U. became unwieldy. Its central organisation was weak, and it was unable to operate effectively among the all-important mine-workers, The employers' control over the African mine-workers was extremely strict. Like its rival, the African National Congress, the I.C.U. was rent by dissensions between Communists and more moderate leaders. It failed to influence the government in labour matters, just as the A.N.C. failed to divert Hertzog from his goal of territorial separation.

Even in 1940 Africans were still remarkably restrained and tolerant towards the white society in which, economically, they were becoming ever more integrated. This was due partly to the fact that South Africa was by far the richest country in Africa, and African wages, low though they were compared with those received by the whites, were still higher than in most of the continent. More money was available in South Africa to spend on African education, which, at the secondary level at least, was of a high standard. Africans therefore demanded no more than to receive a greater share in the wealth of the country, and to be considered as citizens in their own land. Their nationalism was subdued—markedly so in comparison with the strident Afrikaner nationalism which was growing up at the same time. Many young Africans were hopeful about the future. There was still room for political adjustment between the races, and if the white people had earnestly desired to create a multi-racial nation, they could still have done so. But, as we have seen, the opinion of white South Africans was in fact moving rapidly in the opposite direction. To secure election by a white constituency, an ambitious politician had to go one step further than his rivals on the racial issue, and always in the same extreme direction. Therefore, though all seemed peaceful enough on the surface, the sands of goodwill were in fact fast running out.

### South-West Africa

We have noted, in Chapter 13, that the German colony of South-West Africa became a League of Nations mandated territory, administered by South Africa. The country was in fact governed as if it were part of the Union and local resistance was put down by force. In 1922 the Bondelswarts, a Nama group who had lost much of their land to the Germans, opposed the levying of a dog tax. Dogs were of great importance to them for herding and hunting. A police force was sent against them and their village was bombed. The police commented: 'The effects of the lesson taught

in this short campaign will have an indelible impression not only
on the minds of those who resorted to the use of arms in defiance
of lawful authority, but on other native tribes in this territory
as well.'

Land-hungry white South African farmers eagerly bought the
cheap farms in the country, the government providing funds
to enable them to purchase stock and equipment. By 1935 there
were 32,000 settlers in the territory (some of them Germans who
had stayed on), and nearly one-third of the land was in their
possession. Much of the rest was desert. The Africans were forced
to live in reserves, and to labour for the white man to get enough
money to pay their taxes. They had merely exchanged one hard
master—the Germans—for another.

# 16

## THE SECOND WORLD WAR

### *Africa in 1939*

The Second World War is the great turning-point in the history
of modern Africa. Before it broke out, the pace of change in
Africa, since the establishment of colonial rule at the end of the
nineteenth and the beginning of the twentieth century, had been
steady and unhurried. After the war this gradual pace increased
in momentum until it became uncontrollable.

In 1939 the whole of Africa was under European rule. The
Italians were in occupation of Ethiopia. British troops remained
in Egypt, in the Suez Canal Zone. Even Liberia was in practice
dominated by the American Firestone Rubber Company. The
Union of South Africa was an independent Dominion within the
British Commonwealth, but the African population there had less
freedom than the inhabitants of the colonial territories. Everywhere colonial rule appeared to be firmly rooted. Every colonial
territory had by this time police and military forces adequate for all
ordinary situations. With modern, fast communications, reinforcements could have been brought quickly from overseas to deal with
any special emergency. But, for twenty years or more in most colonies, there had been no such emergencies. Colonial governments
had come to be regarded as too strong to be successfully challenged.

UNITED STATES OF AMERICA

HAWAIIAN ISLANDS (USA)
Pearl Harbour (Japanese attacks Dec. 1941)

GREAT BRITAIN

UNION OF SOVIET SOCIALIST REPUBLICS

GERMANY
1941
FRANCE
Vichy Govt.
LIBYA
North African campaigns 1940-43
FWA Vichy

FRENCH EQUATORIAL AFRICA First part of French Empire to join de Gaulle's Free French government

Italian East Africa (Italians driven out 1941)

INDIA
CEYLON
BURMA
CHINA
INDO-CHINA
MALAYA
PHILIPPINES
Vichy officials
DUTCH EAST INDIES

JAPAN
Hiroshima (Atomic bombs Aug 1945)
Nagasaki

AUSTRALIA

NEW ZEALAND

Maximum extent of Nazi German Empire in Europe

Italian Empire (allied to Germany)

French Vichy government (allied to Germany)
—during course of the war French colonies went over to De Gaulle's Free French government

Maximum extent of Japanese conquests

Japanese attacks

British and American attacks against Italian and German armies in Africa

33    The Second World War

NEW ZEALAND (C)

After the war Korea divided between the Communist North and the pro-American South; this division confirmed by Korean War 1950

After French-Indo Chinese conflict Indo-China divided in 1954 between Communist North Vietnam and pro-Western South Vietnam and neutral Laos and Cambodia

KOREA divided N. Korea S. Korea

JAPAN

TAIWAN (Chinese Nationalist Govt. — pro American)

N VIETNAM
S VIETNAM
PHILIPPINE REPUBLIC

CHINA

UNION OF SOVIET SOCIALIST REPUBLICS

INDONESIA

AUSTRALIA (C)

BURMA
INDIA (C)
CEYLON (C)
MALAYSIA (C)

Egypt, Libya, Ethiopia to Bandung,

Bandung (Afro-Asian Conference 1955)

SYRIA
IRAQ
JORDAN
PAKISTAN (C)

UNION OF S. AFRICA (C — until 1961)

Communist countries in East Europe: Poland, Romania, Bulgaria, Hungary, Czechoslovakia, Albania, East Germany, Yugoslavia

After the war Germany divided into East and West

GREAT BRITAIN (C)

Geneva

x Atlantic Charter 1941

New York (UNO headquarters)

(Headquarters of League of Nations; seat of many UNO agencies)

(Communist Govt 1959)

CUBA

CANADA (C)

UNITED STATES OF AMERICA

San Francisco (UNO established 1945)

|||||| Asian countries independent from European control, 1945–54

▨ States with Communist governments, 1965

(C) Commonwealth countries
Those in Africa and West Indies not shown.
Not all Commonwealth countries side with Britain and America against Communist countries

Nevertheless, the concept of trusteeship in colonial policy had begun to produce some practical results during the twenty years since the end of the First World War. Trusteeship was linked with the policy of indirect rule in the British African territories. It had everywhere given African communities a considerable say in the management of their own affairs at the local level and through their traditional authorities. In the West African colonies a start had even been made in the Africanisation of the central institutions of the colonial government. Africans were recruited as administrative officers and some African members were included in the legislative councils and assemblies which advised the governors. Just after the war a former British colonial officer turned writer expressed the opinion that 'We shall not disappear tomorrow, nor the day after tomorrow [he meant for a long time to come], but the Governor of each British colony is in fact presiding over the liquidation of that colony—as a colony. It is to become a self-governing dominion' (W. R. Crocker. *On Governing Colonies*, 1947). The French policies of cultural assimilation and economic association were designed to make France and her colonies permanently interdependent. No Frenchmen seriously thought that any colony would ever achieve a political status independent of France. A few Africans, however, were rising to positions of power in France itself, and were preparing to carry French political party organisation back into the French African territories.

The flaw in all colonial policies was the denial of scope for the political abilities and ambitions of the educated *élite*. In the British territories indirect rule gave status and often considerable power to hereditary chiefs and other members of the traditional, tribal aristocracies. On the other hand it left the new educated professional class without either political influence or social recognition. Under the French system, the educated African could rise higher in the government service and enjoy more social respect. He could do this, however, only at the price of complete identification with France and French culture. He had to cut most of his ties with his fellow Africans. The first generation of educated Africans—men like Casely Heyford of the Gold Coast or Blaise Diagne of Senegal, Herbert Macaulay of Lagos or Tengo Jabavu of the Cape Colony—while pressing for a greater participation in central government by the educated *élite*, accepted the existing gulf between educated and uneducated, between the traditional rural society and the modern, urban society. None of them tried to build up a mass following. Probably they would have been unable to do so had they tried. Certainly the attempt would have brought them into serious trouble with the colonial governments. Among the second generation of educated Africans there were a few, like Azikiwe, who understood that major reforms would not come until the educated had made political contact with the uneducated. Others younger still, like Nkrumah and Senghor, were in 1939 just setting out on their overseas studies, and were to return with the same lesson even more firmly in mind. But, had it not been for the Second World War and for the profound change in the balance of world power that followed it, it is very doubtful whether even Nkrumah's generation would have lived to see African independence, let alone whether they themselves would have brought it about. The educational policies of both France and Britain had made it certain that independence would come to Africa within the twentieth century. The fact that it came in the 1950s and 1960s was due very largely to the five-year struggle around the globe. The colonising nations emerged from this conflict only in the second rank of world powers. America and Russia, the two powers of first rank, had each of them a reason for speeding up the process of decolonisation. Another, though less important, reason why decolonisation came when it did was the direct involvement of large numbers of Africans in the war itself. Therefore, just as we had to look outside Africa in order to understand the beginning of the colonial period, so now we have to look outside Africa in order to understand its end.

## The War, 1939–45

The war that broke out in 1939 was in many ways a continuation of the great struggle of 1914–18. Germany was determined to reverse its military defeat in that war, and to unite all German-speaking people, many of whom lived beyond the frontiers of Germany. Another German grievance was the loss of her African colonies after the First World War. Germany demanded the return of these colonies, so as to give her 'her rightful place in the tropical sun'. In 1933 Adolf Hitler, leader of the National Socialist (Nazi) Party, came to power in Germany. He turned the parliamentary democracy into a dictatorship. Nazi racial attitudes were even more extreme than those of Fascist Italy. German nationalism was stirred up, and was deliberately directed against racial minorities, especially Jews. Britain and France failed either to put a stop to German aggression in its early days or to offer a constructive solution to the problems of Germany's relations with the small states of central Europe. German aggression against these countries led to a general European war, in the first year of which German armies overran most of the continent. France surrendered in June 1940, and was humiliatingly partitioned. The northern and western part was placed under German military rule. The southern part was ruled by the puppet Vichy government, which was subservient to German interests.

In Europe, only Britain and a few small, neutral countries remained outside the new German empire. Mussolini was the ally and tool of Hitler. One British success during the defeats and humiliations of the early years of the war was the expulsion in 1941 of Italy from Eritrea, Somalia and Ethiopia. Many African soldiers took part in the fighting in the Horn of Africa. The Emperor Haile Selassie returned to his kingdom at the beginning of the campaign, and led his own guerrilla band into Addis Ababa. In spite of British attempts to set up a military administration for the period of the war, he was able to reassert his authority. Thus Ethiopia regained its independence after five years of Italian rule. In North Africa the German *Afrika Korps* joined the Italian army in an attack on Egypt and the Suez Canal, which was so vital to British supply lines. Meanwhile the vast military struggle was extending itself still further. In 1941 Hitler invaded Russia, despite an alliance which had been signed between the Soviet state and Nazi Germany as recently as 1939. German armies drove deep into Russia, but were halted short of Moscow by the Red Army and by the terrible Russian winter. Even more fateful was Japan's entry into the war on the side of the Nazis.

The history of modern Japan had until that time provided an object lesson for non-European peoples all over the world. After two centuries of deliberate isolation from European influence, the rulers of Japan in the 1860s realised that the only way to avoid European domination was to modernise their country's economy and society along Western lines—to beat the West at its own game. Consequently Japan became the industrial power of the Far East, and entered upon a stage of imperial expansion similar to that of the West European powers. After defeating Russia in 1905, Japan acquired Korea and Manchuria, and in the 1930s conquered large parts of China. Her attack on the American Pacific

Fleet at Pearl Harbour in the Hawaian Islands in December 1941, however, brought the United States into the war as the ally of Britain. This proved to be the turning-point of the war.

During the early part of 1942 the Japanese overwhelmed the European empires in South-East Asia. Within months of Pearl Harbour the Japanese had driven the British out of their possessions in Malaya and Burma, Sarawak, Borneo and Hong Kong, the Dutch out of Indonesia, and the Americans out of the Philippines. Japan also occupied Indo-China by agreement with the government of Vichy France, whose officials continued to administer the territory under Japanese supervision. India, Ceylon and even Madagascar were threatened with invasion. German and Japanese submarines made the seas of the world unsafe for Allied shipping, At last, however, in 1942, the tide of war started to turn, as Russia and America mobilised their huge resources. The Red Army pushed the Germans out of Russia. American and British forces landed in the Maghrib. They overthrew the Vichy governments of Morocco and Algeria and linked up in Tunisia with the British army that had chased the Germans and Italians out of Cyrenaica and Tripolitania. Then the allies landed in Italy, and fought their way desperately northwards. Mussolini was deposed, and murdered after the Italian government made peace. In June 1944 Hitler's European empire was invaded by a great Anglo-American task-force, which landed in northern France. After a year of bitter fighting and widespread destruction, the Allied and Russian forces met in central Germany. Hitler shot himself, and Germany surrendered in May 1945. In the Far East, America defeated the Japanese in a series of mighty sea-battles, and reoccupied the Philippines. Britain slowly pushed the Japanese out of Burma, using for the purpose many African troops. The war was brought to an abrupt end in August 1945, when the first atomic bombs were dropped on the Japanese cities of Hiroshima and Nagasaki.

### The world after the war

The world of 1939 had been changed almost beyond recognition. Political, economic and military leadership had passed from the West European countries to the two super-states, America and Russia. Both had been dragged by the war out of their previous isolation from international affairs. Europe became divided into their allies or satellites. Eastern Europe passed under Communist control, while Western Europe was defended by American armies and received massive American aid in reviving its shattered economies. The 'hot' war was now transformed into the 'cold' war, because of the enmity between the Capitalist and Communist systems. The 'Iron Curtain' split Europe down the middle. Outside Europe, South America remained under the economic, and, more unwillingly, under the political influence of the United States. Africa was still the colonial possession of the old European states. In Asia, with the defeat of Japan, there developed a political vacuum. The way in which this vacuum was filled was to be of enormous significance for the rest of the world, including Africa.

## The war and Africa

Soldiers from all over Africa were recruited by Britain and France. They went into action in Ethiopia, North Africa and Italy, and against the Japanese in Burma. The colour bar operated in the South African army, as it did in that country's industries. In spite of not being allowed to bear arms, many Africans from the Union were eager to join up as drivers or labourers. As one leader of the African National Congress remarked, 'The country is in danger. Even if a man has quarrelled with his wife, when he sees an enemy approaching his home, he gets up to settle with that enemy.'

Most of the thousands of Africans who became soldiers had never before been out of their native lands. On active service, despite the dangers and hardships, they were well fed and clothed, and comparatively well paid. Many of them learned to read newspapers, to listen to wireless bulletins and to take an interest in world affairs. They learned to see their own countries in perspective, from the outside. On their return home, many of them became dissatisfied with conditions which were not so attractive as army life in countries more developed than their own. With the fighting in North Africa, and with the loss of the rich Far East colonies, Africa had become of vital strategic and economic importance to the Allies. The production of raw materials, such as vegetable oils and minerals, had gone ahead by leaps and bounds. New aerodromes, roads and harbours had been constructed. Labour was in great demand, and hundreds of thousands of people flocked to the towns. But because European and American industries were so closely geared to the war effort, and after the war to their own reconstruction, Africa's growing demand for consumer goods could not be met. The shortage of goods, and their high prices, resulted in disturbances and attacks on foreign shops. In the Gold Coast, for example, economic and political frustrations led to serious riots in 1948. The Watson Commission, which was sent out to investigate the causes of these riots, had this to say about the grievances of the ex-servicemen in particular:

The large number of African soldiers returning from service with the Forces, where they had lived under different and better conditions, made for a general, communicable state of unrest. Such Africans, by reason of their contacts with other peoples, including Europeans, had developed a political and national consciousness. The fact that they were disappointed at conditions on their return, either from specious promises made before demobilisation or a general expectancy of a golden age for heroes, made them the natural focal point for any general movement against authority.

Besides political unrest, the wartime and post-war boom in raw material prices had a most important effect on the economies of African countries. The colonial powers were unable to pay for these raw materials immediately in manufactured goods. Many African colonies became for a time the creditors of their colonial masters. These credits passed mostly into the hands of the colonial governments rather than into the hands of the individual producers. This happened because the colonial governments, in order to prevent rising prices and thus to control inflation, bought produce from the growers at one price, and sold it on the world market at a higher price. The difference between these two prices was retained in government funds. For good or ill, this marked a big step in the direction of socialism. On the one hand it enabled the colonial governments to embark upon big development schemes for the benefit of the community as a whole. On the other hand, by limiting so drastically the prices paid to the growers it probably held back the growth of production, as it certainly did the growth of private savings and investment. Above all, it set a pattern of state control which most independent African governments were to follow.

### The war and European prestige

Most significant for the subsequent spread of nationalism in Africa was what can be termed the psychological effects of the war. The mental attitudes of Europeans and Africans towards each other were greatly changed by the war. Previously Europeans had been able to dominate Africans, not only because of their more advanced military and economic techniques, but also because they *believed* that they were superior and invincible. And most Africans believed this too. The Second World War, even more than the first, completely shattered this myth. Several former colonial powers had been defeated and publicly humiliated. The South-East Asian empires of Britain, France and Holland had collapsed before the Japanese onslaught like straw huts in a storm. The Italian empire in Africa had ceased to exist. The political dissensions which had so weakened France at the beginning of the war had been transferred to the French African colonies. Most of the French officials had sided at first with the racialist Vichy government. Nevertheless, the Governor of Chad, Felix Eboué, by birth a Negro from French Guiana in South America, had supported the Free French resistance to Germany which was led by General de Gaulle. By 1943 the whole of Equatorial Africa had joined de Gaulle, and Eboué had become Governor-General at Brazzaville. Only after much intrigue and squabbling did French West Africa and Madagascar follow suit. In the Maghrib countries the civil war between Free France and Vichy had been even more intense. This dissension among Frenchmen lowered their prestige in the eyes of their African subjects. The Maghribis in particular looked upon the American invaders, with their anti-colonial traditions, as liberators. After Sultan Sidi Muhammad of Morocco had met President Roosevelt at Casablanca in 1943 he began to give open support to the nationalist cause.

In British Africa, the contact with British troops in training or in transit in the various African colonies was an important element in the undermining of colonial prestige. It was quickly noticed that the behaviour of these soldiers towards Africans was not the same as that of the colonial officials and traders. They went out with African girls, in the same way as African troops abroad made friends with local women. As a result the white man —and white woman—ceased to appear as a lofty, superior being, and was seen to be a similar kind of person to the African himself. The Rhodesian African leader, Ndabanangi Sithole, has described in his book *African Nationalism* how the first Europeans contacted by Africans had appeared to them like spirits or like gods:

The African was simply overawed and perplexed. The white man's 'houses that move on the water', his 'bird that is not like other birds', his 'monster that spits fire and smoke' (these are all Sindabele expressions) amazed him. The dynamite that exploded the huge rocks in the mines confirmed the belief that the white man was a god possessing all power and knowledge.

Disillusionment soon set in, but the prestige of the white man was not finally shattered till the Second World War. Sithole went on:

The girls of England, France and Italy who went out with African soldiers, did not help the preservation of the white myth. The African soldiers found themselves at the front line of war with one purpose in view; to kill every white enemy soldier they could get hold of. African soldiers saw white soldiers wounded, dying and dead. The bullet had the same effect on black and white alike. After spending four years hunting white enemy soldiers, the African never again regarded them as gods.

### The independence of Asia, the United Nations and Bandung

After the war was over, by far the most important world event for the future of Africa was the momentous step taken by Britain in 1948 of liquidating her huge Indian empire. The subcontinent was partitioned between India and Pakistan, which became independent states within the Commonwealth. Ceylon did the same. Burma, on becoming independent, did not even join the Commonwealth. These countries between them were inhabited by well over 500 million people, about one-seventh of mankind. Much of the area had been ruled by Britain since the eighteenth century, and many ancient civilisations had flourished there before the British came. To the indigenous traditions of learning there had been added a powerful stream of Western education, beside which the primary and secondary schools of colonial Africa represented the merest trickle. In India and Pakistan, Burma and Ceylon, university graduates existed in tens of thousands. They had long filled the learned professions and occupied all but the very highest positions in the state. Political parties of a modern nationalist kind had been growing up through half a century. The active supporters of these parties amounted to hundreds of thousands or even millions of people. So long as this vast region remained obedient to European rule, it must have seemed hard for any African nationalist to believe that the authority of British or French colonial governments in Africa could be successfully challenged. With the sudden liberation of South Asia the obstacle to African independence at once assumed a completely new look. Not only had the precedents been set, but four powerful outside allies had been added to the cause.

The liberation of the British Indian empire did not carry such revolutionary implications to the colonial powers as it did to Africans. The colonial powers considered that South Asia was ready for independence, but that South-East Asia and Africa were not. In 1941, before America was drawn into the war, Roosevelt and Churchill had met on a battleship off the Canadian coast, and had signed the Atlantic Charter as a statement of their hopes for the future of mankind. They had then declared that they would 'respect the right of all peoples to choose the form of government under which they will live', and that they wished to see 'sovereign rights and self-government restored to those who had been deprived of them'. In Africa, as in Asia, many of the people who were politically conscious imagined that this statement applied to them. Churchill, however, later qualified it, saying 'At the Atlantic meeting we had in mind, primarily, the restoration of sovereignty to the nations of Europe now under Nazi yoke. So that is quite a separate problem from the progressive evolution of self-governing institutions in the regions and peoples which owe allegiance to the British Crown.' In 1944 Arthur Creech Jones, later to be Colonial Secretary in the post-war Labour Government, stated: 'Britain today is in the Colonies and she cannot withdraw; nor do I think it desirable that she should. We are pledged to the pursuit of a policy of constructive trusteeship, a policy which is to lead, we hope, to partnership inside the British Commonwealth.'

France was even more forthright in her intention to remain a colonial power, not only in Africa but in South-East Asia as well. In 1944 de Gaulle replaced the old empire by the new French Union, in which the former colonial 'subjects' now became 'citizens'. In the same year a conference of Free French officials was held at Brazzaville. These officials whole-heartedly agreed with the Colonial Minister, Réné Pléven, when, in a speech to the conference, he said:

We read at one time or another that this war must be ended with what is called a liberation of colonial peoples. In the greater France which includes the colonies there are no peoples to liberate. There are only populations which feel themselves to be French and which wish to take a greater part in the life and democratic institutions of the French community.

In South-East Asia, however, de Gaulle's Free French government took over Indo-China from the discredited Vichy administration, only to become engaged in a long and bitter war against Ho Chi Minh and his Communist guerrillas. This ended in military defeat for the French. In 1954 Indo-China became three independent states, one of which, Vietnam, was further partitioned between the Communist dominated North, and the pro-Western South. In the former Dutch East Indies, Indonesian nationalist groups declared their territory to be independent as early as 1945, and fought against the Dutch when they attempted to move back into their East Indian Empire. After several years of conflict, the Indonesians finally achieved full independence as the result of a series of conferences held between 1949 and 1951. Meanwhile, the British had returned to Hong Kong, and to Malaysia. In Malaya they, too, had had to fight a long war with Communist guerrillas. In this case the colonial power was successful.

During this post-war period the influence of America became decisive for the developing Afro-Asian liberation movement. The main instrument through which American influence operated was the United Nations Organisation, which was founded in 1949 as the successor to the League of Nations. The Charter of the U.N.O. included a comprehensive statement of the rights of all peoples to freedom and justice. This was adopted largely because of American pressure, and against the wishes of the colonial powers. It was likewise agreed that the former Mandated territories should now come under the supervision of the Trusteeship Council of the United Nations, although South Africa refused point blank to make this transfer in respect of the Mandated territory of South-West Africa. One of the conquered Italian colonies—Somaliland—was also placed under the Trusteeship Council, which entrusted it to Italy to administer for a limited period only. Eritrea was joined to Ethiopia. When the smaller countries, such as those of Latin America, took their seats in the United Nations, they fell in enthusiastically behind the attitude of the United States. There is little doubt that the United States encouraged the Indonesian demand for independence, and persuaded the Dutch to give way to it.

The independence of the new Asian states radically altered the composition of the United Nations. There was now a large group of lesser powers at the United Nations which demanded the

speedy end of colonialism everywhere. The undoubted leader of
this group was India. The leaders of India were then developing
the idea of 'positive neutralism' as between the Capitalist and
Communist sides of the Cold War. The first big conference of
these non-aligned nations was held at Bandung in Indonesia in
1955, with Communist China also taking part. The only African
countries then independent were Egypt, Libya and Ethiopia; but
observers were sent by the main nationalist parties in the Sudan,
the Gold Coast, South Africa and Algeria. The conference declared in its manifesto that 'Colonialism in all its manifestations
is an evil, which should be speedily brought to an end', and it
called upon the colonial powers to 'grant freedom and independence to subject peoples'. The sense of solidarity among Asian
and Middle Eastern countries had now spread to nationalists all
over Africa south of the Sahara, who knew that from henceforward they had friends to support them in their struggle. As
one Indonesian commented: 'Before Bandung, many had struggled alone, unaided and often unnoticed, fighting first for independence and then for survival. Now it was clear that these
hitherto disregarded peoples were no longer alone.' For Asian
countries Bandung marked the end of the transition from colonial
rule to independence; for Africans it marked the beginning of the
last, decisive phase in this revolutionary movement.

# 17

## THE LAST YEARS OF COLONIAL RULE,
## 1940–60

### *The new prosperity*

It is very important to remember that the years from 1940 till 1960
were not only the period when African nationalism was building
up to its final triumph. They were also by far the most active
period in the history of colonial rule. To some extent this was a
natural development from what had gone before. During the
period up to 1918, as we have seen, colonial governments had had
to concentrate on making themselves financially self-supporting
on the simplest possible scale. During the 1920s and 1930s there
had at last been a little revenue left over from the basic functions

of government. With this extra money a start had been made in
establishing social services in health, education and welfare. This
start had been terribly slowed up by the world slump of the early
1930s. In the course of the great depression the prices of African
products had fallen to very low levels for four or five years in
succession. The revenues of colonial governments had been
drastically reduced because of this. For example, between 1929
and 1932 the European establishment of the Gold Coast was cut
from 1,281 officers to 427. However, with the booming prices and
revenues of the wartime and post-war years, colonial governments all over Africa could at last make up for 'the years that
the locust had eaten'.

Quite apart from the increasing amount of internal development, colonial governments all over tropical Africa were able,
for the first time in their history, to obtain very large amounts of
financial aid from the colonial powers. The reasons for this are
complex. Perhaps the most important element in the new situation was that during the war Western governments learned to take
a very much larger proportion of their own citizens' incomes in
taxation. After the war was over, instead of lowering this taxation
to its former levels, these governments turned themselves into
'welfare states'. Western governments spent their greatly increased revenues on social benefits. Pensions and unemployment
allowances, health services, subsidised housing, and state education were introduced at all levels. From this vastly expanded
scale of public expenditure it was much easier than formerly to
spare a small proportion for overseas aid. It was consistent with
the philosophy underlying the 'welfare state' that the fortunate
should assist the less fortunate. At the same time there were
reasons of self-interest why colonies should be actively developed
at the expense of the colonial power. Colonialism was under
international attack. Its continuance could only be defended if
the colonies could be shown to be benefiting by the association.
Even so, the continuance of colonialism could only be defended
on a temporary basis. It was clear even to the most reactionary
person in Europe that decolonisation was on the way. In the post-
colonial world, former colonies would be safer neighbours if their
economies were developing than if they were abandoned in a
state of impoverished stagnation. So far as British Africa was
concerned, the Colonial Development and Welfare Act of 1940
expressed the new reforming principles in the following terms:

If full and balanced development is to be obtained, some assistance from outside is necessary at this stage. Few of the colonies possess substantial mineral wealth. The majority are almost wholly dependent on the more limited resources derived from agriculture. Many colonies cannot finance out of their own resources the research and survey work, the schemes of major capital enterprise, and the expansion of administrative and technical staffs which are necessary for their full and vigorous development. Nor can they always afford, in the absence of such development, an adequate standard of health and education services.

A second Colonial Development and Welfare Act passed in 1945 sanctioned the spending of even larger sums of money. Between 1946 and 1955 £210 million, from funds provided by the Act, from private investment, and from money raised by the colonial governments themselves, was spent on development plans in the British territories. Before the war French colonies had been even poorer than the British colonies. Therefore, when money began to pour in, the change was even more startling. Investment came from private sources, and from a government fund set up in 1946. This fund, which was known by the initial letters of its French title as F.I.D.E.S., provided official aid on a scale even larger than the British. The development plans of the nine West African territories alone totalled £277 million for the period 1946–55.

### Economic development

This new flow of money, both from expanding internal revenues and from external aid, revolutionised the activities of colonial governments during the post-war period. From this time every colony had its planning staff and its development programme. Among the more spectacular projects started were the hydro-electric schemes. The largest of these were on the Nile at Jinja in Uganda, at Kariba on the Zambezi between Northern and Southern Rhodesia, on the Volta river at Akasombo in the Gold Coast, and at Fria and Kimbo in Guinea. The main purpose of all these projects was to supply power for industrialisation. Industries supported in this way were cotton-spinning in Uganda; the extension of copper-mining in Northern Rhodesia; factories in Southern Rhodesia; the smelting of bauxite into aluminium, as well as for a whole range of light industries, in the Gold Coast and Guinea. The largest project of all was the Inga scheme for damming the Lower Congo. This was brought to a halt by the crisis that followed the independence of the Congo. The Inga scheme

8

would have supplied half as much electricity as is produced in the whole of western Europe. It would have enabled the Congo to industrialise itself and to export electricity to all the neighbouring countries.

Hydro-electric power for industrialisation was, however, only one particularly striking feature of the development programmes with which every colonial government was concerned after the Second World War. Central to every programme was the expansion and diversification of agricultural production. Not only was the production of cash crops for the world market expanded; even more significantly, food for local consumption, especially by the growing populations of the new towns, was increased and improved. Agricultural and veterinary services extended their operations into almost every administrative district. Strenuous efforts were made to educate farmers to adopt improved methods. These included the rotation of crops, contour-bunding to prevent erosion in hilly areas, the consolidation of scattered holdings, and the introduction of better tools and simple machinery. Pastoral farmers who had hitherto bred cattle largely for prestige, concentrating on numbers rather than on the yield of milk and meat, were persuaded to accept scientific breeding methods and to produce regularly for the market. This meant using co-operative creameries and abbatoirs in the grazing districts instead of moving large herds on the hoof to distant selling-points. Again, fish-marketing organisations were set up in many countries and refrigerated vans began to visit the fishing communities of the seaboard, lakes and rivers to buy their produce and distribute it to the towns. All these activities demanded in turn a corresponding revolution in transport. The old dirt roads of pre-war Africa could no longer stand up to the weight of traffic that now passed over them. A very large proportion of most development budgets was spent on reconstructing and tarring the main trunk roads.

## Progress in education

It was soon realised by all colonial governments in the post-war period that if one limitation on development was money, another and more serious one was the shortage of educated people. Because there had been so few secondary schools in colonial Africa before the war, a large number of Europeans had to be employed to operate the new development plans. These people were expensive. They had to be induced to come to Africa by high salaries, subsidised housing and frequent home leave with free travel. On the political side these new 'invaders' of Africa undid much of the good which they contributed by their skills. Their presence widened the gap between European and Africans. It created the impression that the colonial grip on Africa was tightening, and it intensified political unrest and made all government activities suspect to the people. Education therefore soon became the corner-stone of every development plan.

At the end of the war the vast majority of schools were still mission schools, except in the French territories and in the Muslim parts of British territories. Nearly all of them were primary schools, and most of them provided only four years of education in one or other of the African languages. The first priority for advance was to extend the four-year period to six, the two additional years being devoted very largely to the study of a European language. The main problem here was to train enough primary-school teachers who had the necessary qualifications in English or French. The most significant educational development of the 1940s was the establishment throughout colonial Africa of Primary Teachers Training Centres. In their early days these Training Centres were essentially schools of English or French. This problem of European languages had to be solved before it was possible to press on with the provision of a more adequate number of secondary schools. Before the war these had been very few indeed. Most territories had only two or three secondary schools, staffed mainly by European teachers. Now these schools had to be multiplied. This could only be done very gradually, by bringing in more teachers from Europe, and by employing the fortunate few Africans who had passed through the existing schools. Whereas the reform of primary education had only involved the addition of two years, six new years of education were required for a secondary school. Even if a school was able to add a new class every year, a full secondary school could not be established in less than six years. In fact most schools took much longer than this to grow. Although the 1950s saw a great increase in the number of secondary schools, most of them were dismissing their pupils after only three or four years. The fifth and sixth years of secondary school are still to-day the greatest bottleneck in African education systems.

The secondary-school output determined the possibilities for

8-2

higher education. Nevertheless the British government, at least, did not allow the secondary-school bottleneck to hold up the foundation of universities in colonial Africa. A commission set up in 1943 reported two years later that the development of universities was 'an inescapable corollary of any policy which aims at the achievement of colonial self-government'. During the four years after 1945 four university colleges were set up, at Ibadan in Nigeria, at Khartoum in the Sudan, at Achimota in the Gold Coast and at Makerere in Uganda. Some of the money for these universities came from Colonial Development and Welfare funds. The university college at Salisbury in Southern Rhodesia was added in 1953, and that of Fourah Bay (which had been giving some post-secondary education in Sierra Leone since 1827) in 1960. The entrants to these university colleges were inevitably limited to the young people who had passed through the few long established secondary schools. In all of them fearfully expensive European staffs were built up, while the output of graduates climbed slowly from a hundred to two or three hundred a year. Nevertheless, these were the few hundreds of highly trained people whose existence enabled independence to work when the time arrived. These were the people who would become the senior civil servants, the directors of public corporations, the headmasters and the doctors. The French also trained such people. At this period, however, they trained them almost exclusively in France. It may be that, for those who went, the experience of a great and long-established European university was more worth while from an educational point of view than the somewhat artificial and self-conscious atmosphere of the young universities of British Africa. On the other hand, this policy has left the French-speaking African countries more dependent on France during the period since independence.

It was perhaps in their steady support of educational development at the higher levels that British and French governments showed their awareness of how close they were to decolonisation and their good faith in preparing for it. This was in contrast with the Belgians and Portuguese. The most tragic failure in educational development at this period was the Belgian one. Neither in the Congo nor in Belgium itself was a single Congolese given a university education until the very eve of independence. Even secondary education in the Congo remained much scarcer than elsewhere. What makes it more tragic was that it was not a failure of neglect, but a failure to estimate the pace of history. In 1955 Pierre Ryckmans, who had been Governor-General of the Congo from 1934 until 1947, and who then became the Belgian representative on the United Nations Trusteeship Council, wrote:

Everyone who knows the Congo is convinced that Belgian rule is indispensable there, and that the end of it would be the end of all that we have built up during three quarters of a century. We have preferred to give primary education to the mass of children, and to organise secondary education later, as soon as available resources allow. French West Africa has a thousand young people studying in France, while we have just a handful studying in Belgium. But we have ten times more children than they have in primary schools. I sincerely believe that in thirty years' time we shall have in the Congo at least as many university graduates, and at least as many high-school graduates, and infinitely fewer illiterates than do our French neighbours in West Africa, even though the first university in the Congo opened its doors only last year. But will thirty years of peaceful progress be given us?

Ryckmans answered his question with a cautious affirmative: he was 'full of hope'. In the event, four years later, both he and his government were proved terribly mistaken, when the Congolese were quite unprepared for the responsibilities of an independence which was thrust upon them rather than struggled for.

### *Preparing for democratic self-government*

A field in which nearly all colonial governments were most active during the time that remained to them in the post-war years was that of local government. In the British territories indirect rule was quietly abandoned as too gradual for the world situation. There was clearly not going to be time in which to allow African systems of local government 'to evolve along their own lines'. Democratic local government had to be attained within a very few years. The only thing to do was to follow Western models. Every chief was surrounded by an elected council. The supervision of many local services was handed over to these councils. These services had previously been administered autocratically by the chief or by the District Commissioner. The English county council was the model followed increasingly in British territories. The French aimed to reproduce the system of *communes*, which were the principal units of representative local government in France. Roads, local police, prisons, dispensaries and primary schools became the main concerns of these reformed local authorities. In the employment of the District Councils and *communes* many Africans learned to take administrative responsibility in ways that were not yet open to them in the service of the colonial central governments. Many future national politicans gained their political training through membership of the local councils.

When it came to the creation of representative institutions at the colonial level, British and French policy still showed hesitations and contradictions. It was this that soon caused Britain and France to lose the initiative to the African nationalist movements which we shall be considering in the next two chapters. So far as the British were concerned, the intention to decolonise was not in doubt. Oliver Stanley, the war-time Colonial Secretary, had stated already in June 1943: 'We are pledged to guide colonial peoples along the road to self-government within the British empire.' Whether this meant the full, sovereign independence of every individual colonial unit, large or small, no one yet knew. There were still many people in Britain who hoped that federations of West, East and Central African territories would emerge. But the immediate course seemed clear. It was to repeat the pattern of constitutional development followed earlier in the European-settled lands in Canada, Australia and South Africa. Political power would be given gradually to the Legislative Councils which had already been set up in all the colonies. At the same time the membership of these councils would be widened by increasing African representation, through nominees of the governors and of the chiefs. Later the Legislative Councils would become even more representative by giving the vote to a wider and wider circle of people in the colonies.

Such a plan raised no special difficulties in relation to the West African colonies, where all the British people employed were temporary residents only. The complications arose on the eastern side of Africa. Here, from Kenya all the way down to Southern Rhodesia, there lived small colonies of British settlers. These settlers thought of themselves as permanent residents of these countries. They had already been given varying degrees of privilege in their government. The advance of the African majorities to full voting rights would mean the end of the privileged positions of these settlers. To understand their attitude one has to remember that South Africa had gained independence with a franchise virtually limited to white people, and that in 1923 Southern Rhodesia, with a much smaller proportion of whites to blacks, had gained internal self-government on the same basis. British views had changed greatly since 1923. All the same, the British governments of 1945–55 felt that they had an obligation to protect the settlers of East and Central Africa from a too rapid transference of power to the African majorities. Britain therefore experimented for ten years with a variety of so-called 'multi-racial constitutions' in these areas. The typical 'multi-racial constitution' was one in which each racial group in the community elected a certain fixed number of representatives to the legislature. In this way the various groups were more or less evenly represented, regardless of their actual size. The hope was that a democratic moderation would emerge from the balancing of one group against another in the legislature. As we shall see in Chapter 19, few Africans could see any justice in such a system. Nevertheless, the multi-racial constitutions did perform a useful function in providing a transitional stage between white-settler privilege and majority rule. The great gap between the two might have been very difficult to bridge without this multi-racial stage.

French hesitations and contradictions turned less upon the number of Frenchmen resident in any particular one of their African territories than upon the future relations of the French overseas territories to France. Right up until 1960 the French plan for decolonisation envisaged nothing more than a local autonomy for the ex-colonies within a centralised imperial system. This imperial system was represented first by the French Union and later by the French Community. Whereas the French Union had been intended to include all the French overseas territories, Indo-China as well as Africa, the French Community was limited to Africa south of the Sahara, and to those small island territories, like Martinique (West Indies) and St Pierre et Miquelon (off the coast of Canada), which had accepted full integration with metropolitan France. Algeria was within the Community only while it remained a part of France. Tunisia and Morocco were never members of it. In practice, however, French Africa from 1945 to 1955 was passing through a phase of decolonisation very similar to the 'multi-racial' period in British East Africa. In French West and Equatorial Africa and Madagascar legislative assemblies were being developed both at the federal and at the territorial level. During this transitional stage half the seats in these assemblies were elected by the *citoyens de plein exercise*, that it so say in effect by the locally resident French population.

Except for the Belgian and Portuguese possessions, the rulers of colonial Africa from the Sahara to the Zambezi realised that they had entered into the last period of European colonisation. Yet French and British colonial governments acted their parts in this final act of the imperial drama with unprecedented vigour and even enthusiasm. Development money was being poured into the tropical African colonies. Agriculture and industry were being actively stimulated, and education was being given a decisive push forward. Local government was being made quickly and surely more democratic. Central government was also being made more democratic and representative, but less rapidly and less certainly. The colonial rulers were preparing to leave. There was no more time for political experiments. Therefore Western models were increasingly used for the developing political institutions in the African colonies. All over British Africa Speakers in their traditional wigs presided over the rectangular debating chambers of the Westminster model, in which 'government' and 'opposition' sat facing each other. All over French Africa assemblies sat in semicircular chambers on the Paris model, in which the 'left wing' merged imperceptibly into the 'right wing', without a dividing 'floor'. These were the old 'bottles' imported hastily from Europe to contain the 'new wine' of African nationalism. They were not completely successful, but, as comparison with the Belgian Congo was to prove, they were a great deal better than nothing.

# 18

## THE ROAD TO INDEPENDENCE (1)

### WEST AFRICA

#### *The intellectual roots of African nationalism*

African nationalism is like a great forest tree. Its trunk is the Pan-African movement, which gives a sense of solidarity to all the different people of the continent. Its branches are the independent states of Africa. As the roots of a tree reach deep into the soil, so the origins of African nationalism spread in many directions back into history. We saw in Chapter 12 how nationalism was born in the questioning minds of some of the first mission-educated Africans. In the early days of colonialism a few Africans ceased to think in terms of merely tribal institutions. They began to think of imitating, or of capturing from the inside, Western-type churches and states of a wider than tribal kind. In Chapter 13 we described how some of the earliest generation of Africans to receive a secondary education in colonial schools during the inter-war period later went overseas to continue their studies. Those who then went to America made contact with a large, progressive modern state which had thrown off European colonialism a hundred and fifty years before. They also made contact with a stream of Negro racial consciousness and political discontent which had grown up in the days of slavery and gained strength after emancipation. Those who went to Europe made contact with Socialism and Communism. These radical political movements rose out of the discontents of the underprivileged sections of European societies.

The influence of trans-Atlantic slavery on modern African nationalism has been immense. At a time when Africa was still divided politically and culturally into hundreds of tribal units, Negro slaves in the New World were already detribalised. Nevertheless, because of the sufferings they had all experienced, they remained conscious of their common continent of origin. The idea of emancipation was linked from the first with the idea of a return to Africa, and although only a handful of people actually made the journey, Africa remained as a kind of mystical homeland in the minds of millions more. The symbol of that homeland was colour, the blackness of the Africans' skin. Edward Blyden, the West Indian Negro who settled in Liberia as early as 1850, thought out a philosophy which foreshadowed many of the ideas of present-day African leaders. He was probably the first man to use the term 'African personality'. 'Every race', he wrote, 'has a soul, and the soul of a race finds expression in its institutions.' Or again, 'I would rather be a member of the African race now [he was writing in 1888] than a Greek in the time of Alexander, a Roman in the Augustan period, or an Anglo-Saxon in the nineteenth century.' Blyden, however, could not greatly influence the Africa of his own time, even by going to live there. He was a prophet speaking from Africa to the Negroes of the New World. It was only there that his ideas could be kept alive until the mid-twentieth century.

Throughout the later nineteenth century there was a growing ferment of unrest and discontent among the Negro peoples of the United States and the West Indies. At first religion and politics were indistinguishable. 'The preachers of the Negroes', stated a white observer in Virginia in 1889, 'are their most active politicians. They play alternately upon the political passions and the religious fears of their congregations.' By the end of the century distinctly political movements had arisen. Two of these especially affected the later course of African nationalism. One was the 'Negro Empire' proclaimed by the Jamaican Marcus Aurelius Garvey, with its slogan 'Africa for the Africans' and its plans to transport Negroes back to Africa. Garvey was as racially exclusive as the white settlers in colonial Africa. Despite the failure of all his schemes, he stirred the imagination of Africans as no black man had ever done before. The idea of 'Pan-Africanism' was even more influential. The term was first used in 1900, at a conference summoned in London by a West Indian lawyer to denounce British imperialism. It was not used again, however, until it was revived by William DuBois, a radical American Negro, after the First World War. Throughout the 1920s and 1930s DuBois organised Pan-African Congresses, at which the common sufferings of black people on both sides of the Atlantic were stressed, and also their common cultural background. Unlike Garvey, DuBois did not preach African racialism. He saw the problems of the Negroes of the New World and of the African as part of a world-wide struggle of oppressed, underprivileged people for freedom and justice. Yet both men were working for the same end, 'to raise the status of the Negro, materially and spiritually, in his own eyes and in the eyes of the world at large' (quoted in Shepperson and Price, *Independent African*, p. 435). Many Africans from British territories who were studying in the United States were caught up in the excitement of these ideas and schemes. However, until the Second World War, the majority of those who attended the Pan-African Congresses were American Negroes. Only in the late 1940s did Africans themselves take over DuBois's movement and fully inherit all the diverse strands of thought from across the Atlantic.

The other main strand in the web of African Nationalist ideas was that stemming from European Socialism and Communism. The prophet of both movements was Karl Marx (1818–83), a German Jew, who spent most of his working life as a political refugee in England. Essentially Marx's thought was addressed to the social evils accompanying the spread of industrialism in Europe. He believed that these evils could be cured only if the means of production were taken out of private ownership and put under the control of governments which truly represented 'the workers'. Common ownership was the keystone of Marx's philosophy. In the course of attacking private ownership (Capitalism) he turned against all forms of religion. Religion he described as 'the opium of the people', fostered by 'Capitalists' in order to distract the 'workers' from the evils of their present lot by false hopes of compensation in a future life. The generation following Marx's death saw an increasing division among his followers between Socialists and Communists. Many Socialists kept their religious beliefs and pursued their objectives by peaceful persuasion. The Communists believed that 'socialism' was only attainable by violent revolutions led by carefully indoctrinated, atheist 'party members'. These would seize power, establish a 'dictatorship of the proletariat (workers)' and carry out a fundamental re-education of the whole community. Socialists and Communists agreed in denouncing the colonial system, which they believed to be the creation of capitalist property-owners seeking ever greater numbers of 'workers' on whose labour they could make ever increasing profits. Communists, however, went further than mere condemnation of colonialism. Lenin, the leader of the Russian Communists, demanded the forceful overthrow of colonial rule in the interests of 'world revolution'. As soon as the October Revolution of 1917 had established Communism in power in Russia, the Soviet government, working through its supporters in western Europe, gave not only money but also training in political organisation and revolutionary methods to colonial nationalists who were seeking to overthrow their alien governments. Politically conscious Africans studying in European countries could not fail to be interested in Communism. In the Communist movement they found friends in a world that too often seemed hostile or indifferent to their aims. They found people who sympathised with their humiliations, and a whole philosophy which denounced imperialism as evil. They discovered in Communism techniques of political action suited to their needs, a call to heroism in a world struggle, and a promise of future freedom and prosperity. What is surprising is that so few Africans committed themselves wholeheartedly to the Communist cause, and that for most of them the milder path of Socialism remained the more attractive.

To see how these complex strands were woven together to produce the political activity that resulted in independence, we can look for an example at the early career of Kwame Nkrumah, which is so well told in his autobiography, *Ghana*. Nkrumah was born, probably in 1909, the son of a goldsmith of the Nzima tribe in the south-western corner of the Gold Coast. Members of the Nzima tribe had long been active in the commerce of the west coast. Nkrumah was educated at a Roman Catholic mission school and then at the great secondary school at Achimota, near Accra. He thought of the priesthood, and eventually became a mission teacher, but this did not satisfy his ambitions. In 1935, with the help of an uncle working in Lagos and with the encouragement of the Nigerian nationalist, Dr Azikiwe, he went to the United States. There he spent ten years, first studying and then teaching at Lincoln University in Pennsylvania. He read widely, and stated that the writings of Communists and Socialists did much to influence him in his revolutionary ideas and activities, 'but of all the literature that I studied, the book that did more than any other to fire my enthusiasm was the *Philosophy and Opinions* of Marcus Garvey.' In 1945 Nkrumah left America for London, and there met for the first time the West Indian journalist George Padmore, who became one of his closest friends and advisors. The two men played a prominent part in the Fifth Pan-African Congress held at Manchester in that year. The majority of delegates at this congress were Africans, although it was presided over by DuBois, then seventy-three, the 'Grand Old Man' of the movement. In Padmore's words, DuBois 'had done more than any other to inspire and influence by his writings and political philosophy all the young men who had foregathered from far distant corners of the earth' (*Pan-Africanism or Communism?* p. 161). The congress adopted strongly worded resolutions condemning colonialism: 'We are determined to be free. We want education. We want the right to earn a decent living, the right to express our thoughts and emotions, to adopt and create forms of beauty. We demand for Black Africa autonomy and independence. We will fight in every way we can for freedom, democracy and social betterment.' At the congress, and later in London, Nkrumah worked closely with Jomo Kenyatta, and had meetings with Africans from the French territories, such as Senghor and Houp-

The independence of African States labels (from the map legend):

The Independence of African States

- Independent before 1950
- Independent 1950–1959
- Independent 1960–1966

Rhodesia (Southern)—self-governing in internal affairs: British responsibility internationally

Map annotation boxes:

British Protectorate of Somaliland joined Italian Trust Territory to form Somalia, 1960

Federal Union of Ethiopia and Eritrea, 1954

Italian occupation 1936–1941

1963 resistance to Portuguese

Union of Tanganyika and Zanzibar as Tanzania 1964

1963 Zanzibar

French Somaliland Jibouti

Independent of British control 1922–1936

1961 Revolt against Port. rule

French Soudan and Senegal joined abortive Mali Federation 1959–1960

Bissau: 1961 Revolt against Port. rule

British Trust Territory of Togoland joined independent Ghana 1957

British Trust Territory of Northern Cameroons joined Northern Nigeria 1961: Southern Cameroons joined Republic of Cameroun in a Federal State 1961

Central African Federation 1953–1963 Southern Rhodesia, Northern Rhodesia (Zambia) and Nyasaland (Malawi)

Rhodesia Self-governing colony 1923

South African Mandate under League of Nations; since considered by South African government to be part of the Republic of South Africa

35 The independence of Africa

houet-Boigny. At this stage, most of the political activity among Africans took place in London or Paris, and not in Africa itself. It was then that the foundations of a continent-wide movement were laid. 'The political conscience of African students was aroused, and whenever they met they talked of little else but nationalist politics and colonial liberation movements' (Nkrumah).

## The Gold Coast: the first breakthrough

Until 1947 the Pan-African movement, though it had won the allegiance of the young African intellectuals studying abroad, had achieved little or nothing in Africa itself. Only Dr Azikiwe's newspapers, which were read by a small group of educated people throughout British West Africa, did something to prepare the ground for a more radical approach to politics. The colonial governments, to the extent that they had even heard of Pan-Africanism, thought of it as mere 'students' talk'. The African leaders whom they recognised, and to whom they were preparing to make limited political concessions, were men of an older generation who had done well under colonial rule—the chiefs, lawyers, businessmen and rich farmers. It was men of this sort who in 1947 founded the United Gold Coast Convention, in an attempt to face 'the problem of reconciling the leadership of the intelligentsia with the broad mass of the people' (Nkrumah). These were men of substance and experience. They were Gold Coast patriots too. They looked forward to independence in the shortest possible time—some of them thought in about ten years time. They even realised that, to keep up pressure on the colonial government, it would be necessary to organise widespread support among the people. But they did not themselves know how to do so. They had their own professions to pursue. Politics to them was a spare-time occupation, as it was for most politicians in Europe. In western European countries the only whole-time political organisers were the paid agents of the political parties, who did not themselves stand for election. This was why the U.G.C.C. leaders in 1947 invited Nkrumah to come home and be their General Secretary. Here, they thought, was a man who knew the techniques of organisation, and who would take the rough work off their hands.

No sooner had Nkrumah arrived back in the Gold Coast than he began to pursue an activist policy designed to seize the initiative from the colonial government. He started to reform the inefficient party organisation:

I found on going through the minute book, that thirteen branches had been formed throughout the country. In actual fact just a couple had been established and these were inactive. I saw at once the urgency of a country-wide tour. The results of this were most successful, for within six months I had established 500 branches in the (original) Colony alone. I issued membership cards, collected dues and started raising funds.

The leaders of the U.G.C.C. became involved in violent demonstrations by ex-servicemen in Accra (see Chapter 16). The six top men of the party, including Nkrumah, were placed in detention by the government. This was the beginning of the split between Nkrumah and the U.G.C.C. Nkrumah welcomed such violent activities; his colleagues had second thoughts about their value in achieving independence. The British government responded to the disturbances by inviting an all-African committee under Sir Henley Coussey to make recommendations for constitutional reform. The other five leaders of the U.G.C.C. joined the committee: Nkrumah alone was not invited.,

The Coussey Constitution, which was accepted by the British government, was a real landmark in the history of British moves towards decolonisation in Africa. It was implemented by the new Governor, Sir Charles Arden-Clarke, as soon as he took up his duties in 1949. It provided for an all-African Legislative Assembly, directly elected in the more developed parts of the country and indirectly elected elsewhere. An Executive Council or cabinet was formed with eight ministers chosen from the Assembly and three more to be nominated by the Governor from the ranks of the European civil service. It was in fact the constitution under which Nkrumah was to begin his rule, first as Leader of Government Business and later as Prime Minister, from 1951 till 1954. In 1949, however, Nkrumah had just founded his own Convention Peoples Party in opposition to the U.G.C.C. He denounced the Coussey constitution as 'an imperialist fraud', demanding instead 'Self-Government Now'. He followed up his claim with a campaign of 'Positive Action'. This was a movement of strikes and boycotts, designed to create a sense of struggle throughout the country. For their part in the Positive Action campaign, Nkrumah and other C.P.P. leaders were arrested and condemned to imprisonment on various charges of incitement, libel and sedition. They remained in prison for a year, while the colonial government proceeded with its preparations for a general election in February 1951. This was won by the C.P.P., led during Nkrumah's enforced absence from the scene by K. A. Gbedemah. This electoral victory of the C.P.P. was the result of such political efficiency that the party won the respect and admiration of the formerly very hostile colonial government. Arden-Clarke therefore decided to release Nkrumah and to invite him to form a government. Nkrumah, for his part, agreed to abandon his claim for 'Self-Government Now' and to work for a period under the Coussey constitution. This gave the C.P.P. Ministers the great advantage of learning to operate the machinery of government from the inside before taking the full responsibilities of independence. On Arden-Clarke's side, this bargain, struck in February 1951, committed the colonial government to working, for only a brief transitional period, with the representatives of a radical party with a great popular following. The C.P.P. was very different in its aims and leadership from the moderate, middle-class people to whom the colonial government had previously hoped to hand over power. The government in Britain, and indeed the outside world as a whole, watched with amazement the steadily growing friendship between these two very different men, as they steered the Gold Coast towards independence. Nkrumah tells in moving terms how he received from Arden-Clarke the news of the date, 6 May 1957, fixed by the British government for the Gold Coast's independence under the new name of Ghana:

He handed me a dispatch from the Secretary of State. When I reached the fifth paragraph the tears of joy that I had difficulty in hiding blurred the rest of the document. After a few minutes I raised my eyes to meet those of the Governor. For some moments there was nothing either of us could say. Perhaps we were both looking back over the seven years of our association, beginning with doubts, suspicions and misunderstandings, then acknowledging the growth of trust, sincerity and friendship, and now, finally, this moment of victory for us both, a moment beyond description.

'Prime Minister', the Governor said, as he extended his hand to me, 'This is a great day for you. It is the end of what you have struggled for.'

'It is the end of what *we* have been struggling for, Sir Charles', I corrected him. 'You have contributed a great deal towards this; in fact I might not have succeeded without your help and co-operation. This is a very happy day for us both!'

(Nkrumah, *Ghana*, p. 282.)

### The sequel to Ghana in British West Africa

So far as the rest of British West Africa was concerned, the decision to decolonise followed automatically from the decision to do so in the Gold Coast. In Nigeria the course towards independence was firmly set by a new constitution which came into operation in 1951. This was the same year as Arden-Clarke's bargain with Nkrumah. That the process of independence took three years longer to achieve in Nigeria than in the Gold Coast was due to the special problems created by the differences in education, wealth and outlook between the three regions of Nigeria. The Northern region was largely Muslim and Hausa-speaking. The traditional Fulani ruling class still exercised the predominant influence. The mainly Yoruba-speaking Western region was traditionally organised into a number of states ruled by kingly chiefs, whilst the Eastern region consisted largely of Ibo-speaking people who had never been bound together into powerful political units. The problems created by these differences could not be solved by setting up a unitary state covering the whole of Nigeria. This the 1951 constitution partly tried to do, and was proved to be unworkable. Dr Azikiwe, who had become Chief Minister of the Eastern region, was especially critical of the attempt to minimise regional powers. The problems of Nigeria could only be settled by the compromise solution of a federal system of government. This more complicated structure took longer to develop than the unitary government of independent Ghana. A new constitution came into force in 1954. Under it, Nigeria became a truly federal state, with clearly defined powers granted to the federal government and all other powers given to the regional governments. Each region had to become internally self-governing before the territory as a whole could become independent. The most backward region politically was the North. When, however, this immense region came to play its full part in Nigerian affairs, it dominated the territory politically. No Federal government could be formed without members of the Northern People's Congress party, and the first Federal Prime Minister, Sir Abubakar Tafewa Balewa, was a northerner.

The strains and stresses produced by the interactions of regional interests in Nigeria delayed the granting of full independence until 1960. The major problem in Sierra Leone and, especially, in the Gambia, was the very opposite to Nigeria's. Both territories were very small, and consequently, relatively poor. Nevertheless, the process started in the Gold Coast could not be halted. Sierra Leone became independent in 1961, and the Gambia in 1965. The Gambia is the smallest country in Africa. It is merely the narrow strip of land along the banks of the Gambia river, and is completely surrounded by the French-speaking state of Senegal. The granting of independence to the Gambia raised the question as to whether a country of this size could afford to stand on its own feet as a sovereign state in the modern world.

## The independence of French West Africa

The difference in attitude towards the growth of nationalism between French-speaking and English-speaking West Africans may be seen in a comparison between the life of Senghor and that of Nkrumah. French Africans were at first concerned more with the cultural than with the political aspects of colonialism. English-speaking nationalists, it has been said, wrote constitutions, while their French-speaking contemporaries wrote poetry. Léopold Sédar Senghor was born in 1906 in a coastal village south of Dakar. His prosperous Catholic parents sent him to schools in the colony and later to Paris. The poems he wrote while in France are full of homesick memories of his childhood days. From 1935, after becoming the first African *aggrégé* (qualified secondary-school teacher) in France, he taught in French *lycées* (grammar schools). On the outbreak of the war in 1939 he joined the army, and was captured by the Germans, who tried unsuccessfully to persuade him to turn against France. His years in Paris had brought Senghor into contact with a wealth of political and literary ideas. He knew many outstanding French West Indians, and became the close friend of Aimé Césaire from Martinique, who was to become like himself a poet and a politician. Before directly tackling political problems, these young men felt the need to produce a creed, or statement of cultural values. Between them, Senghor and Césaire created the concept of *Négritude*, 'the affirmation', as they described it, 'of the values of African culture'. In 1947 Senghor and a fellow Senegalese, Alioune Diop, founded *Présence Africaine* in Paris, a magazine devoted to the renewal of these values. Meanwhile, Senghor was turning to practical politics. After the war he returned to Senegal as a Socialist politician, and took part in the events which led up to the formation of the French Union in 1946. He refused to attend the Bamako conference of that year which founded the *Rassemblement Démocratique Africaine*. He rightly believed that the new party would be dominated by Communists. Instead, he led a popular political movement in the Senegal, and was elected as a Deputy to the French Assembly. Under his influence many young

Africans devoted themselves seriously to writing, poetry and the arts. This engagement of some of the best minds in French West Africa with cultural affairs partly explains why, in the early 1950s, these territories were not so politically conscious as their English-speaking neighbours.

Support for Senghor's party extended into Upper Volta and other territories, where it came into direct collision with the R.D.A. The main issue between the two parties from 1955 on-wards was that between the federal policy of Senghor and the territorial policy of Houphouet-Boigny. Houphouet, who was born in the Ivory Coast in 1905, went to France for the first time when elected a Deputy in 1945. Previously he had been a medical assistant, a prosperous cocoa-farmer and a local chief. He had entered politics as the spokesman of a farmers' association. Although a highly sophisticated man, he retained a good measure of the peasant's 'down-to-earth' common sense. He became the first President of the R.D.A. After the breakaway of the R.D.A. from its Communist alliance in 1950, he held Cabinet posts in several French governments. After the war, the Ivory Coast had become the richest of the French West African territories, providing over 40 per cent of the Federation's exports. Houphouet argued that in the federal union, supported by Senghor, the Ivory Coast would always be subsidising its poorer neighbours. As a minister in the French government, therefore, he was influential in preparing the *Loi Cadre* (Outline Law) of 1956. Under the *Loi Cadre* France kept control of foreign policy, defence and overall economic development. All other aspects of government became the responsibility, not of the existing federal governments of French West and Equatorial Africa, but of the twelve individual colonies of which they were composed. The *Loi Cadre* was deeply influenced by the approaching independence of the Gold Coast and Nigeria. France understood that the French Union, the plan for a kind of super-state, would have to be replaced by something much looser and more like the British Commonwealth. But, thanks to Houphouet, the autonomy offered was to units so small (in population, if not in size) that their practical dependence on France was bound to remain very great. Senghor unsuccessfully opposed these constitutional changes, which he considered would result in splitting up West Africa into too many small, weak states. In this opposition he was supported by Sékou Touré of Guinea, a prominent figure in the R.D.A.

Sékou Touré was born in 1922, and was therefore a much younger man than either Senghor or Houphouet. Although he was a descendant of the famous Samory, his family was poor. His first visit to France had been as a delegate to the Communist Trades Union Conference in 1946. Sékou Touré soon became the leading Trades Unionist in French West Africa. In 1956 he led a breakaway movement from the French parent body of the Union, although he still held Communist views, and formed a new Federation of African Trades Unions, free from outside ties. While most of his contemporaries concentrated upon increasing their influence in Paris, Sékou Touré realised that it was in Africa that the foundations of real power were to be laid. He favoured the retention of the Federal government at Dakar. In 1958 it looked as though a regrouping of political parties was about to take place, with Sékou Touré leaving the R.D.A. and joining Senghor. At this moment, however, General de Gaulle came to power in France as a result of the revolt of the French army in Algeria in May 1958. De Gaulle established a new constitution in France, the Fifth Republic. He offered the colonial peoples the choice between autonomy (self-government) as separate republics within a French 'Community', which now replaced the earlier 'Union', or else immediate independence, with the severance of all links with France. In the Referendum held in September 1958, all the colonies of French West and Equatorial Africa voted acceptance of de Gaulle's proposals, except for Guinea, whose people followed Sékou Touré in voting 'No'. Sékou Touré was bitterly disappointed with the failure of French West Africa to achieve independence as a Federation. He considered that the new 'Community' was little more than a disguise for the continuing domination of France.

When Guinea decided to become independent, France immediately stopped all economic aid, and withdrew her civil servants and technicians. Faced with an economic collapse, Sékou Touré turned to Russia and to other Communist countries for assistance. Nkrumah offered him at once a loan of £10 million, and the two statesmen declared the formation of a Union between their two countries. This was a gesture of solidarity, however, rather than a real constitutional measure. As a gesture, it was effective, for the other territories, which had voted 'Yes' in the Referendum, began at once to readjust their positions. Senegal and French Soudan came together to form the Mali Federation, and in 1959 demanded and obtained complete independence, while remaining members of the 'Community'. The Ivory Coast joined in a looser grouping, the 'Entente Council', with Dahomey, Upper Volta and Niger, each member of which demanded its individual independence of France. By November 1960 all the French West and Equatorial African territories had become independent, as had the Malagasy Republic (Madagascar). After a matter of months the Mali Federation divided again into its two parts, French Soudan now taking to itself the name of Mali. The 'Community', as de Gaulle had envisaged it, was a dead letter, though French aid, and therefore French influence, remained very great.

The United Nations Trusteeship Territories in West Africa followed the same broad path as the colonies proper. British Togoland decided by plebiscite (a direct vote of the whole people) to join Ghana in 1957, whilst French Togo became an independent republic in 1960. The history of Cameroon was the stormiest of all West African countries. Civil war between Communist and anti-Communist groups broke out in 1956, and had not been completely resolved when the territory became independent in 1960. In 1961 plebiscites were held in the British Cameroons. The northern part voted to remain within Northern Nigeria. The southern part, however, voted for union with its French-speaking neighbour. Thus the Federal Republic of Cameroun combined for the first time areas which had been under different colonial rules, and defied the language gulf which separates the English-speaking and French-speaking states of West Africa.

# 19

## THE ROAD TO INDEPENDENCE (2)

### NORTH AND NORTH-EAST AFRICA

As we saw in Chapter 14, nationalism in the Muslim north of Africa had developed much earlier than in Africa south of the Sahara. Egypt, indeed, had been self-governing since 1922. Yet it was not until forty years later—after all of West Africa and most of East Africa had become independent—that the emancipation of

North and North-East Africa was completed by the withdrawal of the French from Algeria. The emergence of this region from the colonial period was thus a much longer drawn out and more piecemeal process than that of the regions to the south. And although it became in its final stages increasingly linked with the rest of the Pan-African freedom movement, its origins were different and must be separately treated.

### Egypt and the Sudan

The key country of the North African region was, of course, Egypt. As soon as the British war-time occupation ended in 1944 it was fully independent. A British garrison remained in the Canal Zone, however, in accordance with the terms of the 1936 Treaty. Egypt had by far the largest population and by far the most developed industry and commerce of any Muslim country in Africa. It was also the intellectual capital of the Arabic-speaking world. The two universities of Cairo had between them a student population of 20,000. It was there that Arabic-speaking students from the Maghrib met those from the Sudan and Somalia and formed the same kind of associations as English- and French-speaking African students were forming at the same time in London and Paris. At least for those North African nationalists whose primary loyalty was still to Islam, Egypt was both a place of refuge and a nursery of revolt.

At the same time post-war Egypt itself presented, in the words of John Hatch, 'a classic picture of a society moving inexorably towards revolution'.

Less than five per cent of the total land area of Egypt was productively habitable, the Nile Valley alone providing means of life in this vast desert. Yet, not only were eighty-five per cent of the 19,000,000 inhabitants landless, but over a third of the cultivable land was owned by one half per cent of the population. There were 2,700,000 landowners in the country; of these over 2,000,000 owned less than an acre each. The Eygptian fellahin were among the most downtrodden peoples in the world. Living out their miserable short life in slime and squalor, racked by dysentery, bilharzia and trachoma, existence for the Egyptian masses reached the lowest depths of brutishness in human experience. Yet the ruling class, the land-owning pashas, descended from Turks and without interest in the country which gave them wealth, were among the most ostentatiously opulent group of human beings. King Farouk was the richest, grossest and greediest of them. (John Hatch, *A History of Post-War Africa*, p. 149.)

It was clear that the traditional rulers of such a society would adopt the classic tactics of trying to divert internal discontent into the channels of external aggression. In 1944 they joined with other Arab countries in forming the Arab League, the earliest and most persistent object of which was to prevent the emergence of a Jewish state in Palestine, as soon as Britain fulfilled its declared intention of laying down its Mandate. The United Nations in 1947 decreed the partition of the country between Israel and Jordan. In 1948 the Arab League armies went to war against Israel and were humiliatingly defeated by the one-year-old state. Egyptians especially felt this blow to Muslim prestige, which showed up the corruption and inefficiency of the monarchy and the politicians. Frustrated in their attempts against Israel, the politicians now responded by turning the hatred of the foreigner against the British, in the Canal Zone and in the Sudan. In covert defiance of the 1936 treaty (see p. 182), armed bands of Egyptians were encouraged to attack British troops and installations. In 1951 the Egyptian government declared the 1936 treaty to be at an end. This was important for the Sudan, as well as for Egypt, as the treaty had re-established the condominium over the Sudan. Under pressure from Sudanese nationalists, who were not sure that they wanted to be united with Egypt, Britain responded to the Egyptian move by setting a rapid course towards Sudanese independence.

Meanwhile, British reprisals to Egyptian terrorist attacks led to an outburst of popular feeling in Cairo, in which British and other foreign property was destroyed. Six months later, on 23 July 1952, a group of young army officers seized power. They were led by Colonel Abdul Nasser, but used an older man, General Neguib, as a figurehead. In a short time the revolutionary Army Council swept away the discredited monarchy and parliament. The new rulers of Egypt quickly came to an agreement with Britain over the future of the Sudan. Neguib and Nasser had both served in the Sudan. They knew the strength of Sudanese nationalism. They realised that a friendly Sudan, even though independent of Egypt, was preferable to a hostile dependency. The new Egypt therefore accepted the British proposals. These were that the Sudanese people should hold elections under a constitution providing internal self-government for a period of three years before deciding upon complete independence or union with Egypt. When the time came, in January 1956, the Sudan voted to become an independent republic, though outside the Commonwealth.

By 1954, Nasser had ousted Neguib as President of Egypt. The following year he attended the Bandung Conference. Under his rule Egypt became for the first time openly identified with independence movements in the rest of Africa. Internally, Nasser's Egypt was the first country in Africa to put radical Socialist policies into practice, by limiting severely the amount of land which an individual could own, and by redistributing the large estates among the peasants. Externally, he succeeded in ridding Egypt of the last traces of European domination. Britain agreed to withdraw her troops from the Canal Zone, leaving the canal to be operated as before by the mainly Anglo-French company that had built it. Nasser then turned to his plan for extending the area of irrigated land by building a huge new dam across the Nile at Aswan. This was to have been financed mainly from an American loan. America, however, became increasingly annoyed by his neutralist policies, and in 1956 withdrew its offer of the loan. Nasser responded by nationalising the Suez Canal, announcing that he would finance the 'high dam' from its profits. Britain and France, with Israeli help, thereupon attacked Egypt. They only withdrew under the strongest pressure of international opinion, expressed through the United Nations. Egyptian control over the Canal was confirmed, and Nasser seized British and French property in Egypt. Construction of the new Aswan Dam was begun, financed not so much from canal profits, as from massive Russian aid. The Suez incident proved a sweeping victory for Nasser which greatly enhanced his standing in other African countries.

## Libya, Ethiopia, Somalia

Egypt and the Sudan were bordered both to the west and to the east by countries which had formed the African empire of Italy, and whose independence was determined primarily by the results of the Second World War. The British, during their North African campaigns of 1942 and 1943, had entered into close and secret relations with Sayyid Idris, the temporal head of the Sanusi order, which had organised the Bedouin resistance to the Italians during the 1920s and 1930s (Chapter 14, p. 183). As a result the Sanusi co-operated with the British during the war, and as soon as the Italians had been expelled, Idris returned to his country. There were still, however, a number of problems which had to be solved before he could be recognised as king of a united and independent Libya. The Italians had found their main difficulty in extending their rule from the settled, mainly Berber populations of the coastal cities to the nomadic Arab pastoralists of the interior. Idris now encountered the reverse problem, that of making the rule of the Bedouin acceptable to the more sophisticated and cosmopolitan peoples of the coast. While this problem was being resolved, the country remained, with the consent of the United Nations, under the administration of its war-time conquerors. The southern province of Libya, the Fezzan, had been occupied during the war by the Free French, who had operated a supply road across the desert from Nigeria through Chad to the North African battlefields. This occupation continued after the war and, especially since the Sanusi order was as powerful in Chad as in Libya, the French were in no hurry to move out of the frontier region. The two northern provinces of Cyrenaica and Tripolitania likewise remained under a British administration, which, while strongly favouring Idris's claims, was anxious to keep control until those claims were firmly established. In 1949, therefore, the United Nations began to play a hurrying role, sending its own Commissioner to work out a constitution acceptable to the country as a whole. At last in 1951 a constituent assembly drawn from all three provinces declared Idris King of Libya, and the new state began its independent existence in December of that year.

We have seen (Chapter 16, p. 205) that Ethiopia regained its independence, thanks to the action of British troops, in 1941. The two older Italian colonies of Somalia and Eritrea were conquered by the British during the same campaign, and both of them remained under British administration for the rest of the war and for some time afterwards. Both were the subject of many disputes played out at the United Nations by interested parties. At least three different plans were proposed for Eritrea, with its population of one million people divided almost equally between the hill-dwelling Tigreans, who were Ethiopian Christians, and the Afar and Danakil of the coastal plains, who were Muslims. The Arab countries wanted Eritrea to be independent; the British wanted it partitioned between Ethiopia and the Sudan; the Ethiopians, wishing to recover a sea-port of their own in Massawa, wanted to annex the whole. At length, in 1952, the Ethiopian view prevailed, though under a federal constitution which gave the Eritreans a considerable say in their own affairs. Somalia, after similar disputes, was assigned by the United Nations in 1950 to Italy as a Trust Territory, but for ten years only, at the end of which time it was to become independent. All observers are agreed that Italian rule during this period was exceptionally enlightened and successful.

The Italian Administration showed initiative and courage in opening a School of Politics and Administration at Mogadishu in 1950 as a training centre for Somali officials and political leaders. This bracketing together of the two skills most needed in an emergent country was also reflected in later legislation which, in marked contrast to the British tradition, encouraged members of the civil service to stand as candidates for the legislature, secure in the knowledge that if they failed they could resume their administrative careers without handicap. By 1957 the School of Politics had provided a cadre of officials with basic training in administration, and the emphasis then switched to the concomitant need for technically qualified staff in other fields. The School was transformed into a Technical and Commercial Institute. Meanwhile, in 1954, a Higher Institute of Law and Economics, later to become Somalia's University College, was opened to provide a two-year Rome University diploma course...These developments did much to dissipate what remained of Somali scepticism over Italian intentions, and this effect was greatly enhanced by the progressive opening of senior posts in all branches of the civil service to Somali officials. Here advancement proceeded with rapidity, to such an extent indeed that by 1956 all Districts and Provinces were in the direct charge of Somali administrative officers.

(I. M. Lewis, *The Modern History of Somaliland.*)

Without any doubt the deliberate and rapid decolonisation of Italian Somalia was greatly helped by the fact that all the inhabitants of the country spoke a single language and felt themselves to be a nation. Most African countries had to go through a process of nationalist unification, to which some delaying tactics by the colonial powers was absolutely necessary. With the Somalis the problem was rather that the sense of Somali nationalism existed over a wider area than that of the Trust Territory. It extended clearly over the whole of British Somaliland, where the colonial government, though less active than the Italian Trusteeship administration in its preparations for decolonisation, at least did nothing to prevent the unification of the two territories. Although in a hurried and disorganised way, British Somaliland was brought to independence five days before the Italian Trust Territory, and on 1 July 1960 the legislative assemblies of the two countries met in joint session at Mogadishu and constituted themselves into the National Assembly of the independent and sovereign Republic of Somalia. Still, however, there remained substantial Somali communities outside the boundaries of the new state, in the lowlands of eastern Ethiopia, in the Northern Frontier District of Kenya, and in the tiny, but important French territory of the Somali Coast, whose capital at Jibouti was the coastal terminus of the Addis Ababa railway.

## The independence of the Maghrib

The remaining part of Muslim North Africa was the Maghrib, divided, as we saw in Chapter 14, into Algeria, which was administered as a part of France, and into the two flanking protectorates of Morocco and Tunisia. There was no essential difference between the state of nationalist opinion in the three countries. The vast majority of all their populations were solidly Muslim and Arabic-speaking. Their leaders looked to Cairo and the Arab League for support in their struggle, and were equally affected by developments towards independence in Libya, the Sudan and Somalia. The difference between them was mainly a difference of strategy, which arose from the differing degrees of French commitment. It was obvious to all that if France would adopt delaying tactics in the Protectorates, in Algeria she would fight to the bitter end.

In Morocco, the Sultan had made himself the central figure of the nationalist movement. He refused to give his consent to French laws to ban the Istiqlal and other nationalist parties. In a desperate effort to overcome the resistance to their rule in Morocco, the French sided with the nomadic groups in the Atlas mountains, who were traditionally hostile to the Sultan. In 1953 the French deposed Muhammad V, and exiled him, first to Corsica and then to Madagascar. In his place the tribal *kaid* Thami al-Glawi was made Sultan. This act made Muhammad V the popular hero of Morocco, and more than ever the symbol of the country's hopes. Unrest broke out with the formation of an Army of Liberation by the nationalist groups. The French were forced to acknowledge defeat, and agreed to the principle of independence. In November 1955 Muhammad V returned to his country and was reinstated as Sultan. A broadly representative government under the Sultan, including the Istiqlal Party, negotiated with the French, and Morocco became independent in March 1956. A similar agreement was made with the Spanish government over the northern zone. After only forty-four years under European control, Morocco once more became a united independent monarchy.

Immediately after the war it seemed that France would allow Tunisia to become autonomous within the French Union at a fairly early date. Bourguiba returned to his country in 1949, after four years of self-imposed exile. The following year he was able to state that 'with independence accepted as a principle, there are no more problems'. Such optimism was misplaced. Increasing resistance to constitutional changes came from the French and Italian settlers in Tunisia. It also came from the Governor-General of Algeria. The French in Algeria feared the effect on that country of having an independent Tunisia as a neighbour. In 1952 Bourguiba was arrested, and disturbances broke out which the French were unable to control. By 1954, however, France was fighting a full-scale war against the F.L.N. in Algeria, and had neither the will nor the military forces to break the Tunisian nationalists. As in Morocco, France had to give way to the nationalist movement. In 1955 Bourguiba was released, and Tunisia became independent in March 1956, at the same time as Morocco. Relations with France became strained once more in 1961, when, at the time of the Évian negotiations between France and the Algerian nationalists, Bourguiba demanded the evacuation of French troops from the military base of Bizerta. Violent fighting broke out, and continued until France agreed to the evacuation in June 1962. By that time a large proportion of the European community in Tunisia had left the country. Since the Bizerta crisis, Tunisia and France have grown closer together.

The first outbreak of violence in Algeria occurred within a few days of the end of the war in Europe in 1945, when police fired upon a procession at Sétif. Enraged Muslims turned upon the *colons*, and the French replied with ruthless retaliation; more than one hundred Europeans and many thousands of Muslims were killed. This grim experience gave many Algerians a sense of nationhood for the first time. In 1946 Ferhat Abbas could claim: 'The Algerian personality, the Algerian fatherhood, which I did not find in 1936 among the Muslims [see Chapter 14], I find there today. The change that has taken place is visible to the naked eye, and cannot be ignored.' The French tried to ignore this growing Algerian nationalism. They maintained that Algeria was a part of France. Finally, the nationalist organisation, the *Front de Libération Nationale*, began the Algerian rebellion in November 1954. This uprising was influenced by events in Morocco and Tunisia. In a sense, the French only withdrew from these neighbouring countries with the object of being the better able to hold Algeria. The million Frenchmen in Algeria had relations all over the mother-country. No French ministry in the long series of weak governments which followed one another at frequent intervals from 1945 till 1958 could face the unpopularity of abandoning the hopeless Algerian war. The Egyptian triumph in the Suez crisis encouraged the F.L.N. greatly. It also paved the way for the return to French politics of General de Gaulle. The French people desired a strong ruler, to rescue them from disastrous overseas adventures. They were at last prepared greatly to increase the Presidential powers. During his election campaign the General promised victory in Algeria. No sooner was he in power, however, than he started to pursue his *politique de l'artichoux*. This was his 'artichoke policy' of stripping off, leaf by leaf, the strong combination of right-wing generals, embattled settlers and reactionary administrators which had defied the peace-making efforts of all his predecessors. A cease-fire was finally arranged with the F.L.N. at Évian in 1962, after seven and a half years of bitter fighting. By this time older leaders like Ferhat Abbas had been pushed aside by younger, more radical men. After a short period of civil war, during which most of the French settlers left the country, Muhammad Ben Bella emerged as the strong man of independent Algeria.

Under Ben Bella's leadership Algeria achieved a prominent position in the Pan-African movement and in the affairs of the Organisation for African Unity (see Chapter 22). As one of the few African countries to gain independence by means of violent revolution, it was only natural that Algeria should adopt sweeping Socialist policies to cope with the many problems left by the long war against France. Ben Bella was an outspoken critic of all manifestations of neo-colonialism and was particularly hostile to the European minority governments of southern Africa. He aligned himself closely with Russia and with her Communist allies, especially Cuba. Yet despite embittering memories of the recent struggle, Algeria retained many links with France. Several thousand French teachers were employed in the schools, and the French continued to exploit the oil of the Algerian Sahara.

In spite of his great international prestige, however, Ben Bella's position within Algeria soon became less secure. The civil war which had followed the winning of independence had left wounds in many parts of the country, particularly among the freedom-loving Berbers of the Kabylia district, whose opposition had been ruthlessly crushed by Ben Bella. There were, besides, many other Algerians who resented his dictatorial methods and his increasing reliance on the help of Communist countries. Ben Bella, who had spent most of the Algerian war in a French jail, had never really won the confidence of the former soldiers of the F.L.N., who disliked taking orders from one whom they regarded as a non-combatant. All these groups of dissatisfied people found a rallying point in the person of Colonel Boumedienne, who early in 1965 staged an almost bloodless *coup d'état*, which toppled Ben Bella from power. The new government represented a compromise in Algerian politics. It contained members of Ben Bella's former administration, as well as army leaders and representatives of other sectional interests. Still, Boumedienne pursued a noticeably less radical course than his predecessor. Internal problems were given more attention and foreign policy much less. The *coup d'état* led to the indefinite postponement of the much heralded conference of Afro-Asian countries, which was to have been a second Bandung and which was to have been held in Algiers in June 1965. China and other countries of the extreme left now refused to attend, claiming that there were too many deep divisions among the Afro-Asian states for such a large-scale meeting to produce any useful results. What they really meant was that it was no longer possible to imagine Algeria as the bridgehead for violent revolutionary movements in Africa.

# 20

## THE ROAD TO INDEPENDENCE (3)

### EAST AFRICA AND THE CONGO

The timing of independence in East and Central Africa was influenced to some extent by developments in North Africa, particularly by the achievement of independence in Somalia. But these influences were late ones. The beginnings of the freedom movement in East Africa were much more closely connected with events in West Africa than in North Africa.

### The influence of Nkrumah

Nkrumah had always made it clear that, once Ghana had achieved its independence, it would be his main objective to lead the rest of Africa to independence and unity. Accordingly, in December 1958 he invited representatives of nationalist movements in twenty-eight territories still under colonial rule to meet at Accra for the first All-African Peoples Conference. Nkrumah was at that time at the height of his influence. He was the undisputed leader of the Pan-African movement. At the Conference, however, he deliberately shared the limelight with Tom Mboya of Kenya, who proved to be a brilliant Chairman. This was the first real demonstration that East Africa was beginning to play a significant part in the African revolution. A few months before, Mboya and Julius Nyerere of Tanganyika had formed the Pan-African Freedom Movement of East and Central Africa, which sent its own delegate to Accra. Kenya and Tanganyika were both, according to Mboya, 'facing a rough patch in the independence struggle', and felt the need for Pan-African support. The Accra Conference set up a body to direct and assist anti-colonial struggles, and planned to establish other regional organisations on the same lines as P.A.F.M.E.C.A. Some African leaders, previously unknown to one another, came away from Accra with a new sense of solidarity and purpose. In particular, Patrice Lumumba returned to the Belgian Congo tremendously impressed by the contacts he had made. The Belgians later admitted that the Accra Conference 'brought decisive results for the Congo. There Lumumba got the support which he needed to implement his demand for independence.'

### East Africa: Mau Mau and multi-racialism

The 'rough patch in the independence struggle' alluded to by Tom Mboya was largely the result of the uncertainty of British policy towards East Africa during the years 1948–58. The British government was slow to understand that the appeal and compulsion of African nationalism were bound to spread from one end of the continent to the other. It knew that the East African territories were economically much poorer, and educationally more backward, than the West African countries. Britain therefore assumed that nationalism in East Africa would be correspondingly slower to develop. Moreover, British thinking about its East African policy was complicated by the settler problem. It was considered that the presence of the settlers demanded that some alternative should be found to the normal pattern of one-man one-vote democracy. This alternative was to be along the lines of the 'multi-racial' type of constitution which we described in Chapter 17. It was thought that this stage of political development would need to last for at least twenty years. This meant for as long ahead as anyone needed to think.

This distinction between the preparedness of West and East Africa for independence seemed to most European minds to be fully justified when, in 1951, there broke out in Kenya the violent insurrection of the Kikuyu people, known as Mau Mau. No observer of the situation denied that the Kikuyu had exceptional grievances. Their numbers had grown steadily throughout the colonial period, and yet the land into which they might have expanded was occupied by settlers' farms. As the East African Royal Commission of 1955 reported, 'Throughout our inquiry we were impressed by the recurring evidence that particular areas were carrying so large a population that agricultural production in them was being retarded, that the natural resources were being destroyed, and that families were unable to find access to new land.' In face of this land shortage large numbers of Kikuyu were driven to seek inadequately paid jobs in the towns, or else on the European farms. In the towns many were unemployed and took to living by crime. These poverty-stricken and land-hungry people looked with understandable envy and resentment upon the settlers' estates. These were large, well-tended and rich. Many of them nevertheless included large areas of uncultivated land.

The Mau Mau rebellion began with the murder of a few British farmers. Their cattle were mutilated, and other acts of violence carried out. All these demonstrations were intended to instil such terror into the settler community that most would leave the country. Very similar events had taken place in Ireland during the nineteenth century. There the landlords had been Englishmen, and the Irish peasants poor and landless. In Kenya the government responded by arresting Jomo Kenyatta and other well-known Kikuyu leaders. They were charged with organising the revolt and were condemned to long terms of imprisonment. Kenyatta strenuously denied the accusation. Certainly his removal from the scene had no obvious effect on the course of events. The active insurgents were comparatively few in number.

They had their bases in the almost impenetrable forests high up the slopes of Mount Kenya and the Aberdare range. From these forests they ventured forth in small bands at the dead of night to swoop on outlying farms, to attack the soldiers who had been sent against them, and, very frequently, to take bloody reprisals against fellow Kikuyu suspected of co-operating with the government. The British would not give way in the face of such tactics. The fact that the enemy was unseen made a resort to counter-terrorism almost inevitable. The Kikuyu peasantry were rounded up from their scattered homesteads and made to live in villages which could be defended and policed. People suspected of collaborating with the insurgents were very roughly interrogated in the attempt to get information. The detention camps for captured insurgents used brutal methods to break the psychological resistance of their inmates—that is, their clinging to ideas that the government considered dangerous. Such is the nature of all secret warfare—it is the same in South Africa today. By the end of 1955 the back of the revolt had been broken, at a cost to Britain of more than £20 million and some hundred British lives. The casualties of the civil war between insurgents and collaborators among the Kikuyu was officially estimated at three thousand, but was reckoned by some reputable observers at ten times that number. Nothing like this had ever happened in West Africa. It was akin to the war in Algeria between the nationalists and the French. Obviously not much progress towards self-government was possible in Kenya while the struggle lasted. On the other hand, the Mau Mau revolt did serve to demonstrate that small bodies of British settlers, like those in Kenya, Tanganyika, Nyasaland and Northern Rhodesia were quite incapable of defending themselves. It also showed that the multi-racial constitutions in these countries would be effective only for so long as British force was available to keep them in being.

Immediately, the most important effect of the Mau Mau revolt on political development in Kenya was to prevent the emergence (until after independence) of a single mass party. While the insurrection lasted, the colonial government, fearing that it would spread to the whole country, permitted political organisations on a regional basis only. By the time the emergency was over, regionalism had developed so far that a deep rift had opened between the Kikuyu and the Luo politicians on the one hand and those of the Kalenjin (Nilo-Hamitic) and coastal Bantu peoples

9                                                                    O & A

on the other. When national politics were again permitted, two rival parties emerged—the Kenya African National Union (K.A.N.U.), and the Kenya African Democratic Union (K.A.D.U.). Because of their mutual distrust, Kenya, which might have been the first, proved in fact to be the last of the East African countries to achieve independence.

Although for different reasons, Uganda was almost as deeply divided as Kenya. There were three contending interests in the territory. The first was the exclusiveness of the kingdom of Buganda. Buganda feared to lose its privileged position in the territory, which it owed to the settlement established by the colonial power. Most of the Buganda politicians found it difficult to work with those from other parts of the country. Secondly, there was the moderate nationalism of the other traditional kingdoms of the south and west. They resented the privileges and aloofness of Buganda, yet felt that they, too, had much to lose from rapid change. Thirdly, there was the less hesitant radicalism of the north and east, where the socialist Uganda Peoples Congress soon found its main support. The alliance which eventually brought about the independence of Uganda was one between the first of these three interests and the third. This, however, was slow to emerge. So Uganda, despite the absence of a settler problem, was by no means in the forefront of the nationalist struggle in East Africa.

The pace-maker on the eastern side of Africa turned out, surprisingly enough, to be Tanganyika, which was economically and educationally far behind its two northern neighbours. Also political consciousness had been much slower to emerge in Tanganyika during the early years of the African revolution. Yet, between 1956 and 1959, Tanganyika not only pushed through from the backward ranks of colonies to the front, but actually set the pattern for all the British territories from Kenya to the Zambezi. Without any doubt, Tanganyika's sudden success was due to the fact that the Tanganyika African National Union (T.A.N.U.), founded by Julius Nyerere in 1954, was by far the most efficiently organised mass party to emerge anywhere in Africa since Nkrumah's C.P.P. Within three or four years of returning to Tanganyika from his studies in Edinburgh, Nyerere had created a nation-wide party structure, with active branches in almost every district in the country. He was helped, as he said himself, by the fact that the population was divided among more than 120 tribal groupings, of which none had been large enough, or central enough, to acquire a predominant position. He was helped, too, by the Swahili language. As a result of the Arab penetration of the nineteenth century and the educational policies of the German and British colonial governments, Swahili was understood throughout the length and breadth of the land. He was helped, finally, by the fact that so little in the way of political organisation had been attempted before. He was able to start with 'a clean slate'.

From the first, the weight of Nyerere's attack was directed against the 'multi-racial' conception of constitutional advance. As the United Nations Mission of 1954 stated in its report, 'The Africans of this country would like to be assured, both by the United Nations Organisation and by the Administering Authority, that this territory, though multi-racial in population, is primarily an African country and must be developed as such.' During the next four years Nyerere strove by a remarkable moderation to show that, while T.A.N.U. stood for government by the African majority, non-Africans would have nothing to fear from such a government. Nyerere preached this doctrine with such success that in the elections of 1958, held under the existing 'multi-racial' constitution, all the contested seats were won either by T.A.N.U. candidates or by those non-Africans who received T.A.N.U. support in exchange for an undertaking to collaborate with T.A.N.U. when elected. The result of the elections coincided with the appointment of a new Governor, Sir Richard Turnbull, who saw, as Arden-Clarke had seen in the Gold Coast in 1951, that the turning-point in the country's development had now been reached. In October 1958 Turnbull announced that, when self-government was attained, Tanganyika would be ruled by its African majority. Nyerere enthusiastically welcomed this statement saying:

We have always waited for a Governor of this country even to indicate that it was the government's policy that, when self-government is eventually achieved, the Africans will have a predominant say in the affairs of the country. Now the Africans have this assurance, I am confident that it is going to be the endeavour of the Africans, if non-Africans have any fears left, to remove them quickly.

Under the guidance of Nyerere and Turnbull, who worked together in the same spirit as Nkrumah and Arden-Clarke, Tanganyika fairly rushed out of the colonial era. Full independence was achieved in December 1961, after an apprenticeship of little more than three years. This was in a country with a population larger than Ghana's, but with less than a tenth of the number of university and secondary-school graduates.

Obviously, once the multi-racial system had been abandoned in Tanganyika, it could do longer be seriously defended in Kenya or Uganda. Nor could it be defended in Nyasaland or Northern Rhodesia, the two northern territories of the Central African Federation which had been formed in 1953 (see Chapter 21). The new trend in British policy as a whole was recognised when, early in 1959, Iain Macleod succeeded Alan Lennox Boyd as Colonial Secretary. Whereas Lennox Boyd's policy had been to strive for every additional year of colonial rule that could be gained, Macleod's was to free Britain from responsibilities in Africa with all possible speed. The 1960 Kenya Constitution which bears his name provided for an African majority in the Legislative Assembly. 'At one swift blow,' said a leader of the settlers, 'power was transferred to the Africans.' Further political changes in Kenya, as also in Uganda, were delayed only by disagreements among the Africans themselves. In Kenya, not even the release of Kenyatta in August 1961 could break the deadlock between K.A.N.U. and K.A.D.U. When the country became independent in December 1963, it was under a compromise constitution which provided for considerable regional autonomy. In Uganda Milton Obote, the founder of the Uganda Peoples Congress, succeeded in 1962 in making an alliance with the royalist Buganda Kabaka Yekka Party. This alliance at last carried the country to independence with the Kabaka of Buganda as head of state.

Britain completed her decolonisation of East Africa in December 1963 by granting independence to Zanzibar under a constitution which left the Arab Sultan as head of state. The government was formed by an obviously precarious alliance between the political party directed by the old Arab ruling minority and the smaller of two parties representing the African majority of the population. As we shall see in Chapter 22, this government was to last less than two months before being violently overthrown by a Communist-inspired revolution. Here at least, the British were to blame for moving out too soon.

## The Congo

While East Africa was hurrying along the path to independence, an even more sudden and perilous emancipation from colonial rule was taking place in the Congo. Until 1957 the Belgians had continued to rule their huge colony as if it were completely isolated from the changes taking place elsewhere in Africa. When in 1956 a Lecturer at the Colonial University in Antwerp, Dr A. A. J. van Bilsen, published a 'Thirty Year Plan for the Political Emancipation of Belgian Africa' he was attacked in Belgium as a dangerous revolutionary. Van Bilsen based his time-table on the perfectly correct notion that 'in the Congo and Ruanda-Urundi the formation of an *élite* and of responsible, directing *cadres* is a generation behind the British and French territories'. Yet, four years after van Bilsen had made this statement, the Belgian authorities who had attacked him for his imprudent haste had left the Congo to fend for itself. On the eve of Congo independence in 1960, the Belgian Prime Minister implicitly acknowledged his country's failure: 'if we could have counted at this moment on proper organisations at a provincial level, the political solutions for the Congo would have been greatly facilitated'.

The independence of the Congo was in fact far from being a triumph of African nationalism. It was, rather, a result of Belgian irresolution, and of the inability of a small country like Belgium to stand up to international pressures. The first crack in the wall of Belgian paternalism came in 1957, when Africans took part for the first time in municipal elections. Kasabuvu, who had built up a position of political leadership among the Bakongo people of the lower Congo, was returned as Mayor of one of the Leopoldville *communes* (municipalities). This was typical of what happened elsewhere. An American observer wrote: 'Almost every party formed in the Congo had its origin in a tribal group, and since there were many tribes, there were many parties. Local interests were paramount and never ceased to be a powerful factor in politics.' Patrice Lumumba, who emerged at the same period as a political leader in Stanleyville, was the only Congolese politician who had a clear vision of the importance of creating a single, nationwide party. To succeed, he would have needed not only time, but also some prolonged resistance from the Belgian colonial government, in order to force other Congolese politicians to see the necessity for such a party. This resistance, however, was not forthcoming.

In August 1958 de Gaulle visited Brazzaville, just across the river from Leopoldville, to proclaim autonomy within the French Community for the four colonies which had formed the Federation of French Equatorial Africa. Naturally, this provoked unrest on the Belgian side. Many of the little tribal parties began to demand independence for the Congo. Strikes and disorders broke out, and in January 1959, less than a month after Lumumba's return from the Accra Conference, there was a serious riot in Leopoldville. Mobs of unemployed people sacked European shops and mission schools. The situation in the capital was brought under control in less than a week, but the blow to Belgian prestige was great. During the year that followed it became evident that law and order in many parts of the country was on the verge of breakdown. Some of the most dangerous situations were the result of tension between rival groups of Congolese. In the Kasai Province, for example, a civil war threatened between the Kasai Baluba, who were employed in the diamond mines, and the Benelulua, who worked on the oil-palm plantations. The Benelulua regarded the Baluba as intruders into their country. Again, in the Mandated Territory of Ruanda-Urundi an extreme state of tension was developing between the Batutsi ruling class and the Bahutu majority of the population. The Batutsi had maintained their social and political predominance under both German and Belgian rule, and their object, like that of the settlers in Rhodesia, was to gain political independence for the territory before the introduction of a universal franchise destroyed their ascendancy. The Belgians reacted to the steadily growing defiance of the Batutsi by suddenly switching their support to the newly formed Bahutu political movement, but they were unable to control the situation which resulted. All over the country, but especially in the north, the Batutsi were massacred by their former subjects, their houses burnt, their possessions looted, while the Belgian administration looked on, unable or unwilling to intervene. By the end of 1959, therefore, Belgian Africa presented a very different picture from that of 1956. It is true that the disorders had all been local ones. It is also true that to a larger power than Belgium these disorders would not have appeared impossible to suppress. But to Belgium, in the words of a government spokesman, they presented a terrifying alternative: 'to try to organise independence as quickly as possible, or to accept responsibility for the bloodshed which any delay would probably bring about. A colonial war entails heavy financial losses, which a small nation cannot afford. We are fearful lest another Algeria might develop in the Congo.'

At the beginning of 1960, therefore, the Belgian government summoned a group of Congolese political leaders to a 'Round Table Conference' in Ostend. Several of the Africans who took part have stated that they went to Belgium expecting to settle for a five-year transitional period leading up to independence. They would have been willing to accept this. But Belgium was by this time disillusioned with the Congo. It was not prepared to take the responsibility of continuing to govern the country while Congolese political parties united themselves, or while Congolese civil servants were trained to take over administrative duties from the Belgians. Above all, Belgium was not prepared to send any more troops to suppress the disorders that would certainly grow worse. While the conference was meeting, a cry went up throughout the country of 'Pas un soldat au Congo' ('Not a single soldier to Congo'), The Congolese negotiators at the Round Table Conference found no resistance against which they could bargain, no strength that would force them to unite. They came away with a date for independence which was less than six months away— 30 June 1960.

In May 1960 there were held the first national elections ever to take place in the Congo. The results were indecisive, but a few days before the end of Belgian rule Lumumba, after lengthy negotiations, succeeded in forming a government with himself as Prime Minister, and Kasavubu, his chief rival, as President. Even the independence ceremonies were a disaster. A paternal speech from King Baudouin provoked the bitter reply from Lumumba, 'Nous ne sommes plus vos singes' ('We are no longer your monkeys'). Six days later the Congolese army, the *Force Publique*, mutinied. 'It all started', said Lumumba, 'when General Janssens, the Belgian Commander, refused to promote Congolese to the rank of officer.' The soldiers turned upon the Belgian officers and their families. Whereupon Belgian troops intervened to protect Europeans and their property. With the collapse of law and order, all the old hatreds and humiliations came to the surface. Africans avenged themselves on Europeans, and different peoples within the Congo fought each other. The worst inter-African conflict took place in the Kasai, where the tension between Baluba and Benelulua now broke out into open warfare. The political struggle between the regionalists and the centralists, which was so much a feature of this period of African history (in Kenya and French West Africa, for example) became charged with danger in the Congo. Kasavubu of the Bakongo, Kalonji of the Baluba and Tshombe in Katanga all wanted to set up a loose federal structure, in which real power would reside with the provincial and tribal groups. Lumumba, on the other hand, tried to work for a strong, centralised state. On 11 July Tshombe withdrew Katanga from the Congo, and declared its independence. This move received the backing of the *Union Minière*, the huge company which controlled the Katanga copper mines. The Congo government thus lost the greater part of its revenues. Lumumba called upon the United Nations for military help to halt the disintegration of the country and to rid the country of the Belgian troops which had intervened in the mutiny. Thus the United Nations entered the most critical operation in its history. Wisely, it called for most of its contingents of soldiers to be sent from the African states. But when these forces did not do exactly as Lumumba wished, he turned to Russia for assistance. The chaotic situation in the Congo thus became a matter for world-wide concern, introducing the rivalries between Communism and Capitalism into the heart of the African continent. This made the African states more determined to follow a neutral path, but the Congo crisis produced deep divisions in their ranks, as we shall see in the concluding chapter. As early as 1960 Nkrumah remarked prophetically, 'Once we admit our impotence to solve the question of the Congo primarily with our African resources, we tacitly admit that real self-government on the African continent is impossible.'

The calling in of the Russians proved the downfall of Lumumba. Hitherto Belgian and other Western influences had been confined to a veiled support of Tshombe's secessionist movement in Katanga. Henceforward, these influences, with American backing, began to intervene in the affairs of the central Congolese government. Lumumba was overthrown by an alliance between the army, led by Colonel Mobutu, and many of the regional politicians, headed by Kasabuvu. The Russians were expelled. Lumumba was arrested and handed over to Tshombe, in whose custody he was murdered in March 1961. Faced with the problem of the central government's bankruptcy, the United Nations at last began to intervene more forcefully to break the secession of Katanga. It was only in 1963, however, after much heavy fighting, that this province was occupied and reunited with the Congo state. By this time it was the United Nations that was bankrupt.

A number of its richer member states, including Russia and France, had refused to contribute to the Congo operations. Those who did contribute (Britain and America especially) were suspected of paying the piper in order to call the tune; that is, of using the United Nations in order to achieve their own aims. The United Nations had no option but to withdraw from the Congo. Left to itself, the central government could not hope to hold the all-important Katanga region by force. The unity and the solvency of the country could only be maintained by admitting Tshombe and his supporters to the central government on their own terms.

Meanwhile in Rwanda, and to a lesser extent in Burundi, tension between the Batutsi and the Bahutu continued to grow. Attempts to form the two little countries into one independent state failed, and they went their separate ways. The United Nations supervised the final stages of the transition to independence. In Rwanda the previously subservient majority of the population overthrew with fearful violence the Batutsi monarchy and proclaimed a republic. In Burundi the monarchy survived, but was constitutionalised. Both states achieved independence in 1962. In Rwanda this at first served merely to intensify the harrying of the Batutsi, most of whom were driven as refugees into neighbouring countries.

## Madagascar

As we have seen in previous chapters, Madagascar has had in many ways a history rather separate from that of the African mainland. The population of the island is largely non-African, the language entirely so. At least since the beginning of the nineteenth century there has been little coming and going across the Mozambique Channel. During the colonial period, when it was under French rule, Madagascar was a kind of half-way house between the French territories in West Africa and those in South-East Asia and the Pacific. From the time of the Second World War, however, the isolation of Madagascar from the rest of Africa began at last to be broken down. During the war the island experienced the occupation of British forces, many of them African. After the war Malagasy students began to go in some numbers to France. There they encountered French-speaking students from the West African territories, with whom they felt more akin than with the South-East Asians. Most important of all, perhaps, was the fact that the timing of Madagascar's struggle for independence coincided with the African revolution rather than with the Asian one. The first modern political party with independence as its object was founded in 1946. This party had its first trial of strength with the French in the following year, when a famine caused by the mismanagement of the government-controlled Rice Board gave rise to a violent rebellion. The revolt sprang up all over the island, among many different groups, including the aristocratic Hova, as a spontaneous reaction to colonial rule. The ferocity of the French military action against the rebels led to a still more widespread insurrection, which took nearly a year to repress. Many aspects of the Malagasy rebellion were similar to the earliest anti-colonial rebellions, such as the Maji–Maji outbreak in German East Africa in 1905–6. The Maji-Maji rebels thought that the German bullets would be harmlessly turned into water. Similarly, during the Malagasy rebellion:

When the rebels, armed only with pointed sticks, went in to attack troops armed with rifles and machine-guns, they advanced in step in serried ranks shouting '*Rano, Rano*', which means 'Water, Water', as a magical formula intended to turn the bullets into water as they left the guns. Even some of the French soldiers began to have doubts and to panic when their fire proved ineffective through faulty aiming or the use of old cartridges.

(O. Mannoni, *Prospero and Caliban*, p. 59.)

After the great rebellion, Madagascar entered upon a remarkably smooth transition from colonial rule to self-government, and then to independence. Much of the credit for this is due to the moderation of one remarkable personality, Philibert Tsiranana, who, in common with many other African leaders, began his career as a teacher. He was opposed to the rebellion and, after its repression, used all his gifts to heal the deep scars. His Social Democratic Party co-operated with the French in implementing reforms introduced under the *Loi Cadre* of 1956, and some of the Malagasy who had been sentenced by the French to long terms of imprisonment for instigating the rebellion became ministers in his Cabinet. In the de Gaulle Referendum of 1958 he was supported, not only by the Malagasy, but also by many of the 80,000 French settlers on the island. When the country became independent in June 1960, Tsiranana became the first President. The only serious opposition to his government has come from the Hova people of the highlands around the capital. These former rulers of the island are still the best educated and the most sophisticated group. They are mainly Protestant, while the majority of the population is

Roman Catholic. These religious and social tensions have not yet been resolved. Nevertheless Madagascar, as we shall see in the final chapter of this book, is now an important and unequivocal member of the community of African states. It plays a leading part both in the union of French-speaking African states (the *Union Africaine et Malgache*) and also in the Organisation for African Unity. These ancient colonists from across the Indian Ocean have at long last been assimiliated into Africa.

## 21

## THE WHITE-DOMINATED SOUTH

During the years between 1960 and 1965, while the rest of Africa was moving rapidly towards independence under African governments, most of southern Africa was moving still further in the opposite direction. To understand why this was so, one has first of all to imagine the difference in outlook between a colonial power based in Europe and a self-governing community of white people living as a ruling minority in an African country. The government of a colonial power has many other things to worry about besides its colonies. It has to rule its own country to the satisfaction of the electorate, and it has to conduct its relations successfully with the outside world. Its colonies are a very marginal interest. Colonial affairs do not sway many votes at a general election, and if colonies are troubled, the government is more likely to lose votes on their account than to gain them. Troubled colonies are expensive. Colonial wars are unpopular, both internally with the electorate and externally with foreign powers. It is difficult to recruit civil servants to go and work in troubled colonies. For all these reasons the staying-power of a European-based colonial system is very slight. As soon as a colony becomes more troublesome to rule than it is worth, the politicians of the colonising country will want to cut their losses and leave.

The outlook of a self-governing minority is quite different. Here the centre of power is locally based. Here the soldiers, the policemen and the civil servants are all employed by the local government, which is elected by the local white community. This local community has one overriding interest, which is the maintenance

of its own highly privileged way of life. Beside this all other considerations are subsidiary. It does not mind using forceful methods
in suppressing revolt. It does not mind antagonising the outside
world. In the transfer of power to the black majority it sees
the certain end of the life it has always known. It sees the
abolition of privilege, the confiscation of property, and a general
turning of the tables which will leave most of its members with
no option but to try and start life afresh as refugees in another
continent. To prevent this, it is prepared to fight and to kill, and
if need be to be killed. If there are a few people in such a community who can see further then their own immediate interests,
their voices are not heard and they do not become members of
parliament. It is therefore not surprising that in southern Africa
the main result of the African revolution in the lands to the north
was to stiffen the forces of white supremacy. Only in Northern
Rhodesia and Nyasaland, where the British Colonial Office still
shared power with the government of the Central African Federation, did African majorities succeed in winning independence and
majority rule.

### South Africa: apartheid

South Africa, it has been said, has suffered from the effects of
three evils—Land, Labour and Legislation. In Chapter 15 it was
shown how the Africans, who formed over two-thirds of the
population, were allowed the use of less than 13 per cent of the
land. It was also shown how their labour, so vital to the economy
of South Africa, was paid at a far lower rate than white workmen
received. As to legislation, there were many discriminatory laws
before 1948. During the eighteen years (to 1966) of National
Party rule, however, the volume of *apartheid* legislation has been
almost incredible. *Apartheid* (Afrikaans, separation) was the
political slogan of the National Party, but there was little that was
new about the idea. The South African Bureau of Race Relations,
which was closely connected with Dr Verwoerd, defined *apartheid*
as: 'The territorial separation of Europeans and Bantu, and the
provision of areas which must serve as national and political
homes for the different Bantu communities and as permanent
residential areas for the Bantu population or the major proportion
of it.' This was an idealistic way of looking at *apartheid*. Strijdom,
the Prime Minister before Verwoerd, was more frank and
realistic: 'Call it paramountcy, *baaskap* or what you will, it is
still domination. I am being as blunt as I can. I am making no

excuses. Either the white man dominates or the black man takes over.'

The National Party's combination of White South African racialism and Afrikaner nationalism made it electorally unbeatable, as some three-fifths of the White population are Afrikaans-speakers. The National Party has gained support in every election since 1948. By the end of the 1950s the government had eliminated all non-white people from exercising the right to vote even in the Cape Province. Political rights in the country as a whole are for whites only. Faced with mounting criticism from the Asian and African members, Verwoerd withdrew South Africa, which had become a republic in 1960, from the Commonwealth in 1961. This had long been the aim of many Afrikaners, ever since their own traditional republics had been brought under British rule in the 1899–1902 war, and so into the Union.

The great mass of *apartheid* legislation affected the daily lives of every African, Indian and coloured person in the country. The different races were forced to move to separate areas in the towns, and the non-whites were not allowed to use the same transport and other facilities as the white people. They were not permitted to compete with them for jobs. Opposition, from the small group of liberal Europeans, as well as from the other peoples, was suppressed under a variety of new laws. White South Africans developed a fear of Communism which was hardly justified by the actual threat of Communists to their rule. The Communist Party was declared illegal. Any criticism of the government's racial policies was considered to be Communist inspired, whether the criticism came from professed Communists or not. By naming any opponent as a Communist, the Minister of Justice could ban him from all public affairs. People were imprisoned without trial, or kept under house-arrest. One of the most far-reaching *apartheid* measures was the Bantu Education Act of 1953, which took African education out of missionary control, and made it an instrument of government policy in reshaping men's minds. Verwoerd, then Minister of Native Affairs, said of the Act:

Racial relations cannot improve if the wrong type of education is given to the Natives. They cannot improve if the result of Native education is the creation of frustrated people who as a result of the education they receive have expectations in life which circumstances in South Africa do not allow to be fulfilled immediately, when it creates people who are trained for professions not open to them.

Africans, therefore, were to be given an inferior kind of education, to fit them for their chief function in South Africa, that of labourers. The frustrations endured by Africans led to a series of disturbances in 1959–60, which culminated in March 1960 when Africans demonstrating against the Pass Laws at Sharpeville were fired upon by the police.

Moderate African opposition was ruthlessly swept aside. By 1959 initiative in the resistance to European domination had passed from Luthuli's African National Congress to the Pan-Africanist Congress, which believed in militant action, or to even more extreme groups. The African leaders who might still have attempted to come to terms with white South Africans, such as Nelson Mandela, were imprisoned for life following the Rivonia trial of 1964–5. Increasingly, African opposition has taken the only course open to it, that of violence and terrorism. Faced with outspoken criticism from the rest of the world, Verwoerd, far from relenting, pressed on with what were called the positive aspects of *apartheid*. These were the creation of African 'home-lands' or Bantustans, for the various African language groups. This was a mid-twentieth century application of the old colonial policy of 'divide and rule'. The government was at pains to explain its policy:

The right to self-determination, like liberty, is indivisible. If all African peoples are entitled to self-determination, it is true also for the White South African nation. In the South African situation a way has to be found in which hitherto dependent Bantu peoples can achieve their autonomy without jeopardising the independent nationhood of the Whites. The ultimate aim is the co-operative association of independent Bantu states and a White nation—a Commonwealth of South Africa.

The first such territory, the Xhosa-speaking Transkei, was established in 1963. The following year elections were held, in which a political group which supported the *apartheid* principle was narrowly returned. But Africans in the Transkei enjoyed only a limited form of self-government. Real power remained with the white South African Government. The dilemma that faced the upholders of *apartheid* was that economically South Africa was an integrated society. On the one hand the towns and industrial areas were considered to belong to white South Africans. Nevertheless, very large numbers of Africans and other groups permanently resided in these towns and industrial regions, which were economically dependent upon cheap African labour. On the other hand Africans in the overcrowded 'homelands' relied upon money sent to them by their relatives and friends who worked in the mines and factories. They could not stand economically upon their own feet.

Since the Second World War the South African government has looked upon the Mandated territory of South-West Africa as a fifth province of South Africa. It has refused to acknowledge the United Nations' rights and responsibilities in the territory. In 1960 Ethiopia and Liberia, the only black African states which had been members of the League of Nations, brought a suit in the International Court to test South Africa's right to rule South-West Africa. In July 1966, after six years of proceedings, the Court decided by one vote that Ethiopia and Liberia had no right to bring the case. Meanwhile the territory has been to all intents incorporated within South Africa. *Apartheid* measures, including plans to set up Bantustans, have been applied extensively in South-West Africa.

The British Protectorates of Basutoland, Swaziland and Bechuanaland are situated within South Africa, or are neighbouring to it. They were developed by Britain along constitutional lines towards self-government in spite of their poverty and small size or small population. All three attained internal self-government by 1964–5. In 1966 Basutoland became independent under the name of Lesotho, and Bechuanaland under the name of Botswana. Swaziland became independent in 1968. All three territories, however, will remain in practice dependent, economically and for their communications with the outside world, upon South Africa. Nevertheless, in spite of their vulnerability Lesotho, Botswana and Swaziland will be hopeful examples of self-governing states to Africans in the Republic of South Africa.

## The Central African Federation

The coming to power of the National Party in 1948 finally alienated English-speaking Rhodesians from the idea of joining South Africa. This had been considered off and on for many years, especially in the early 1920s, as a solution to their basic problem, that of being outnumbered by about fifteen to one by the African population. White Rhodesian settlers objected not so much to the extreme racial policies of the South African government, but to its anti-British and republican sentiments. Sir Godfrey Huggins (later Lord Malvern), leader of the South Rhodesians, now joined forces with Sir Roy Welensky of Northern Rhodesia in reviving schemes for the union of their territories. They argued that although in Northern Rhodesia and Nyasaland the European populations were even smaller than in Southern Rhodesia, it would be preferable to control these predominantly African lands, difficult though this might be, than have them as independent neighbours. The settlers hoped that a large Federation would soon become a fully amalgamated Dominion free from British control. They also wanted the economic benefits that were expected to result from a federation of the three territories, with the opportunities for further white settlement which this would create.

The British government supported the federal scheme for wider reasons. Certainly the economic advantages counted for much and were used to try to persuade Africans to consent to the plan. It was stressed how interdependent the three territories had become. The Rhodesias were dependent upon Nyasaland for labour, the two northern countries upon Southern Rhodesia for manufactured goods and some agricultural products, and the copper mines upon Southern Rhodesian coal and transportation. An even closer economic union, it was argued, must result in improved living standards for all the inhabitants, African as well as European. Further, Britain was genuinely concerned to develop a large multi-racial community as a bastion of good sense and moderation against the harsh racial policies of South Africa. This was the period of multi-racial constitutions in the East African territories (see Chapter 17), and the Federation that came into being in 1953 was an attempt to swing Central Africa out of the South African into the East African orbit. Britain was aware of the racialism of the Rhodesian settlers, and of the opposition of the majority of Africans to the idea of Federation. In spite of warnings of European intentions and of African fears, the British government sincerely hoped that the benefits of political stability and economic expansion would soften the former and allay the latter. Moreover, by stopping short of amalgamation, at Federation, it kept a live interest in the administration of the two northern territories, which gave it the ultimate power to put the process into reverse.

The economic growth of the Federation was, as expected, rapid. New industries were developed in Southern Rhodesia, and towns (especially Salisbury, the Federal capital) increased in size. One of the world's largest dams was constructed at Kariba on the Zambezi, to provide cheap electricity for the copper mines of Northern Rhodesia and the industries of Southern Rhodesia. Africans shared less in this expansion than did Europeans. In 1961 the average annual income of wage-earning Europeans was estimated at £1,209, whilst the average for wage-earning Africans was £87. Many Africans were not even wage-earners. Economically, Nyasaland, especially, had reasons to be dissatisfied. 'Federation,' wrote the Canadian economist Thomas Franck in 1960,

has meant to Nyasaland nothing more than a paltry subsidy—less than £4 million a year—from the Federal Government. Is it for that that the proud people of Nyasaland have been asked to give up their hopes of national independence and told to throw in their lot with a handful of white rulers living hundreds of miles away?

(Franck, *Race and Nationalism*, p. 324.)

Within ten years the two contending forces of settler intransigence and African nationalism destroyed the new state. The European politicians who controlled both the Federal and the Southern Rhodesian Parliaments were determined to maintain European supremacy. 'Political control,' wrote Lord Malvern in 1956, 'must remain in the hands of civilised people, which for the foreseeable future means the Europeans.' Welensky likened the Federation not to a partnership of equals, but to the relationship existing between rider and horse, the African being the horse! He was a skilful politician, and when the franchise qualifications were amended in 1957, he appeared to give Africans a greater representation, while in fact decreasing the value of the African vote. He made it clear that, at the 1960 conference to revise the Federal Constitution, he would demand independence from the last traces of British control. African resentment at Welensky's past performance and future threats came to a head early in 1959, soon after the return of Dr Banda to Nyasaland after an absence of over forty years. Demonstrations, strikes and riots led to States of Emergency being proclaimed in Southern Rhodesia and Nyasaland, and to the detention without trial of many African nationalist politicians.

The settlers maintained that opposition to the Federation came only from a handful of 'extremists'. Many people in Britain shared this belief. The Devlin Commission, which inquired into the Nyasaland troubles, rejected it:

The government's view is that these nationalist aspirations are the thoughts of only a small minority of political Africans, mainly of self-seekers who think their prospects of office will be worse under Federation; and that the great majority of the people are indifferent to the issue. We have not found this to be so. It was generally acknowledged that the opposition to Federation was there, that it was deeply rooted and almost universally held.

The 1959 Emergencies were the dividing line in the fortunes of the Federation. Early the following year the Belgians decided to pull out of the neighbouring Congo. By this time the British government had lost faith in the multi-racial experiments in Tanganyika and Kenya. Harold Macmillan, the British Prime Minister, during his 1960 African tour, was critical of the lack of progress towards genuine partnership in the Federation. He ended his tour in Cape Town, where he delivered his famous 'Wind of Change' speech before the white South African members of parliament:

We have seen the awakening of national consciousness in peoples who have for centuries lived in dependence upon some other power. Fifteen years ago this movement spread through Asia. Many countries there of different races and civilizations pressed their claim to an independent life. Today the same thing is happening in Africa and the most striking of all the impressions I have formed since I left London a month ago is of the strength of this African national consciousness. The wind of change is blowing through this continent, and whether we like it or not this growth of national consciousness is a political fact, and our national policies must take account of it.

Macmillan's speech surprised and annoyed white South Africans, but it did not produce any results in that country. North of the Limpopo it marked a further stage in the decline of the Federation. The Monckton Commission, which was sent to look into the workings of the Federation, considered that, for Africans, 'partnership was a sham'. The commission recommended that if all else failed, the territories should have the right to secede. Iain Macleod, the Colonial Secretary who was responsible for the departure from the multi-racial idea in Kenya (see Chapter 20), decided that the Federation should not stand in the way of the two northern territories attaining African majority rule. Under Banda's leadership, Africans in Nyasaland achieved this in 1961. The Northern Rhodesian settlers, with Welensky's help, delayed a similar development in that country. By 1963, however, Kenneth Kaunda, who had built up a great reputation for his statesmanship, led Northern Rhodesia to this position. He and Banda made it clear that they would take the earliest opportunity to withdraw from the Federation. The British government appointed R. A. Butler as a special minister to preside over its dismantling. On the last day of 1963 the Federation came to an end. Nyasaland became independent as Malawi. Northern Rhodesia followed as the Republic of Zambia in October 1964. The Rhodesian settlers, who from now on left the 'Southern' out of the name of their country, retained an even stronger hold over the Africans living between the Zambezi and the Limpopo. At the same time they demanded that Britain should grant the European dominated government of Rhodesia its independence.

Britain had entered into the Federal scheme sincere in its hopes that it would solve the racial as well as the economic problems of Central Africa. When it became clear that the Federal government was pursuing policies which resulted in an increase of racial tensions, Britain moved decisively to bring the association to an end. In the event, Malawi and Zambia followed quickly in the footsteps of the West African states in becoming fully independent. Rhodesia (Southern) reverted to its pre-1953 position, but in a continent that was much more hostile to it.

Within Rhodesia, the break-up of the Federation had destroyed the credit of the white politicians who had supported it, and this cleared the way for the emergence of more extreme leaders who wanted to consolidate white power along South African lines by closing the possibility of even a slow advance by Africans towards a voting majority. Since such a course would involve the passing of discriminatory legislation, which would certainly be vetoed by the British government under the powers reserved to it in 1923, it followed that the first aim of the new leaders must be to gain their total independence from Britain. For two and a half years successive Rhodesian governments attempted to secure this independence by negotiation, but without success. Finally, on 11 November 1965, the government of Mr Ian Smith attempted to seize it by a long-threatened unilateral declaration. The opening paragraph of the declaration intentionally echoed the United States' Declaration of Independence of 1776:

Whereas in the course of human affairs history has shown it may become necessary for a people to resolve the political affiliations which have connected them with another people and to assume among other nations the separate and equal status to which they are entitled...

These and other statements in Smith's declaration must have seemed bitterly ironic to the African majority of Rhodesians.

The Rhodesian U.D.I., as was to be expected, produced a crisis of world-wide proportions. Here, as the finale to the long chapter of African liberation movements, was a minority of 250,000 white Rhodesians asserting their right to rule in independence over four million black fellow-citizens. Yet no country in the outside world was prepared to intervene by force of arms. The British government refused to recognise the act, and successfully prevented its recognition in all other capitals of the world including those of South Africa and Portugal. Working through the United Nations, it went on to organise a series of financial and commercial sanctions, which were agreed to by most governments, but which were not always enforced by those governments upon their own citizens. The sanctions war reached a climax in April 1966, when the United Nations authorised Britain to use force against tankers carrying oil for Rhodesia to the Mozambique port of Beira. A year after U.D.I., however, it seemed that sanctions were not affecting the Rhodesian economy drastically enough to bring down the Smith government in any near future. Essential supplies, including oil, were still flowing into Rhodesia from South Africa. A successful blockade of South African ports would have involved a substantial proportion of the navies of the great powers, and no such solution was attempted.

Meanwhile the Rhodesian U.D.I. was, needless to say, provoking a crisis of unprecedented intensity in the African states to the north of the Zambezi. But it was primarily a crisis of frustration. The African states knew that they did not have the strength to intervene militarily in Rhodesia by themselves. The country most closely affected was of course Zambia, which was dependent on the Rhodesian railways for the export of most of its copper and for most of its essential imports. Zambia was also the only African-ruled country through which Rhodesia could be invaded. The Zambian government found itself under heavy pressure from the more militant African states to receive contingents of 'freedom fighters', who would attempt to stir the African population of Rhodesia into active resistance to the Smith regime. This Zambia, for reasons of her own internal security, was unwilling to permit. President Kaunda therefore took his stand on the proposition that Rhodesia was a British responsibility, and offered his territory as the base for a British attack. Most other African states joined

Zambia in pressing Britain by every means to suppress the Rhodesian rebellion by force. Following a meeting of the O.A.U. in December 1965, some of them, perhaps too hastily, broke off diplomatic relations. Others threatened, and still threaten, to leave the Commonwealth. At the time of writing, however, Britain seems no more likely to use force against Rhodesia than she ever did. To do so would be a major operation, entailing sacrifices which the majority of her electorate would not support. The Rhodesian crisis, therefore, seems more likely to poison the relations of African states with Britain than to bring any immediate relief to the black Rhodesians. Zambia is determined to forge new road and rail links with Tanzania, which will reduce her economic dependence on Rhodesia. If these measures are successful, the Zambezi will become the economic as well as the political dividing-line between white and black Africa until such time as the black Rhodesians are able to take the lead in freeing themselves.

## Portuguese Africa

In this period at least, the Portuguese empire in Africa proved an exception to the rule that a colonial system based in Europe would not resist the onslaught of African nationalism. The reasons for this are interesting. First, Portugal is one of the poorest countries of Europe. It has few industries, and a standard of living not much higher than many African countries. Unlike other colonial powers, its colonial interests are not marginal, but central to its economic existence. Secondly, the Portuguese state is a dictatorship. The Portuguese people, accustomed to authoritarianism at home, are unmoved by authoritarian rule in the colonies. Dr Salazar, who has been Prime Minister of Portugal since 1932, has consistently played upon feelings of national pride and glorified the achievements of the Portuguese imperial past as an inducement to future greatness. As long ago as 1934 he announced:

The prestige of Portugal will shine forever. Everywhere the pride of being Portuguese will quicken the life-blood of the people and will vouchsafe peace and repose to the ashes of our heroes who are no longer with us. To reach our goal we have to experience a far-reaching revolution in economics, politics, ideas, customs, institutions, and in our collective life.

This programme was to apply to the colonies as to Portugal itself. Portuguese Africa was at that time almost completely undeveloped, and was a financial burden to Portugal. Public works, sugar and other estates, and the few mines, were operated largely by forced labour. In the 1930s and 1940s a spate of colonial legislation from Lisbon gave the impression of great change, but merely laid the foundations for future growth. The development of Angola and Mozambique in the 1950s was considerable. The motives for this development were suggested by Salazar in 1943: 'The rich, extensive colonial lands, under-developed and sparsely populated, are the natural complement for metropolitan agriculture. In addition they will take care of Portugal's excessive population.' Large numbers of Portuguese migrated to the African territories. By 1960 there were over 200,000 settlers in Angola, and 90,000 in Mozambique. The African populations were 4,500,000 and 6,200,000 respectively. Both colonies had become settler territories, in many ways like Southern Rhodesia, though without self-government. Agricultural and mining development (the most important being the Angolan diamond mines) remained firmly in European hands. Portugal's racial policy was in theory similar to the French policy of assimilation. The status of citizen, however, conferred few political rights, in Portugal or in the colonies. To become a citizen an African had to comply with a whole range of educational, economic and religious tests. Schools, moreover, were so few, and economic opportunities for Africans so lacking, that only a small number of Africans became *assimilados* (assimilated people). By 1950 there were only 30,000 *assimilados* in Angola and 25,000 in Mozambique. The vast majority of the population were *indigenas* (natives), whose main function in the eyes of the administration was to provide labour. Much was made of the virtue of work. In 1943 a Colonial Minister said, 'If we want to civilise the native we must make him adopt, as an elementary moral precept, the notion that he has no right to live without working.' The economic expansion of the colonies greatly benefited Portugal itself, about 25 per cent of the national budget being derived from Africa. In 1951 the colonies were theoretically incorporated into Portugal as overseas 'provinces', but the inferior status of the African *indigenas* continued.

Like the Belgians in the Congo, but with far more determination, the Portuguese refused to heed the course of events in the rest of Africa. In November 1960, a few months after Macmillan's 'Wind of Change' speech, it was declared: 'We are not in Africa like so many others. We will continue as always our policy of integration. To this end it is necessary for us to be what we have always been, and we will not change.' In February 1961 serious rioting occurred in Luanda, and in March a widespread revolt broke out in northern Angola; there was a similar uprising in Portuguese Guinea. Forty thousand Portuguese troops were used to crush the Angolan rebellion, which received support from the neighbouring Congo, as well as from other African states. Most of the fighting was over by the end of 1963. It was perhaps the most bitter experience in modern African history, except for the Algerian war. Fortunately for Portugal, the Angolan nationalist groups were divided by rivalries, as were the groups that formed the Mozambique Liberation Front in 1963. Portuguese colonial policy was attacked by all countries except South Africa in the United Nations. A United Nations Sub-Committee (which was not allowed to enter Angola) reported: 'The Portuguese authorities face a historic choice; whether to continue to rely on the use of force, with its inevitable miseries, or to respond to world opinion and take measures to build a new relationship with the people of Angola. What is needed is readiness to understand the new forces in the world.' Portugal has shown few signs of understanding these new forces. After the outbreak of the revolt, reforming legislation was rushed through by the government. The status of *indigenas* was abolished, and all inhabitants became Portuguese citizens. The local Legislative Councils were given slightly increased powers. Yet further immigration was encouraged. 'We believe it necessary,' said the Minister for the Overseas Provinces, 'to continue the settlement of our Africa by European Portuguese, who will make their homes there and find in Africa a true extension of their country.' Experience elsewhere in Africa has shown that political and racial tensions increase in direct proportion to the number of white settlers in a territory. It remains to be seen whether Portuguese reforms are not too few and too late; and whether Portugal can by sheer force and determination put up the same kind of resistance to African nationalism as may be expected from the self-governing white communities of Rhodesia and South Africa.

## 22

## INDEPENDENT AFRICA IN THE MODERN WORLD

*The colonial legacy*

The lives of individual Africans and of the states of which they are citizens are rooted in the manners and customs, and the political and religious ideas of the pre-colonial past. Measured on the time-scale of history, the colonial period was but an interlude of comparatively short duration. But it was an interlude that radically changed the direction and the momentum of African history. It would be unwise to neglect the positive contribution of this period while denouncing the unpleasant—and inevitable— aspects of alien rule. The Rhodesian nationalist Ndabaningi Sithole has generously acknowledged the debt to colonialism:

It has given to Africa a new vigorous industrial pattern, a new social consciousness, new insights and visions. It has created a new environment. It has annihilated many tribal and linguistic barriers and divisions. The European colonial powers are to be praised for the work they have done in helping the emergence of African nationalism. It is only a blind man who will not appreciate the fact that colonialism has stimulated and shaped African nationalism. The twentieth century African nationalism is indeed a child of European colonialism.

(*African Nationalism*, 1959, p. 74.)

Foremost among the legacies bequeathed to independent Africa are the political boundaries created by the colonial powers. Many African leaders have spoken of the 'balkanisation' of Africa under colonialism. It is important to understand what this means. Thanks to the colonial partition of Africa, most of the modern African countries are much larger than the pre-colonial political units. Although a few, like Gambia and Togo, are still inconveniently small, countries the size of Nigeria, Congo, Sudan or Tanzania, to name only a few, have far greater potentialities— political, social and economic—than even the largest of the old African kingdoms.

The negative side of the colonial legacy was largely expressed by Sylvanus Olympio, the first President of the Togo Republic, who, until he was assassinated in 1963, was one of the shrewdest of African leaders.

The effect of the policy of the colonial powers [he wrote] has been the economic isolation of peoples who live side by side, in some instances within a few miles of each other, while directing the flow of resources to the metropolitan countries. For example, although I can call Paris from my office telephone here in Lome, I cannot place a call to Lagos in Nigeria only 250 miles away. Again, while it takes a short time to send an air-mail letter to Paris it takes several days for the same letter to reach Accra, a mere 132 miles away. Railways rarely connect at international boundaries. Roads have been constructed from the coast inland but very few join economic centres of trade. The productive central regions of Togo, Dahomey and Ghana are as remote from each other as if they were separate continents.

According to this line of thought, what was needed was not a grand political union of African states as advocated by Nkrumah, but rather the establishment of closer communications between neighbouring African states on a regional basis. President Houphouet of the Ivory Coast, was even more outspoken. He maintained that a political union of African states would do nothing to solve Africa's main problem which was one of economic poverty. A union between poor countries would not make any of them richer, and might actually impede their relations with the richer countries which could help them. Referring to the neutralist position adopted by the countries attending the Afro-Asian Conferences at Bandung and Cairo (1958), he warned his audience against:

a spirit of hate which severs the under-developed countries from the powers to which they were attached and finally dooms them, on the one hand to a regrouping in misery and mediocrity, on the other to a kind of perpetual auction, in which a majority of the non-committed countries live, which gives them some short-lived successes but which cannot guarantee them the satisfaction of their constant needs.

Although few African statesmen agreed with Houphouet, the years since 1959 have in fact seen a strengthening rather than a weakening of the frontiers between African countries. The reasons for this have been partly economic. African countries have found it easier to get the outside aid which they all need on a country-by-country basis. More important still, however, have been the internal political problems which have forced every newly independent government to concentrate its main attention on its own affairs. To these problems we must now turn.

### Tribalism and nationalism

Africans entered upon their independence full of hope for the future. Their optimism was shared by outside well-wishers, including the former colonial powers. The difficulties and complexities of the immediate post-independence situation, however, were underestimated both in Africa and elsewhere. With independence it became clear that the impressive unity with which African peoples had faced their colonial rulers had been a deceptive facade. It had been a unity of anti-colonialism rather than a unity of real nationalism. Despite the seventy years of colonial rule, tribalism was still in most places a potentially stronger force than nationalism. Throughout the continent local or regional interests, based mainly on tribal or language groups, threatened the security and stability of the new states. All governments had to take drastic measures to meet these early crises, and in doing so they incurred the criticism of using non-democratic methods. Some countries were successful in controlling or curbing these dangerous forces; others were less so, and some suffered a breakdown of law and order.

The strife in the Congo became chronic. It showed no sign of abating even after the forced re-incorporation of the Katanga in 1963. The United Nations forces withdrew, but the Congolese army could not keep the peace throughout the huge country. The governments appointed by President Kasavubu depended upon Western, especially American, military and economic aid. The Communist countries and several African states supported the followers of the murdered Lumumba (who had achieved a martyr's reputation). By 1964 most of the eastern regions of the Congo were in open revolt. Tshombe reappeared upon the political scene and formed a government. He employed white soldiers—the so-called mercenaries—to stiffen the Congolese army. Militarily they proved successful, and by mid-1965 most of the country had been reconquered from the rebel forces; but this use of white mercenaries made Tshombe extremely unpopular with most other African leaders, and contributed to his downfall. After a brief period of political manoeuvring at the end of 1965, a military clique under General Mobutu finally seized power, overthrowing even Kasavubu, who had succeeded in holding on to the Presidency since independence. At the time of writing, however, the state of the Congo was still very disturbed.

In neighbouring Rwanda the civil war between the Batutsi and the Bahutu became even more violent after independence than before. By 1964 tens of thousands of people had been killed and more than 100,000 Batutsi refugees had fled to Uganda and Tanganyika.

Yet another country to experience grave internal disorders was the Sudan. The differences between the Arabic-speaking Muslim northerners, who ruled the country, and the pagan and Christian peoples of the south, were more extreme than those between groups in most other states. The British had in fact ruled the two halves of the country in almost separate compartments. After independence, northern administrators and northern troops moved into the south and pursued an injudicious policy of Islamisation and Arabicisation. To the southerners this appeared like a new form of colonialism. At last in 1962, after several years of unrest, the southerners rose against the Khartoum government, which suppressed them with a heavy hand. Since then more than a quarter of a million southern Sudanese have taken refuge in Uganda, the Congo, Ethiopia and Chad, while many of those remaining in the country have retreated into the bush, leaving only the towns and administrative centres in government control. Like the Africans in the European-dominated parts of central and southern Africa, the southerners formed liberation movements and demanded either secession from the Sudan, or, at the very least, an autonomous position within it.

### One-party rule and African Socialism

Even those African governments which did not have to face open acts of separatism knew well that the surviving forces of tribalism were a grave threat to the unity of their new states. They knew also that they must somehow satisfy the demands of the mass of the people for rapid changes following independence. People were not prepared to exchange a set of white rulers for a set of black rulers who might become just as remote from their daily lives as their predecessors. Popular aspirations were reflected among the younger government supporters, who pressed for ever more radical policies to eradicate poverty and ignorance. In order to survive in power, the leaders had to satisfy these demands, and to channel the ambitions of the younger politicians into purposeful action. Throughout most of independent Africa the response to these pressures was the formation of one-party states with socialist programmes, in which the nation-building activity of the party organisation was seen as much more important than the deliberative and restraining functions of a Western-type democratic legislature.

The constitutional systems set up in some haste by France and Britain during the last years of their rule in Africa (see Chapter 17) nearly everywhere underwent radical changes during the early years of independence. Opposition parties, being viewed not merely as political rivals but as divisive and therefore dangerous elements within the state, were threatened, harried and finally suppressed. The French-speaking West African states were the first to establish one-party rule. They had the beginnings of an example in France itself, where since 1958 President de Gaulle had enjoyed wide powers and where political activity was much restricted. Except for Nigeria where until early 1966, a multi-party system seemed to be a condition of the Federation's survival, most of the former British colonies followed suit. In the absence of recognised oppositions, the formal meetings of parliaments and legislative assemblies became much less important than they had been. More and more powers passed into the hands of presidents and ministers. More and more of the making of policy went on behind the scenes in cabinets and party committees.

Side by side with the elimination of parliamentary opposition went the strengthening of the government and the dominant party organisation in relation to the civil service, the judicature (the courts and the judges), the armed forces, the police, the trade unions and the press. Fundamental to a two-party system in western Europe is the political neutrality of the public services: it is this, and this alone, which enables them to work under successive governments with differing points of view. In newly independent Africa, however, many members of the public services were expatriates, and many more were members of the old *élites* which had grown up under colonial rule. These men were not trusted by the new rulers, who did not feel secure until men of strong and tested party allegiance had been placed in key positions throughout these services.

Our conception of the President's office [wrote Julius Nyerere] is obviously incompatible with the theory that the public services are, and ought to be, politically impartial. Civil servants are human beings; they have political views and this must affect their work. Policies they like are executed with enthusiasm, those of which they disapprove are implemented reluctantly, or may even be slowed down. But in Tanganyika enthusiasm is a most important national asset. We cannot afford the luxury of administrators who are neutral.

And so the District and Provincial Commissioners of colonial times were succeeded, not by politically neutral African civil servants, but by party officials. Recruits from party youth organisations were sent for training as army and police officers. Trade unions were brought under government control. So was broadcasting. Presidential powers were extended to include the right to detain and imprison without trial people suspected of political subversion, and the right to remove judges who returned politically unacceptable verdicts. Nkrumah, at least, had forecast developments of this kind. In his autobiography, published on the eve of independence, he had written: 'Even a system based on social justice and a democratic constitution may need backing up, during the period following independence, by emergency measures of a totalitarian kind. Without discipline, freedom cannot survive.' It was inevitable that the movement towards strong, one-party government in the independent African states should incur criticism in the western countries, whose peoples prided themselves above all else on the political liberties which they had won in the past from the over-strong, monarchical governments under which their own national unity had once been established. Most Westerners did not understand the need for strong government in independent Africa. They assumed that the movement towards one-party states showed nothing but the determination of those who had won power to keep it by any means. Communist countries on the whole welcomed the new political trends, which seemed to be bringing the African countries nearer to their own systems of government. The idea of the single revolutionary party was indeed one which had been adopted by many African leaders from the Communist example, although many of them were careful to explain that their acceptance of it did not commit them to a full imitation of the Communist system. Nyerere argued that:

The British and American tradition of a two-party system is a reflection of the society from which it evolved. The existence of distinct classes and the struggle between them resulted in the growth of this system. In Africa the Nationalist movements were fighting a battle for freedom from foreign domination, not from domination by any ruling class of our own. Once the foreign power—'the other Party'—has been expelled, there is no ready-made division among the people. The Nationalist movements must inevitably form the first Governments of the new states. Once a free Government is formed, its supreme task lies ahead—the building up of the country's economy. This, no less than the struggle against colonialism, calls for the maximum united effort by the whole country if it is to succeed. *There can be no room for difference or division.*

Both Nyerere and Nkrumah stressed that the struggle against poverty is similar to a state of war, when, even in western countries, 'national' governments chosen from all parties are held to represent the will of the people. The one-party state is a kind of 'national' government, and Nyerere and others have claimed that it follows the tradition of African life, in which 'the elders sit under the big tree and talk until they agree'. In Tanzania the system of elections adopted in 1965, when voters were asked to choose between rival candidates both representing the single party, has gone far to meet the main objection to one-party rule, which is that governments can only be changed by plots or violence. Eight ministers lost their seats in this election.

Not all African one-party states adopted Socialism. Houphouet for example, firmly believed in a 'liberal economy', under which the Ivory Coast expanded rapidly, financed mainly by France. Most African leaders, however, considered this dependence upon a single source of foreign aid as a form of 'neo-colonialism', and have permitted only a certain amount of direct capitalist participation in their economies. Nkrumah held that: 'Capitalism is too complicated a system for a newly independent nation. Hence the need for a socialist society.' And a Ghanaian report added: 'Independent African states are faced with urgent and pressing problems of reconstruction, for the solution of which all the available national resources both human and otherwise must be mobilized.' In the former British colonies the foundations of a Socialist economy were laid during and after the war, when government agencies undertook much of the economic development. African leaders, however, claimed that their Socialism (like their one-party states) was rooted in the tribal past.

### The Pan-African movement in independent Africa

We have seen that the major pre-occupation of the newly independent states was to convert a merely negative anti-colonialism into a positive sense of nationalism co-extensive with their own boundaries. It was an obvious consequence of this preoccupation that Pan-Africanism should assume a lower place than it had held when colonial peoples, struggling for their freedom, had seen in continental unity the key to success. The largest appeal of Pan-Africanism was, and still is, to the unfree. Political leaders in unfree territories had welcomed Nkrumah's guidance and help, but as rulers of independent states they were concerned with the immediate problems of consolidating their power within their own countries, and they resented his attempts to retain the leadership of the continent. At the first conference of Independent African States held at Accra in 1958, Nkrumah received nothing but applause. At the second conference, held only two years later in Addis Ababa, the Nigerian delegate spoke for many when he said: 'If anyone makes the mistake of feeling that he is a Messiah who has got a mission to lead Africa, the whole purpose of Pan-Africanism will, I fear, be defeated.'

Most of the former French colonies retained their close links with France, and were especially cautious in their approach to international problems. These countries (the Brazzaville group) were joined by Ethiopia and Nigeria and by other non-socialist states to form the Monrovia Group in 1961. They stressed the need for 'non-interference in the internal affairs of states'. The only former French colonies that were more radically inclined were Guinea, which had opted out of the French community in 1958, and Mali. These now joined Ghana and some of the Arab North African countries to form the Casablanca group. The prolonged Congo crisis widened the gulf between the two groups, the Monrovia states supporting the United Nations' efforts and the governments set up under Kasavubu, the Casablanca states supporting Lumumba's party.

In 1958, the East African countries set up their own regional organisation, the Pan-African Freedom Movement of East and Central Africa (PAFMECA), which was attacked by Nkrumah as yet another obstacle to the achievement of African unity. Ghana, however, was becoming increasingly isolated, even within the Casablanca group. Ghana, Guinea and Mali had formed in December 1960 the nucleus of a Union of African States. But in 1962 the socialist government of Mali re-established close economic links with France, and patched up its quarrel with Senegal. Later the same year Sékou Touré and de Gaulle healed the breach that had existed between Guinea and France since 1958, and came to an agreement on economic aid and technical

Somalian claims to French Somaliland, Haud and Ogaden (in Ethiopia) and Northern Frontier District of Kenya

Somalian–Ethiopian and Somalian–Kenyan conflicts 1960-1965

FR. SOMALILAND

Haud
Ogaden
SOMALIA

Casablanca January 1961

1964 Moroccan-Algerian frontier war

MOROCCO

Frontier undefined

SPANISH SAHARA

ALGERIA (FLN)

LIBYA

July 1952 Egyptian Army Revolution (Nasser)

Cairo 1958 Afro-Asian Solidarity Conference

EGYPT (UNITED ARAB REPUBLIC with Syria: 1958-1961)

United Arab Republic (Egypt) has close ties with Iraq and the Republican forces in the Yemen

French Soudan and Senegal formed Mali Federation 1959-1960

MAURITANIA claimed by Morocco

MALI

NIGER

CHAD

SUDAN

1962-1965 Revolt of Southern Sudanese against Arabic-speaking Northern government

YEMEN

ERITREA

SENEGAL

GAMBIA

PORT. GUINEA

Conakry Afro-Asian Solidarity Conference 1960

1961 Revolt against Portuguese rule

GUINEA

SIERRA LEONE

LIBERIA

Monrovia May 1961

IVORY COAST

VOLTA

GHANA

TOGO

DAHOMEY

NIGERIA

Accra : first conference of Independent African States 1958

CAMEROUN

CENTRAL AFRICAN REPUBLIC

CONGO

ETHIOPIA

Addis Ababa Feb 1962—PAFMECSA May 1963—OAU

N.F.D.

KENYA

UGANDA

Ivory Coast, Volta, Niger and Dahomey formed Entente Council 1959

Ghana-Guinea Union 1958; joined by Mali as the Union of African States 1961. Dissolved 1963

GABON

Brazzaville Dec 1960

SpG

CONGO (Kinshasa)

Internal conflicts 1960 to 1966

RUANDA

BURUNDI

Mwanza Sept 1958 Moshi PAFMECSA Afro-Asian Conference 1963

Kenya Uganda

TANZANIA

Tanzania member of East African Common Services Organization

||||||| Casablanca Powers (Algeria—FLN government in exile)

/////// Brazzaville group (Union Africaine et Malgasy—UAM)

\\\\\\\ Joined Brazzaville group to form Monrovia Powers (Libya detached from Casablanca group) Monrovia group formed the Inter-African and Malagasy States Organisation (IAMO)

≡≡≡≡≡ Pan-African Freedom Movement of Eastern, Central and Southern Africa: member states nationalist movements in Mozambique, Angola, Rhodesia, South West Africa, South Africa, Botswana, Lesotho and Swaziland sent delegates (PAFMECSA)

Casablanca and Monrovia groups and PAFMECSA absorbed into the Organisation of African Unity (OAU), 1963.

Most other independent African states joined the OAU.

:::::::: Union Africaine et Malgache (UAM) reconstructed 1964, joined by Congo (Kinshasa)

ANGOLA

1961 Angolan revolt against Portuguese rule

ZAMBIA

MALAWI

MOZAMBIQUE

RHODESIA

SOUTH WEST AFRICA

BOTSWANA

SWAZILAND

LESOTHO

SOUTH AFRICA

MALAGASY REPUBLIC

**36   African unity and disunity since independence**

assistance. Guinea no longer had to rely solely upon Communist aid. Nkrumah's immediate recognition of the Togo government that seized power after the assassination of President Olympio in January 1963 led to the dissolution of the Union of African States. Modibo Keita of Mali and Sékou Touré of Guinea now worked with the East African leaders to bring the two blocs together. Their efforts were successful in that, at Addis Ababa in May 1963, all the independent states came together to found the Organization of African Unity. However, the Secretariat of the O.A.U. and its economic, military and other commissions fell far short of the political union demanded by Nkrumah. Hardened nationalists like Ben Bella frankly stated their views: 'I have not come here because of any special interest in African charters. My primary aim is to help liberate those parts of Africa not yet liberated. If this conference doesn't share my concern, I will refuse to be a signatory to any charter.'

A nine nation Liberation Sub-committee was set up with its headquarters at Dar es Salaam, but it proved unable to pursue a single-minded course. The liberation movements in the Portuguese possessions, in Rhodesia and in South Africa, were themselves divided into contending groups, all vying for support from O.A.U. Disputes among the O.A.U. countries dashed its founders' high hopes. The Monrovia states re-established their own organisation early in 1965. This time they were joined by Tshombe's Congolese government.

The ideals of Pan-Africanism, as they developed after the war, seem thus as far from realisation as they have ever been. The difficulties in the way of a United States of Africa, in a huge continent with poor communications, large sparsely populated areas and fragmented economies, seem overwhelming. The first considerations of most African leaders are for their own states. It was the view of Nigeria's Sir Abubakar Tafawa Balewa, and not that of Nkrumah, that was adopted by O.A.U.: 'African unity must be based on the sovereignty of all African countries, whatever their size, population, and social level.' Nyerere in a speech at the end of 1963 which referred pointedly to the 'pretensions that have been made from outside Africa', stated:

One of the hard facts we have to face in the way to African unity is that this unity means on the part of countries the surrender of sovereignty and on the part of individual leaders the surrender of high positions. We must face quite squarely the fact that so far there has been no such surrender in the name of African unity.

In East and West Africa, in the countries of the Maghrib and in Egypt, the nationalism of each state was becoming a more potent political force than Pan-African sentiment. What now mattered to a man was that he was a Kenyan, a Nigerian or a Senegalese, and not that his government was a member of O.A.U. Hostility to white rule in Southern Africa remained as the largest surviving force uniting all the African-ruled states, but even this is a unity of sentiment rather than of action. In 1965, while Tanzania was training freedom fighters from Mozambique, Tshombe was intercepting arms destined for the freedom movement in Angola.

### 1965–66: the year of the military revolutions

As we have seen, the states of Africa have behaved since independence very much like states the world over. State interests have been the primary concern. Minor wars have already blown up between African states—between Morocco and Algeria over their ill-defined southern frontiers, and between Somalia and her neighbours, Ethiopia and Kenya. Nearly all African states have entered upon the dangerous and vastly expensive game of increasing their armaments. Inevitably, as in all young states, this has increased the power of the armed forces to intervene in the political affairs of their own countries. Egypt, as we have seen, became a military dictatorship only six years after the British had evacuated the country at the end of the war. In the Sudan, General Abboud and his leading officers seized power from the politicians only two years after independence. It is significant that these were the first two ex-colonial states whose armies were officered by their own nationals. Elsewhere, the politicians unconsciously enjoyed for several years the protection of expatriate commanders and police-chiefs.

The warning note was struck in East Africa, where, early in January 1964, a Communist inspired revolution overthrew the four-week-old government of Zanzibar. A few days later the armed forces in Tanganyika, led by some of the younger African officers, mutinied and rioters looted the streets of Dar es Salaam. The army mutinies spread to Uganda and Kenya. All three governments took the wise yet humiliating step of recalling British troops to disarm the mutineers and restore order. Later in 1964 Tanganyika joined with Zanzibar in a new union called Tanzania. This union restrained to some extent the revolutionary ardour of the Zanzibaris, but conversely it resulted in Nyerere adopting even more extreme Socialist policies. Nyerere, who was considered in 1961 to be one of the most moderate leaders in Africa, moved under the pressure of events step by step away from that position, so that by 1965 Tanzania had become one of the most radical and militant of African states.

The extreme difficulties, however, for the leaders of poor states recently emerged from colonialism in coping with the problems of governing their own countries while at the same time trying to play a part in international affairs, came to a head in 1965 and 1966. During this year a wave of military revolutions swept over Africa. In June 1965, as we have seen, Boumedienne overthrew Ben Bella in Algeria. In November Mobutu seized power from Kasavubu in the Congo, at the same time as Smith made his illegal declaration of independence in Rhodesia. Dahomey followed at the end of the year, when the army Chief of Staff took over the government (for the third time in two years). Then, in January 1966, the army seized power in the Central African Republic and Upper Volta. During the same month Nigeria suffered the bloodiest and most tragic of all these revolutions, when the army staged a simultaneous coup in all three regions, murdering, amongst many others, the Federal Prime Minister, the universally respected Sir Abubakar Tafawa Balewa, and the premiers of the Western and Northern Regions. It is true that the political situation in Western Nigeria had been dangerous for some three years past, in that the Federal government had been keeping in power there a political party which had not been elected by the people of the Region. Nevertheless, the military coup does not seem to have originated in the West, but rather among a group of young officers, including many from the Eastern Region, who were out to unify the country and to reform the corruption of Nigerian politics in general. Certainly, their action gained them at first wide popular support, and under the leadership of General Ironsi the military government which they had set up made a sensible and businesslike beginning in reform, making full use of the efficient Nigerian civil service.

The most spectacular of all the military revolutions, however, was that which in February 1966 toppled Nkrumah from the Presidency of Ghana. This occurred while Nkrumah was absent from the country on a state visit to China, and, in contrast with the Nigerian coup, it was nearly bloodless. The Kumasi garrison, which was on manoeuvres in the north of the country, was

ordered by its commander to drive straight to Accra, where it
achieved complete surprise. Like Ironsi in Nigeria, General
Ankrah, who headed the new government, was not one of the
instigators, but a senior officer who took charge of the movement
once it had started. As in Nigeria, the military government of
Ghana has been level-headed and appears to enjoy wide popular
support. The fall of Nkrumah marks a turning-point in the history
of independent Africa, for Nkrumah was perhaps the most typical
African leader of his time—the lonely student abroad, the strident
young politician in constant trouble with the colonial authorities,
the prime minister who brilliantly guided his country through the
troubled waters of independence, the dictator whose continent-
wide ambitions proved too great a burden for his people to bear.
The twenty years or so of African history from the end of the
Second World War until 1965 could be called, without too much
exaggeration, the age of Nkrumah.

In yet another African country the army, while not forming a
military government, has been used to effect a revolution. This
was in Uganda, where the Prime Minister, Milton Obote, facing
dissension within his Cabinet, arrested five of his colleagues,
including those nearest to the Kabaka Yekka element in the
ruling alliance. He next introduced and unconstitutionally drove
through parliament a new and unitary constitution, doing away
with the privileged position of Buganda within the country, and,
on meeting with defiance from the Kabaka and his Council, the
Lukiiko, sent in the army to attack the Kabaka's palace and the
Buganda government headquarters. The Kabaka fled the country,
and was deposed and succeeded in the Presidency by Obote.

So far as we know, none of these revolutions except that in
Zanzibar was inspired from outside Africa. On the contrary, it
seems that each of the others was the result of tensions and conflicts peculiar to the state in which it occurred. In Ghana it had
long been realised that only a military coup would be capable of
unseating Nkrumah and the single-party government of the
C.P.P., under which elections had become a meaningless farce. In
Nigeria and Uganda military action was inspired by the desire to
overthrow divisive federal constitutions which were judged to be
a barrier to the work of nation-building. In the Congo Mobutu's
seizure of power was an attempt to end the factional feuds which
had brought the country down in six short years from the wealthiest
colonial territory in Africa to one of the least solvent and stable

of independent African states. Indigenous army commanders were the new element in all these situations. Yet soldiers do not usually exert their power in politics unless they feel sure of public support. It may be said that in all these countries military action represented to some extent a judgment by the people that the first generation of nationalist politicians had failed them. It may also be said that the issue that gave rise to these military actions were *internal* issues, which made it less and less possible for African states to engage in Pan-African pursuits outside their own borders. The new military leaders are aware that in the long run they are no less dependent than their predecessors on public good will. They know that they will be judged primarily by what they achieve at home.

In world politics the African determination to avoid alignment has succeeded in so far as none of the great powers now sees in Africa the main scene of future conflict. The East-West rivalry has become vastly more complex than it was in 1960. The attention of America is increasingly taken up in Vietnam, and America's former allies, especially the French, have tended to follow their own independent policies. On the other hand, the Communist world has been rent by a great ideological rift between Russia, where the standard of living and therefore the desire for stability now approaches that of Western Europe, and China, which has become the chief exponent of militant revolution in the under-developed world. The main scene of conflict has shifted unequivocally to Asia. Individual African states may look to one or another of the developed countries for the economic aid which they all so desperately need. But there is no longer in the outside world the sense of a 'battle for Africa' in which any of the great powers is likely to spend vast sums and risk its security by intervening, for example, in South Africa, or Portuguese Africa, or even in Rhodesia. Africa is no longer the 'dark continent' of the nineteenth-century European imagination. But nor is it any longer the 'dark continent' of the Pan-Africanist's dreamland. It is, like every other continent, a cockpit of jostling interests, some internal, some external, each seeking its own advantage in whatever direction the opportunities of the passing moment seem to dictate.

## FEDERAL GROUPINGS AND PAN-AFRICAN ORGANISATIONS

GHANA–GUINEA UNION, 1958; became the *Union of African States*— Ghana, Guinea and Mali. Founded 1961, dissolved 1963.

MALI FEDERATION—Soudan and Senegal, 1959–60.

ENTENTE COUNCIL—Ivory Coast, Dahomey, Upper Volta and Niger, 1959.

AFRO-ASIAN SOLIDARITY CONFERENCES: Bandung (1956), Cairo (1958), Conakry (1960), Moshi (Tanganyika, 1963).

CONFERENCE OF INDEPENDENT AFRICAN STATES: Accra (1958, 8 states), Addis Ababa (1960, 13 states), Addis Ababa (1963, O.A.U. Conference).

ALL AFRICAN PEOPLE'S ORGANIZATION: conferences at: Accra (1958), Tunis (1960), Cairo (1961).

PAN-AFRICAN FREEDOM MOVEMENT: for Eastern and Central Africa 1958, for Eastern, Central and Southern Africa, 1962. Kenya, Uganda, Tanganyika, Zanzibar, Somalia, Ethiopia and Nationalist movements in Central and Southern Africa. PAFMECA and PAFMECSA absorbed into O.A.U. 1963.

BRAZZAVILLE GROUP (Union Africaine et Malgache—UAM) 1960. Senegal, Mauritania, Ivory Coast, Dahomey, Upper Volta, Niger, Cameroun, Gabon, Chad, Congo (Brazzaville), Central African Republic, Madagascar.

CASABLANCA GROUP, 1961: Ghana, Guinea, Mali, Morocco, U.A.R. (Egypt), Libya, Algerian Government in exile (F.L.N.).

MONROVIA GROUP, 1961: the twelve Brazzaville states, plus Liberia, Nigeria, Sierra Leone, Togo, Ethiopia and Libya (from Casablanca Group). Formed the Inter-African and Malagasy States Organization —IAMO.

ORGANIZATION OF AFRICAN UNITY—OAU, 1963: Addis Ababa. Absorbed PAFMECSA, IAMO, Casabalanca Organization. Set up Nine-Nation Liberation Committee, Dar es Salaam: Algeria, Congo (Léo), Ethiopia, Guinea, Nigeria, Senegal, Tanzania, Uganda and U.A.R.

African and Malagasy Union—UAM (see above)—dissolved after formation of OAU, later reconstituted (1964), joined by Congo (Léo) 1965.

## SUGGESTIONS FOR FURTHER READING

This is not intended to be an exhaustive list of works on modern African history, but only a brief guide to further reading. We hope that *Africa since 1800* has itself acted like a signpost at a busy cross-roads; that it has stimulated readers' interests in various directions, to study a whole range of topics far more deeply than the brief space that we have been able to give them. Most of the works mentioned contain bibliographies, which will carry the inquiring reader still further on his way. First we suggest some works on a few wide topics that cover all, or most of, the continent; then, further reading on each of the main regions of Africa.

## Pre-nineteenth century African history

For those readers who wish to pursue the study of African history before the beginning of the nineteenth century, the earlier chapters of Roland Oliver and J. D. Fage, *A Short History of Africa* (Penguin, 1962), provide the necessary outline material. If read in conjunction with this introduction, Basil Davidon, *Old Africa Rediscovered* (1959), is a useful popular account of the results of archaeological work, mainly on the Iron Age. The same author's *Black Mother* (1961) deals with the effect on Africa of the slave-trade, and his *The African Past* (1964) is an anthology of readings on pre-nineteenth-century African history. Other aspects of the slave-trade are covered by Daniel P. Mannix and Malcolm Cowley, *Black Cargoes* (1964), a fairly lightweight work, and, more seriously, in R. Coupland, *The British Anti-Slavery Movement* (1933) and in H. A. Wyndham, *The Atlantic and Slavery* (1935).

For those students who wish to read deeper into the origins of African peoples and their cultures and institutions, G. P. Murdock, *Africa—Its Peoples and Their Culture History* (1959), is a provocative work which should, however, be treated with care. C. G. Seligman, *Races of Africa* (3rd ed., 1957), is still one of the best short introductions to this subject. A larger work is H. Baumann and D. Westermann, *Volkerkunde Afrikas*, which has been translated into French as *Les peuples et les civilisations de l'Afrique* (1948). Readers might find parts of Robert Cornevin, *Histoire des peuples de l'Afrique noire* (1960) and *Histoire de l'Afrique* (1964), of interest, but neither book is entirely reliable. Articles by J. H. Greenberg collected in *Studies in African Linguistic Classification* (1955) and *The Languages of Africa* (1963) are important specialised studies; the latter is critically reviewed by Malcolm Guthrie in *The Journal of African History*, vol. v (1964), no. 1. J. D. Fage, *An Atlas of African History* (1963), is an indispensable companion to all the works mentioned in this section.

## Islam and Christianity in Africa

There is no general history of Islam in Africa. The little book by Bernard Lewis, *The Arabs in History* (7th ed., 1962), is an excellent short guide to the history of the Middle East and North Africa during the Muslim period, whilst a good brief historical introduction to Islam is the English translation of D. Sourdel, *Islam* (1962). H. A. R. Gibb, *Mohammedanism, an Historical Survey* (2nd ed., 1953), is concerned with the evolution of Muslim religious thought and institutions. J. Spencer Trimingham's works are detailed studies of Islam in various regions of Africa: *Islam in the Sudan*

(1949), *Islam in Ethiopia* (1952), *A History of Islam in West Africa* (1962), and *Islam in East Africa* (1964).

C. P. Groves, *The Planting of Christianity in Africa*, is a monumental work summarising the early periods of the Christian Church in northern Africa and Ethiopia, but dwelling especially on the development of European Christian missionary activity during the nineteenth and twentieth centuries. Volume ɪ (1948) takes the story up to 1840, volume ɪɪ (1954) from 1840 to 1878, volume ɪɪɪ (1955) from 1878 to 1914, and volume ɪv (1958) from 1914. Some aspects of this 'planting' of Christianity are treated in Bengt Sundkler, *Bantu, Prophets of South Africa* (1948), F. Welbourn, *East African Rebels* (1961)—a study of African reactions to Christianity, and George Shepperson and Thomas Price, *Independent African* (1958). This last is the story of the Chilembwe uprising in Nyasaland, and is a classic study of the influence of Christianity in the origins of African nationalism.

## European exploration

It is impossible here to more than touch upon the vast literature of this subject. The best short anthology of the writings of the principal British explorers is Margery Perham and Jack Simmons, *African Discovery* (first published in 1942 and often reprinted); this may be supplemented by C. Howard and J. H. Plumb, *West African Explorers* (1951), and C. Richards and J. Place, *East African Explorers* (1960), which, however, is not so satisfactory. Recent compilations or re-issues include: C. F. Beckingham (ed.), James Bruce, *Travels to Discover the Source of the Nile* (1964); J. Simmons, *Livingstone and Africa* (1955); I. Schapera (ed.), *Livingstone: Missionary Correspondence* (1961); Richard Burton, *The Lake Regions of Central Africa*; A. H. M. Kirk-Greene, *Barth's Travels in Nigeria* (1962). Rather different from these earlier explorers are the two works of Mary Kingsley, republished with introductions by J. E. Flint, *West African Studies* (1964), and *West African Travels* (1965). Philip Curtin, *The Image of Africa: British Ideas and Action, 1780–1850* (1964), presents a fascinating picture of what British people thought about Africa and its inhabitants in the period before the partition; in spite of its title, the material is drawn from West Africa.

## The partition

The question of why Africa was partitioned by the European powers, when, and in the manner it was, has exercised a number of historians. Their answers vary according to the region of Africa in which they have made a specialist study and the European archival material with which they are most familiar. Ronald Robinson and John Gallagher in *Africa and the Victorians* (1961), see Britain's presence in Egypt as playing the vital role in the scramble. Henri Brunschwig, *L'Avènement de l'Afrique noire* (1963), considers that the activity of de Brazza in the Bateke region really sparked off the indecent rush. J. D. Hargreaves, *Prelude to the Partition of West Africa* (1963), and C. W. Newbury, 'Victorians, republicans, and the partition of West Africa', *Journal of African History*, vol. III (1962), no. 3 (a review of Robinson and Gallagher), see the growing economic competition between Britain and France in West Africa as moving inexorably towards partition. Further reviews in the *Journal of African History* should be consulted: Jean Stengers, 'L'impérialisme colonial de la fin du XIXᵉ siècle: mythe ou réalité (vol. III (1962), no. 3), also a review of Robinson and Gallagher, from the 'King Leopold' point of view; Henri Brunschwig, 'Les origines du partage de l'Afrique occidentale' (vol. V (1964), no. 1), on Hargreaves's work; and finally Roland Oliver, 'Europe and Africa', in the same volume of the *Journal*, on Brunschwig's book.

Robinson and Gallagher do not give sufficient attention to the aims and diplomacy of France and Germany and other European powers, and from this point of view should be read in conjunction with W. L. Langer, *The Diplomacy of Imperialism* (2nd ed., 1950), A. J. P. Taylor, *The Struggle for Mastery in Europe* (1954) and P. Renouvin (ed.), *Les Politiques d'expansion impérialiste* (1949).

Biographies of the leading European figures in the partition 'on the ground' will be referred to in the sections on each region in Africa. Here may be mentioned Roland Oliver, *Sir Harry Johnston and the Scramble for Africa* (1957), as the ubiquitous Johnston appears all over the continent. The first volume of Margery Perham's great biography, *Lugard* (two vols., 1956 and 1960) also covers East and West Africa in this period.

### The colonial period

Lord Lugard's *The Dual Mandate in British Tropical Africa* (4th ed., 1929), and Albert Sarraut's *La mise en valeur des colonies françaises* (1941), are the classic statements of the British and French colonial policies. Margery Perham's work on *Lugard* is essential reading. Lord Hailey's monumental *African Survey* is a mine of information on the colonial period. Changes in political policies, and economic and cultural developments within the period are strikingly illustrated by a comparison of the 1938 and the 1957 editions. The two volumes of R. L. Buell's *The Native Problem in Africa* (1928, re-issued 1965), is a historical source of great importance on the policies of the European powers towards their colonial subjects. S. H. Frankel, *Capital Investment in Africa* (1938), is an economic study which should be consulted in conjunction with the *African Survey*. W. K. Hancock's *A Survey of British Commonwealth Affairs* (vol. II, part ii, 1942, n. ed. 1964) is another work essential to an understanding of the effects of white settler expansion in southern and eastern Africa, and the advance of European capitalism in West Africa. W. M. Macmillan, *African Emergent* (Penguin, 1949), is an indication of British colonial attitudes after the Second World

War. R. Delavignette, *Service Africaine* (1946, translated into English as *Freedom and Authority in French West Africa*), contains a valuable discussion of French colonial policy between the two World Wars.

## African nationalism

Shepperson and Price, *Independent African* (see section on Christianity above), is a fascinating study of some of the many strands that produced African nationalism. Shepperson has further studied some of these aspects in an article, 'Notes on Negro American influence on the emergence of African nationalism', in the *Journal of African History*, vol. I, (1960), no. 2. George Padmore, *Pan-Africanism or Communism?* (1956), was written from personal experience in the Pan-African movement. Thomas Hodgkin, *Nationalism in Colonial Africa* (1956), is a first-rate work from the earlier years of post-war (mainly West African) nationalism. If available, W. E. B. DuBois, *The World and Africa* (1947), should be consulted. The writings of Nkrumah and Senghor make an interesting comparison of the different backgrounds of foremost English-speaking and French-speaking nationalist leaders. While not a profound statement, Ndabaningi Sithole's *African Nationalism* (1959) has the virtues of simplicity and wit.

Bernard Lewis, *The Middle East and the West* (1963 and 1964), is an excellent short account of the Middle Eastern background to the nationalism of North Africa.

## Independence and after

Most of the books on contemporary Africa are inevitably the works of journalists rather than trained historians, sociologists or political scientists. Such books, therefore, are useful for the information they convey rather than for their balanced interpretation of the facts. Extremely useful guides through the jungle of recent events are Colin Legum (ed.), *Africa: a Handbook to the Continent* (1961), and *Political Africa* by Ronald Segal (1961). A shorter version of this last has appeared as a Penguin, *African Profiles* (1963). Gwendolen M. Carter's *Independence for Africa* (1960) and *Transition in Africa* (with W. O. Brown, eds., 1958) contain much useful material. The books of Jack Woddis, including *The Roots of Revolt* (1960), are rich in quotations, although his interpretations are at times open to question. Thomas Hodgkin, *African Political Parties* (Penguin, 1961), Colin Legum, *Pan-Africanism* (1962), Ph. Decraene, *Le Panafricanisme* (2nd ed., 1961), and the same author's *Tableau des partis politiques de l'Afrique au sud du Sahara* (1963), all provide much information, as does Helen Kitchen, *Handbook of African Affairs* (1964), which contains information on the armed forces of the African states. *African One-Party States*, ed. Gwendolen M. Carter (1962), is a detailed examination of a selection of these new nations. African statements which should be consulted include Nkrumah's books, such as *I Speak of Freedom* (1961), and *Africa Must Unite* (1963), Julius Nyerere, *Democracy and the Party System*

(1963), and Mamadou Dia, *The African Nations and World Solidarity* (translated by M. Cook, 1962). Looking ahead is Dunduza Chisiza, *Africa—What Lies Ahead?* (1962), as is Basil Davidson's *Which Way Africa?* (Penguin, 1964).

This is a good place to mention the paper-back series run by some publishers on contemporary African affairs, Outstanding in Britain are the Penguin African Library, and the series published by the Oxford University Press for the Institute of Race Relations. Naturally the standard of individual titles in these series varies considerably; but in general it is high, and students are able to build up an invaluable collection of books on Africa at comparatively little cost. Other books worthy of mention are: Immanuel Wallerstein, *Africa: The Politics of Independence* (1961), Guy Hunter, *The New Societies of Tropical Africa* (1962), Melville J. Herskovits, *The Human Factor in Changing Africa* (1962), and John Hatch, *A History of Post-War Africa* (1965).

## Africa region by region

There are great gaps in our detailed knowledge of many aspects of the history of modern Africa. In this respect, some regions are better served than others, at least in works of sound and reputable scholarship. We will begin our survey of some of the books on the different parts of the continent in the European-dominated south, and move northwards until we reach Arabic-speaking Egypt.

### South Africa

E. A. Walker, *A History of Southern Africa* (3rd and revised edition, 1957), is the standard single-volume work, but is concerned mainly with the history of the relationships between the two white groups in South Africa. This bias is apparent throughout South African historical writing. There is no good history of the African peoples in South Africa in any period, nor is there any satisfactory attempt to view South African history as a whole. The re-issued volume VIII of the *Cambridge History of the British Empire* (1963) is disappointing; little new has been added to it since it first appeared in 1936. C. W. de Kiewiet, *A History of South Africa, Social and Economic* (1951), pointed the way towards a wider appraisal of South African history. A fascinating insight into the earlier growth of Afrikaner racial attitudes is given in the historical section of the psychologist I. D. MacCrone's *Race Attitudes in South Africa* (1937 and 1957). For the period of the Cape Frontier wars and the Great Trek, John S. Galbraith, *Reluctant Empire, 1834–54* (1963), is an essential contrast to W. M. Macmillan, *Bantu, Boer and Briton* (1929, new edition 1964). C. W. de Kiewiet, *The Imperial Factor in South Africa* (1937), covers the third quarter of the nineteenth century. The fifteen crucial years from 1895 to 1910 in South African History are, not unnaturally, a happy hunting ground for historians, beginning with J. van der Poel, *The Jameson Raid* (1951). J. S. Marais,

*The Fall of Kruger's Republic* (1961), and G. H. L. Le May, *British Supremacy in South Africa, 1899–1907* (1965), are excellent studies of the Anglo-Boer conflict. G. B. Pyrah, *Imperial Policy in South Africa, 1902–10* (1955), deals with the events leading up to the Act of Union, while L. M. Thompson, *The Unification of South Africa, 1902–10* (1960), is a masterly work. J. Omer-Cooper, *The Zulu Aftermath* (1966) is a study of the consequences of the Shakan revolution.

The social and economic results of the mineral development in South Africa on African life are admirably examined in J. van der Horst, *Native Labour in South Africa* (1942). Mary Benson's *The African Patriots* (1963) is about the African National Congress in South Africa, by a white sympathiser, and Edward Roux's *Time Longer than Rope* (1948 and 1964), a history of African political and trade union reactions to European rule, especially during the period between the two wars, is the work of an active political figure; it must be treated with great caution. L. M. Neame, *The History of Apartheid* (1962), is a useful general account of the policy of the present government of the Republic. Pienaar's contribution to S. Pienaar and Anthony Sampson, *South Africa: Two Views of Separate Development* (1960), is an interesting statement in English of the Afrikaner point of view. An insight into the African side of the picture is presented with great dignity by A. J. Luthuli in *Let my People Go* (1962), and by Govan Mbeki, *South Africa: The Peasants' Revolt* (Penguin, 1964). A vast study of the political structure of South Africa after the Second World War is Gwendolen M. Carter, *The Politics of Inequality* (1958).

South Africa is well served with biographical works. Edwin Smith's *The Mabilles of Basutoland* (1934); a missionary family in Basutoland contains the best short study of Moshesh. The first volume of Sir Keith Hancock's biography of Smuts, entitled *The Sanguine Years, 1870–1919* (1962), and Alan Paton's study of the younger *Hofmeyr* (1964) are first-rate.

The only short introduction to the history of South-West Africa is Ruth First, *South West Africa* (Penguin, 1963). H. Vedder, *South-West Africa in Early Times* (1938), is a much more detailed history up to the end of the nineteenth century.

### Central Africa

There are several introductory histories of the lands which briefly made up the Central African Federation: A. J. Hanna, *The Story of the Rhodesias and Nyasaland* (1960), and A. J. Wills, *An Introduction to the History of Central Africa*, (1964), are both useful. Three works published under the auspices of the Institute of Race Relations, London, approach the history of Rhodesia (Southern) in more detail: Philip Mason, *The Birth of a Dilemma* (1958), takes the story through to 1918; Richard Gray, *The Two Nations* (1960), covers the period from the end of the First World War to 1953; and Philip Mason, *Year of Decision* (1960), deals with the Federation up to 1960. Recent books by white and black inhabitants of these lands are understandably controversial—a few may be mentioned: Colin Leys and Cranford Pratt, *A New Deal in Central Africa* (1960); L. H. Gann and Peter Duignan, *White Settlers in Tropical Africa* (Penguin, 1962); and Kenneth Kaunda, *Zambia Shall be Free* (1962). Sithole's work on African Nationalism has already been commented upon in the section on Nationalism. Patrick Keatley, *The Politics of Partnership* (Penguin, 1963) is a journalist's rousing account of the interconnections of British and Rhodesian politics. Thomas Franck, *Race and Nationalism* (1960), is an interesting study by a Canadian economist of the Federation. Robert I. Rotberg, *The Rise of Nationalism in Central Africa, 1873–1964* (1966) is concerned with Zambia and Malawi.

A. J. Hanna, *The Beginnings of Nyasaland and North-eastern Rhodesia, 1859–1895* (1956), should be supplemented by the relevant chapters in Roland Oliver, *Sir Harry Johnston and the Scramble for Africa* (1957). Shepperson and Price's *Independent African*, which we have already mentioned, is essential reading for the early history of Nyasaland. L. H. Gann, *A History of Northern Rhodesia, Early Days to 1953* (1964), is extremely good. A wholly satisfactory biography of Rhodes has yet to appear. J. G. Lockhart and C. M. Woodhouse, *Rhodes* (1963), does not bring us much closer to appreciating Rhodes in his Central as well as South African setting than earlier studies, such as Basil Williams, *Cecil Rhodes* (1921). G. Oudard, *Cecil Rhodes* (1939), presents a French view of the empire builder.

### Madagascar

The best work on the subject is Hubert Deschamps' magnificent *Histoire de Madagascar* (1960), especially for the pre-colonial period. F. Boiteau, *Contribution à l'histoire de la nation malgache* (1958), is useful. There is little useful in English on the history of the island. O. Mannoni, *Prospero and Caliban* (1956), is a psychological study of the relationships between Europeans and Malagasies on the island in the colonial period. Gallieni's methods of 'pacification' are described in S. H. Roberts, *History of French Colonial Policy* (1929 and 1963).

### Portuguese territories

The best account of the Portuguese activities in Angola and Mozambique in English is James Duffy, *Portuguese Africa* (1959). A shortened version appeared in the Penguin series as *Portugal in Africa* (1962).

### East Africa

The *History of East Africa*, when it is completed by the publication of the third volume (edited by Margery Perham and R. E. Robinson), will provide a comprehensive study of the history of this area by experts in their various fields. Volume I, edited by Roland Oliver and Gervase Mathew, takes the story from the earliest times to the period immediately following the partition. The chapters in this volume dealing with the history of the African peoples in the first three-quarters of the nineteenth century, and of the Arab penetration of East Africa, treat these subjects more fully than the works of R. Coupland, *East Africa and Its Invaders . . . to 1856* (1938) and *The Exploitation of East Africa, 1856–90* (1939). These however, are still good on British policy towards this area. Norman R. Bennett, *Studies in East African History* (1964), contains useful material, particularly a study of Mirambo. Other works on the pre-colonial period include Roland Oliver, *The Missionary Factor in East Africa* (2nd ed., 1965), J. F. Faupel, *African Holocaust* (1962); about the persecution of the Christians in Buganda in 1886 see also the article by J. A. Rowe, 'The purge of Christians at Mwanga's Court', in the *Journal of African History*, vol. v (1964), part 1, and Kenneth Ingham, *The Making of Modern Uganda* (1959), which needs to be read in conjunction with the relevant chapters in volume I of *The History of East Africa*. Volume II of this *History* (1965), edited by Vincent Harlow and E. M. Chilver, covers the colonial period. Elspeth Huxley, *White Man's Country* (2 vols., 1953), is a study of the achievements of Lord Delemere in Kenya; Elspeth Huxley and Margery Perham, *Race and Politics in Kenya* (2nd ed. 1953), is useful.

D. A. Low and R. C. Pratt, *Buganda and British Overrule, 1900–1955* (1960), is especially valuable on the events leading up to the Agreement of 1900. George Bennett, *Kenya, A Political History: The Colonial Phase* (1963), is an excellent short study. Susan Wood, *Kenya: The Tensions of Progress* (1960), and Clagett Taylor, *The Political Development of Tanganyika* (1963), are of value. Even more so is the *East Africa Royal Commission Report, 1953–55* (Cmd 9475 of 1955), which provides the economic and social background essential for an understanding of the transition period from colonial rule to independence. A. J. Hughes, *East Africa: The Search for Unity* (Penguin, 1963), is a study of this transition, but is not as good as other books in the Penguin series. On Mau Mau, L. S. B. Leakey, *Mau Mau and the Kikuyu* (1952) and *Defeating Mau Mau* (1954), should be compared with J. M. Kariuki, '*Mau Mau*' *Detainee* (1963; Penguin, 1965). Tom Mboya's autobiography, *Freedom and After* (1963), is most entertaining.

### The Congo

Roger Anstey, *Britain and the Congo in the Nineteenth Century* (1962), is a penetrating study of British trading activities around the Congo estuary, and of the abortive Anglo-Portuguese Treaty which led up to the Berlin Conference. The best work in English on Leopold and the setting up of the Congo Free State is Ruth Slade, *King Leopold's Congo* (1962). P. Ceulemans, *La question arabe et le Congo (1882–1892)* (1959), is of great importance for an estimation of the achievement of the Arabs in the eastern Congo on the eve of the colonial period. If it is available, E. D. Morel's *Red Rubber* (1906) should be read as an outstanding example of humanitarian propaganda. A statement of Belgian colonial policy is Pierre Ryckmans, *Dominer pour servir* (1948). On the events leading up to independence, and subsequently, Ruth Slade, *The Belgian Congo* (1960), Colin Legum, *Congo Disaster* (Penguin, 1961), and Alan P. Merriam, *Congo: Background of Conflict* (1961), are useful.

### Ethiopia and the Horn of Africa

The best summary of early Ethiopian history is that by Jean Doresse, of which the first volume is called *Le Royaume de la Reine de Saba* and the second *L'Empire du Prêtre Jean*. There is no up-to-date, satisfactory history of Ethiopia in English. A. M. Jones and E. Monroe, *The History of Ethiopia* (1960), is an unrevised new edition of the work which first appeared in 1935, and contains some inaccurate material. David Mathew, *Ethiopia*, is of great interest for the little-known period from the late seventeenth to the early nineteenth century. J. Spencer Trimingham, *Islam in Ethiopia* (1952), which has already been mentioned, is concerned with the Muslim states to the east and south of the Christian empire. Edward Ullendorff, *The Ethiopians* (1960), provides some useful social and cultural background material.

On Eritrea there are Stephen H. Longrigg, *A Short History of Eritrea* (1945), and on the more modern period, G. K. N. Trevaskis, *Eritrea, A Colony in Transition, 1941–52* (1960). I. M. Lewis, *A Modern History of Somalia* (1965), is the only useful work in English. John Drysdale, *The Somali Dispite* (1964), sketches the backgound to contemporary Somali frontier problems.

Compared with Ethiopia, the Sudan is well provided with recent books on its history. P. M. Holt, *A Modern History of the Sudan, from the Funj Sultanate to the Present Day*, is an excellent short introduction. Richard Hill, *Egypt in the Sudan, 1820–81* (1959), and P. M. Holt, *The Mahdist State in the Sudan, 1881–98*, fill in the nineteenth-century details. The Egyptian penetration into the Negro south is dealt with in Richard Gray, *A History of the Southern Sudan, 1839–89* (1961). The successor to this work, R. O. Collins, *The Southern Sudan, 1883–98; a Struggle for Control* (1962), is not so satisfactory.

### West Africa (including ex-French Equatorial Africa)

J. D. Fage, *An Introduction to the History of West Africa* (3rd ed., 1962), is the best short history of the region in English, especially for the period of European penetration and colonial rule. Material on the Jihad movement at the end of the eighteenth century and the beginning of the nineteenth is somewhat scattered. J. Spencer Trimingham, *A History of Islam in West Africa* (1962), is very useful, as are parts of A. Adu Boahen's masterly study, *Britain, the Sahara, and the Western Sudan, 1788–1861* (1964). There is a chapter on Usuman dan Fodio in Michael Crowder, *History of Nigeria* (1962). E. W. Bovill's two books, *Caravans of the Old*

*Sahara* (1933) and *The Golden Trade of the Moors* (1958), the latter a complete revision of the former, are concerned with the trans-Saharan trade of the Sudanic states throughout their history, and end with accounts of the jihads. In French, Y. Urvoy, *Histoire des populations du Soudan Central* (1936) and *Histoire de l'empire du Bornou* (1949), are most informative. Thomas Hodgkin, *Nigerian Perspectives* (1960), uses contemporary sources to present a fascinating picture of the whole range of Nigerian history, including the Fulani jihads.

Turning to the states of the forest regions, S. Johnson, *The History of the Yorubas* (reprinted 1956), is a sound account of traditional history. M. G. Smith, *Government in Zazzau...1800 to 1950* (1960), is a most interesting detailed study. R. E. Bradbury, *The Benin Kingdom* (1957), and a revised edition of Jacob Egharevba's *A Short History of Benin* (1960), deal rather with the great age of this state, before the beginning of the period covered by this book. Michael Crowder's history covers the whole range of Nigerian history. Abbé M'Veng, *Histoire du Cameroun* (1963), might be useful. Moving westwards, there is Melville J. Herskovits, *Dahomey* (1938), and Robert Cornevin, *Histoire du Togo* (1959). J. D. Fage, *Ghana, an Historical Interpretation* (1959), sets the emergence of modern Ghana against the background of its past. W. E. F. Ward, *A History of Ghana* (2nd ed., 1958), is useful. R. L. Buell, *Liberia: a Century of Survival, 1848–1947* (1948), is the best short history. Christopher Fyfe, *A History of Sierra Leone*, is a thorough work on the nineteenth-century history of this territory. On the French West African territories, the historical section of the two West African volumes of the *Encylopédie de l'Empire Française* (1949), and volume IV, by M. Delefosse, of G. Hanotaux and A. Martineau (eds.), *Histoire des colonies françaises* 1931), are valuable. The short book of H. Deschamps, *Le Sénégal et la Gambie* (1964) is excellent on the ex-French colony, but weak on the ex-British one.

There are a growing number of more specialist studies, especially from the Nigerian region, many by African historians. These include K. Onwuka Dike, *Trade and Politics in the Niger Delta, 1830–85* (1957), S.O. Biobaku, *The Egba and their Neighbours, 1842–72* (1957), C. W. Newbury, *The Western Slave Coast and its Rulers* (1961), G. I. Jones, *The Trading States of the Oil Rivers* (1963), and J. F. Ade Ajayi and Robert S. Smith, *Yoruba Warfare in the Nineteenth Century* (1964), and J. F. Ade Ajayi, *Christian Missions in Nigeria 1831–1881*, (1965).

John Flint, *Sir George Goldie and the Making of Nigeria* (1960), and Margery Perham's *Lugard*, already mentioned, are two fine biographies concerned with leading figures in the partition of West Africa. The general works listed above cover the colonial period and the rise of African nationalism. Additional material can be found in S. H. Roberts, *History of French Colonial Policy, 1870–1925*, and R. Delavignette, *Freedom and Authority in French West Africa*, which have both been previously mentioned; H. R. Rudin, *Germans in the Cameroons, 1884–1914* (1938); F. M.

Bourret, *Ghana: the Road to Independence, 1919–57* (2nd ed., 1960); David Apter, *The Gold Coast in Transition* (1955); David Kimble, *A Political History of Ghana, 1850–1928*, (1963; see on this the review article by Adu Boahen, 'The roots of Ghanaian nationalism' in the *Journal of African History*, vol. v (1964), no. 1); and Michael Crowder, *Senegal: a Study of French Assimilation Policy* (1962). V. Thompson and R. Adloff's *French West Africa* (1958) and *The Emerging States of French Equatorial Africa* (1960) are encyclopaedic works, with useful historical sections.

Many West African political leaders have launched into print, and have thereby added a personal testament to the record of the nationalist movement. Kwame Nkrumah's autobiography and other works have been noted in an earlier section. Chief Awolowo's autobiography, *Awo*, appeared in 1960, as did a collection of Azikiwe's speeches. Sir Ahmadu Bello, *My Life*, was published in 1962.

The best short guide to the period after independence is Ken Post, *The New States of West Africa* (Penguin, 1964). Philip Neres, *French-speaking West Africa* (1962), and Ruth Morgenthau, *Political Parties in French-Speaking West Africa* (1964) are both useful. Aristide R. Zolberg, *One-Party Government in the Ivory Coast* (1964), is a fine study of the party controlled by Houphouet.

## The Maghrib

There is no satisfactory history in English of the Maghrib as a whole, or of any of the countries comprising it. Nevill Barbour (ed.), *Survey of North West Africa* (1959), is valuable mainly for more recent events. C. A. Julien, *Histoire de l'Afrique du Nord jusqu'en 1830*, vol. II (2nd ed., 1956), is a useful introduction which takes the story up to the French occupation of Algiers. The collective works *Initiation au Maroc* (1938), *Initiation à la Tunisie* (1950) and *Initiation à l'Algérie* (1957) are extremely useful, as is Jacques Berque, *Le Maghreb entre deux guerres* (1962).

On Algeria, Y. Lacoste, A. Nouschi and A. Prenant, *L'Algérie passé et présent*, (1961), is a very thorough study. An article by Douglas Johnson, 'Algeria: some problems of modern history' in the *Journal of African History*, vol. v (1964), no. 2, is of outstanding importance for an understanding of the main trends of Algerian history. Marcel Emerit, *L'Algérie à l'époque d'Abd el-Kader* (1951), is excellent, whilst Philippe d'Estailleur Chantereine, *Abd el-Kader le Croyant* (1959), is a more popular account of the Muslim hero. Jacques Carret, *Le Maraboutisme et les confrèries musulmanes en Algérie* (1959), is a study of the religious orders in Algeria, and of their relationship with the rise of nationalism.

Henri Terrasse, *Histoire du Maroc jusqu'au protectorat français* (2 vols., 1949 and 1950), is the standard history of Morocco. Robert Montagne, *Les Berbers et le Makhzen dans le sud du Maroc* (1930), is an interesting study of the struggle between the Sultan's government and the nomadic groups. E. Aubin, *Le Maroc d'aujourd'hui* (English translation, *Morocco*

*Today,* 1906), is an eyewitness account of the last years of independence of the old sultanate. On the work of Lyautey in Morocco, there is Roberts, *History of French Colonial Policy,* noted in earlier sections, and G. Catroux, *Lyautey le Marocain* (1952), the work of a fellow soldier and admirer; also Robert Montagne, *Révolution au Maroc* (1953). Rom Landau, *Moroccan Drama, 1900–55* (1958), is fascinating, but should be treated with some caution. On Tunisia, P. Sebag, *La Tunisie* (1951), and A. Raymond, *La Tunisie* (1961), contain useful material. The period of British influence in Tunisia in the mid-nineteenth century is covered by Adu Boahen's *Britain, the Sahara and the Western Sudan,* which has already been commented upon. This work is also of great importance for the history of Tripoli during this period. E. E. Evans-Pritchard, *The Sanusi of Cyrenaica* (1949), is extremely valuable, covering both the genesis of the order and the Italian invasion and colonisation of North Africa.

Maghribi nationalism and independence have been studied in some detail. Among the best, or most accessible, books, are Ch. A. Julien, *L'Afrique du Nord en marche* (1952), Roger Le Tourneau, *Évolution politique de l'Afrique du Nord musulmane, 1920–1961* (1962), and A. Nouschi, *La Naissance du nationalisme algérien, 1914–1954* (1962). Ferhat Abbas, *La Nuit Coloniale* (1962), is a statement from one of the leaders of the F.L.N. Lorna Hahn, *North Africa: Nationalism to Nationhood* (1960) is useful.

## Egypt

A really good history of modern Egypt in any language remains to be written. F. J. Charles Roux, *L'Egypte de 1801 à 1882* (vol. VI of G. Hanotaux (ed.), *Histoire de la nation égyptienne,* 1948), and F. J. Charles-Roux and H. Dehérain in volume VII of the *Histoire* (1941), are rather old-fashioned, but still useful. H. H. Dodwell, *The Founder of Modern Egypt: Muhammad Ali* (1931), presents a very inadequate view of the great viceroy. There is good material on Muhammad Ali in A. E. Crouchley, *The Economic Development of Modern Egypt* (1938), and John Marlowe, *Anglo-Egyptian Relations, 1800–1953* (1954), is a very good over-all study. If available, Lord Cromer, *Modern Egypt* (1911), and Lord Lloyd, *Egypt since Cromer* (2 vols., 1933–4), are very interesting documents. For Egyptian reactions there are M. Rifaat Bey, *The Awakening of Modern Egypt* (1947), and N. Safran, *Egypt in Search of Political Community: An Analysis of the Intellectual and Political Evolution of Egypt, 1804–1952* (1961). Recent Egyptian history is covered by C. Issawi, *Egypt at Mid-Century* (1954), Jean and Simonne Lacouture, *Egypt in Transition* (1958), and Anwar El Sadat, *Revolt on the Nile* (1957). John Marlowe, *Arab Nationalism and British Imperialism* (1961), deals with Britain's relations with the Middle Eastern countries in the twentieth century. A good introduction to the army revolution in Egypt is P. J. Vatikiotis, *The Egyptian Army in Politics* (1964); also recommended is M. Berger, *Military Elite and Social Change: Egypt since Napoleon* (1960).

# SHORT READING LIST

Roland Oliver and J. D. Fage, *A Short History of Africa* (Penguin, 1962, 1966).

Bernard Lewis, *The Arabs in History*, 7th ed., 1962.

Roland Oliver, *Sir Harry Johnston and the Scramble for Africa*, 1957.

Ronald Robinson and John Gallagher, *Africa and the Victorians*, 1961.

J. D. Hargreaves, *Prelude to the Partition of West Africa*, 1963.

Ruth Slade, *King Leopold's Congo*, 1962.

George Shepperson and Thomas Price, *Independent African*, 1958.

J. D. Fage, *An Introduction to the History of West Africa*, 3rd ed., 1962.

*Oxford History of East Africa*, vols I and II.

A. J. Wills, *Introduction to the History of Central Africa*, 1964.

C. W. de Kiewiet, *A History of South Africa, Social and Economic*, 1941.

L. M. Neame, *The History of Apartheid*, 1962.

P. M. Holt, *A Modern History of the Sudan*, 1961.

A. Adu Boahen, *Britain, the Sahara, and the Western Sudan, 1788–1861*, 1964.

John Marlowe, *Anglo-Egyptian Relations, 1800–1953*, 1954.

Colin Legum (ed.), *Africa: a Handbook to the Continent*, 1961.

John Hatch, *A History of Post-War Africa*, 1956.

J. D. Omer-Cooper, *The Zulu Aftermath*, 1966.

# INDEX